D1569060

When Children Kill

When Children Kill

The Dynamics of
Juvenile Homicide

Charles Patrick Ewing

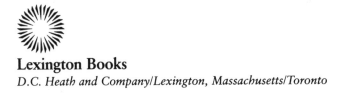

Lexington Books
D.C. Heath and Company/Lexington, Massachusetts/Toronto

Library of Congress Cataloging-in-Publication Data

Ewing, Charles Patrick, 1949–
    When children kill: the dynamics of juvenile homicide / Charles Patrick Ewing.
      p.   cm.
    Includes bibliographical references.
    ISBN 0-669-21883-9 (alk. paper)
    1. Juvenile homicide—United States. I. Title.
  HV9067.H6E95   1990
  364.1′523′083—dc20   89-48514
                                                          CIP

Published simultaneously in Canada
Printed in the United States of America
Casebound International Standard Book Number: 0-669-21883-9
Library of Congress Catalog Card Number: 89-48514

The paper used in this publication meets the minimum requirements of American National Standard for Information Sciences—Permanence of Paper for Printed Library Materials, ANSI Z39.48-1984. ∞™

Year and number of this printing:

91 92 10 9 8 7 6 5 4 3 2

This one is for you, Ben—with the hope that your generation will see the solutions mine could not or would not see.

Contents

Tables

Acknowledgments

The idea for this book first arose in discussions I had with my research partners Simon Singer and John Rowley. Our joint work, which culminated in several earlier articles on juvenile justice and juvenile homicide, has proven invaluable in this project. Much of the credit for the literature review goes to John, who tracked down, photocopied, organized, and—most important—saved dozens of articles. For Simon's part, he tried to help me see the problem—indeed, all problems—more scientifically. Any failure in that regard is more my fault than his.

Others who helped in the research leading to this book, and who deserve special thanks, include Lori Battistoni, a former student, who helped with the research on girls who kill; Maurice Recchia, my research assistant, who spent countless hours in the library, at the computer, and on the phone tracking down names, numbers, dates, et cetera; and Betsy Kizis, Chief Homicide Investigator with the New Hampshire Public Defender Program, my friend and colleague, who read and criticized portions of the manuscript.

Immersing oneself for several years in a topic as grim as juvenile homicide without losing perspective requires a great deal of emotional support from loved ones. As always, my work on this project has been supported—in more ways than she knows or I can count—by my wife, Sharon Harris-Ewing. Elaine Harris Ewing and Benjamin Harris Ewing also made their contributions by never allowing me to spend as much time as I might have on this project.

Introduction: The Dynamics of Juvenile Homicide

N ew York: A four-year-old girl awakens before dawn and finds her 3 week-old-twin brothers asleep in their cribs. She picks up one brother and drops him to the floor. She picks up the other. When he starts to cry, she throws him back into his crib. Moments later, the girl's parents find both twins dead from fractured skulls.[1]

Alabama: Two seventeen-year-olds and a fourteen-year-old agree to play "Top Secret," a fantasy game in which the players roll dice and act out roles. Several of the fantasy roles selected involve robbing stores and killing people. After agreeing to live out these fantasy roles in reality and then kill themselves, the three boys rob a convenience store of $700, then shoot and kill the night clerk as they leave.[2]

South Carolina: A seventeen-year-old drops a boulder off a highway overpass while his seventeen-year-old friend watches. The boulder tears through the roof of a passing car, killing a sleeping three-year-old boy.[3]

Georgia: Two sisters, seventeen and fourteen, frequently beaten by their mother and sexually abused by her boyfriend, shoot and kill her to prevent her from beating one of them with a yardstick.[4]

Oregon: A Boy Scout leader is convicted of sexually abusing two teenage boys and is sentenced to serve fifteen days in jail. A week later, he is shot and killed by one of the boys, age seventeen.[5]

Massachusetts: Two neighbors, a fourteen-year-old and a five-year-old, argue over a Halloween pumpkin. The fourteen-year-old beats and drowns the five-year-old, then stuffs his body into a plastic bag in the older boy's closet.[6]

California: A gunfight between rival Los Angeles street gangs in a neighborhood park leaves dead a nine-year-old boy who, caught in the cross fire, was hit by a stray bullet fired by a seventeen-year-old gang member.[7]

Missouri: The battered body of a nineteen-year-old male is found in a cistern, along with a dead cat. Four baseball bats are found nearby. Evidence indicates that the youth was beaten with the bats as many as fifty times by three boys, all seventeen years old, as part of a satanic sacrifice.[8]

Wisconsin: A sixteen-year-old girl, who no one knows is pregnant, gives birth to a baby, repeatedly stabs the newborn, and then puts the body in a plastic bag before depositing it in a garbage can.[9]

Florida: A five-year-old boy pushes a three-year-old playmate from a stairwell. The playmate grabs onto a ledge, but the five-year-old pries the boy's hands loose, and the three-year-old plunges to his death.[10]

Indiana: A sixteen-year-old boy shoots and kills his sleeping father after his mother tells him she will kill herself if he does not slay his father.[11]

New Jersey: A fifteen-year-old boy rapes, sodomizes, and bludgeons a thirteen-year-old girl from his neighborhood. He then drags her facedown across the street and several hundred feet through the woods before dumping her into a swamp, where she drowns. After the incident, the boy goes home, cleans up, and attends a birthday party for a girl he has been dating.[12]

Indiana: Four teenage girls set about to rob a seventy-eight-year-old Bible teacher. One of the girls, age fifteen, stabs the elderly woman thirty-three times with a foot-long butcher knife while the victim recites the Lord's Prayer. All four girls then flee with $10 in cash and the victim's car.[13]

Florida: Two brothers, eighteen and sixteen, both "skinheads" (members of a neo-Nazi gang known for hatred of Blacks and homosexuals), beat and stab to death a forty-one-year-old Black man.[14]

New York: A seventeen-year-old boy shoots and kills his mother, then tells authorities that she had sexually abused him for years prior to the killing.[15]

Louisiana: Three boys, ages sixteen, fourteen, and thirteen, kidnap, rape, beat, and drown a six-year-old boy, whose body is later found at the bottom of a swimming pool.[16]

Pennsylvania: A sixteen-year-old and his twenty-two-year-old companion are confronted by a man whose apartment they are burglarizing. They beat the man, behead him, and then use his blood to write "redrum" (murder spelled backward) on the wall.[17]

Georgia: A thirteen-year-old stabs his grammar school principal to death with a nail file after the principal spanks him.[18]

Georgia: In April, a sixteen-year-old boy robs and beats to death a retired couple in their home. Four months later, he robs and beats to death three women. A short while later, the local police find him driving a car belonging to one of the victims.[19]

Massachusetts: A fifteen-year-old boy bludgeons a classmate to death with a baseball bat. Later he tells witnesses he did so because he wanted to see what it would feel like to kill someone.[20]

Colorado: A fifteen-year-old and his friend, age fourteen, brutally beat and stab to death the fifteen-year-old's mother. Another teenage friend says "boredom" was the probable cause: "All we want is something to do, somewhere to go."[21]

Oregon: Fired from his job at an ice cream store, a seventeen-year-old and his eighteen-year-old friend return to the store and commit a robbery. They then force the manager to kneel in an ice cream freezer and shoot him in the head.[22]

Massachusetts: A sixteen-year-old is charged with terrorizing a local family with a hatchet. A year later, he enters another family's home, shoots a mother, and strangles her two children.[23]

Every year, at least 1,000 and often more than 1,500 American youngsters under the age of eighteen intentionally take the lives of others and are arrested on charges of murder or manslaughter. As the above sampling of cases makes clear, these homicides vary greatly. Some are crimes of premeditated violence motivated by greed, lust, or a desire for revenge. Others seem to be crimes of passion: unpremeditated impulsive overresponses to provocation by the victim or to some explosive drive within the killer. Still others lack apparent motivation and seem utterly senseless, perhaps the products of insanity.

This volume examines the phenomenon of juvenile homicide from a variety of perspectives. Chapter 1 examines the incidence and prevalence of juvenile homicide, reporting a variety of statistics on juveniles who kill. For example: How many juveniles kill each year? How do the numbers of juvenile homicides compare to the numbers of adult homicides each year? How many juveniles who kill are boys? How many are girls? Do boys and girls differ in their homicides? What are the ages of juveniles who kill? Who do juveniles kill, and under what circumstances do they kill?

Chapter 2 critically reviews the existing research base on juveniles who kill. What have the various studies of juvenile homicide discovered to date about this phenomenon? What remains to be discovered? What have been the limitations of existing research approaches, and what must be done to overcome these limitations?

Chapters 3 through 8 each deal with a specific type of juvenile homicide. Chapter 3 examines intrafamilial homicides: juveniles who kill their parents and/or siblings. Chapter 4 considers homicides committed by juveniles in the course of perpetrating other crimes, primarily theft crimes (such as robbery and burglary) and sex crimes (such as rape and sexual abuse). Chapter 5 examines apparently senseless, unusual, highly deviant, or bizarre juvenile homicides, as well as homicides perpetrated by juveniles who appear to be psychotic or suffering from some other form of serious mental illness.

Chapter 6 examines what has recently become one of the most visible and troubling forms of juvenile homicide in America: killings committed by groups or gangs of youths, acting together—killings that are almost always senseless and often related to drug trafficking. Chapter 7 deals with homicides committed by very young children, essentially those under the age of ten. As detailed in chapter 1, children under the age of ten commit only a miniscule percentage of all juvenile homicides, but these killings are often the most disturbing. Chapter 8 also deals with a minority group among juveniles who kill: girls. As indicated in chapter 1, girls generally account for less than 10 percent of all homicides committed by American juveniles annually.

Chapter 9 examines the general legal structure for dealing with juveniles who kill, specifically the statutory provisions in every American jurisdiction that allow some juvenile killers to be tried as adults, sent to prison, and, in some cases, even executed. Finally, chapter 10 considers the future of juvenile homicide in America, specifically what the incidence of juvenile homicide is likely to be between now and the turn of the century.

1
A Statistical Overview

H omicides committed by children and adolescents fascinate the public and generate significant media attention, but such homicides are
relatively rare. Indeed, it may be the relative infrequency of juvenile
homicides as much as anything else that contributes to the fascination and
attention. People younger than eighteen constitute roughly 26 percent of the
total resident population of the United States.[1] Yet annually for the past decade or so, consistently less than 11 percent of those persons arrested in the
United States for murder or non-negligent manslaughter have been under the
age of eighteen (see Table 1–1).

The number of juveniles arrested for homicide is a rough indicator of the
incidence of juvenile homicide, but not of the rate of such homicide. Calcu-
lating the approximate rate at which juveniles kill requires dividing the number of arrests by the number of persons in the juvenile age group. As shown
in Table 1–1, over the last five years for which such data are available (1984–
1988), the number of juvenile arrests for murder and non-negligent manslaughter has shown a steady annual increase.[3] At the same time, population
data indicate that there has been a steady annual decrease in the number of
juveniles in the United States.[4] Putting the two statistics (arrest and population data) together, it is clear that both the number of juvenile homicides and
also the rate at which juveniles kill have been increasing in recent years.

Using FBI arrest data and U.S. Census Bureau statistics, Cornell calculated the approximate rate at which juveniles in the ten- to seventeen-year-
old age range committed murder or non-negligent manslaughter over a ten-
year period from 1977–1986.[5] Cornell eliminated youngsters under ten years
of age because of the extremely low frequency with which they are arrested
for these homicide crimes. He also calculated a similar approximate rate for
adults (i.e., those age eighteen and older). His findings, displayed in Table
1–2, demonstrate that since 1984, the annual rate of juvenile homicides has
shown a small but steady annual increase, and that has generally been highly
correlated with the rate for adult homicides.

Table 1–1
Murder and Non-Negligent Manslaughter Arrests by
Age Group 1979–1988[2]

Year	Total Arrests	Number below 18	Percentage below 18	Number 18 and Older	Percentage 18 and Older
1979	18,264	1,707	9.3	16,557	90.7
1980	18,745	1,742	9.3	17,003	90.7
1981	20,432	1,858	9.1	18,574	90.9
1982	18,511	1,579	8.5	16,932	91.5
1983	18,064	1,345	7.4	16,719	92.6
1984	13,676	1,004	7.3	12,672	92.7
1985	15,777	1,311	8.3	14,466	91.7
1986	16,066	1,396	8.7	14,670	91.3
1987	16,714	1,592	9.5	15,122	90.5
1988	16,326	1,765	10.8	14,561	89.2

Table 1–2
Rates per 100,000 of Murder and Non-Negligent Manslaughter Arrests for
Juveniles and Adults 1977–1986[6]

Year	Rate of Arrests/ 100,000 Juveniles	Rate of Arrests/ 100,000 Adults
1977	4.5	10.0
1978	4.8	10.8
1979	4.8	10.3
1980	5.0	10.4
1981	5.4	11.1
1982	4.7	8.6
1983	4.1	9.7
1984	3.1	7.2
1985	4.1	8.2
1986	4.4	8.3

As Cornell observed, the rate of homicide arrests for juveniles has typically been roughly half the rate of such arrests for adults. However, for this particular decade, the correlation between the two rates was extremely high—approximately 0.81—thus "suggesting that whatever factors affect the homicide rate similarly affect adults and juveniles."[7]

Age

If homicides committed by those under eighteen are rare, those committed by younger youths are even rarer. The vast majority (generally more than 85 percent) of juveniles who kill are fifteen, sixteen, or seventeen years old.[8] Annually, for the past decade or so, less than 1 percent of those persons arrested for murder or non-negligent manslaughter have been under the age of fifteen.[9] Moreover, during this same time period, only a handful of the annual number of arrests for these crimes have involved perpetrators under the age of ten.[10] Arrest data may underestimate the number of very young children who kill, since at least some of these youngsters are probably never formally arrested. Indeed, in most jurisdictions, children under the age of seven are deemed incapable of criminal conduct.[11] Still, it seems fair to say that very few homicides are committed by children under the age of ten.

Overall, as shown in Table 1–3, the incidence of juvenile homicide seems to vary directly and positively as a function of age. As age levels rise, so do the annual number of arrests for murder and non-negligent manslaughter. Interestingly, other crimes committed by juveniles do not show nearly so clear a positive correlation between incidence and age.[12]

Although juveniles rarely kill, their commission of other crimes is not nearly so unusual. In the United States, annually, youths under the age of eighteen consistently account for about 17 percent of all reported arrests, about a third of arrests for serious property crimes (burglary, larceny-theft, motor vehicle theft, and arson), and 16–17 percent of arrests for all major

Table 1–3
Murder and Non-Negligent Manslaughter Arrests of Juveniles by
Age Group 1984–1988[13]

Year	Total Arrests	Age					
		<10	10–12	13–14	15	16	17
1984	1,004	6	25	107	156	288	422
1985	1,311	3	18	144	216	391	539
1986	1,396	7	15	134	245	443	552
1987	1,592	14	25	164	216	451	722
1988	1,765	7	27	167	273	461	830
Total	6,648	38	103	678	1,044	1,973	2,812
Percent of total		0.6	1.5	10.2	15.7	29.7	42.3

violent crimes combined (i.e., murder, forcible rape, robbery, and aggravated assault).[14] Similarly, youths under the age of fifteen account for about 5 percent of all reported arrests, 13–14 percent of arrests for serious property crimes, and just under 5 percent of arrests for all major violent crimes combined.[15] Even children below the age of ten, who almost never kill, regularly comprise about 1 percent of the annual number of arrests for all major crimes combined and just under half a percent of all arrests.[16]

Gender

Juvenile homicide, like most crimes at all ages, is much more likely to be perpetrated by males than females.[17] Just as younger juveniles rarely kill, girls of any age are extremely unlikely to commit homicide. As Table 1–4 demonstrates, at all age levels under eighteen years, the vast majority of those arrested for murder or non-negligent manslaughter are males. As Table 1–3 also shows, however, these data, while striking, are quite consistent with statistics on homicides committed by adults. On an annual basis, men consistently comprise nearly 90 percent of *all* persons arrested for murder or non-negligent homicide. Similar data also obtain for both juveniles and adults for most major crimes and many minor crimes.[18]

Race

Black youths are vastly overrepresented among those juveniles arrested for murder or non-negligent manslaughter. Only about one sixth of all Americans under the age of eighteen are Black, yet in recent years roughly half the juveniles arrested for these homicide crimes have been Black.[20] Indeed, as Table 1–5 indicates, in some recent years, Black youths have constituted the majority of those arrested for murder and non-negligent manslaughter in the under-eighteen age bracket.

Undoubtedly these figures reflect to some extent the existence of racial discrimination in the criminal justice system. There is no question that Blacks are more likely than Whites to be arrested for the crimes they commit. However, even allowing for such discrimination, there also seems to be no question that Black youths are disproportionately involved in the commission of criminal homicides. In short, Black youths are much more likely than White youths to kill.

It is also worth noting that these figures are consistent with both juvenile arrest data for other violent crimes and adult arrest data for murder and non-negligent manslaughter. Blacks are disproportionately represented not only

Table 1–4
Percentage of Murder and Non-Negligent Manslaughter Arrests by
Gender and Age 1984–1988[19]

Year	Gender	Age							
		<10	10–12	13–14	15	16	17	< 18	18 +
1984	Male	83	76	87	88	89	93	90	86
	Female	17	24	13	12	11	7	10	14
1985	Male	100	78	88	88	92	92	91	87
	Female	0	22	12	12	8	8	9	13
1986	Male	86	87	96	93	89	97	93	87
	Female	14	13	4	7	11	3	7	13
1987	Male	93	72	85	92	90	94	91	87
	Female	7	28	15	8	10	6	9	13
1988	Male	71	96	92	91	93	94	93	87
	Female	29	4	8	9	7	6	7	13

Table 1–5
Number and Percentage of Murder and Non-Negligent Manslaughter
Arrests (under Age 18) by Race 1984–1988[21]

Year		Whites[a]	Blacks[a]	Native Americans[b]	Asians[c]
1984	Number	539	454	7	4
	Percent	53.7	45.2	0.7	0.4
1985	Number	629	661	3	12
	Percent	48.2	50.7	0.2	0.9
1986	Number	689	671	13	22
	Percent	49.4	48.1	0.9	1.6
1987	Number	671	880	16	24
	Percent	42.2	55.3	1.0	1.5
1988	Number	720	997	7	23
	Percent	41.2	57.1	0.4	1.3

[a]Includes some Hispanics
[b]Includes American Indians and Alaskan Natives
[c]Includes Asians and Pacific Islanders

among juveniles arrested for murder and non-negligent manslaughter, but
also among those arrested for other major crimes of violence, including rape,
robbery, and aggravated assault.[22] Blacks are also vastly overrepresented
among adults (i.e., individuals eighteen and older) arrested for murder and
non-negligent manslaughter.[23]

Although Black youths are disproportionately represented among homicide arrestees under eighteen, the ratio of juvenile to adult murder and non-negligent manslaughter arrestees has been virtually the same for both racial groups for at least the past five years. Roughly 8 percent of the homicides committed by members of both races have been committed by persons under the age of eighteen.[24]

Ethnicity

Hispanics constitute probably the largest identified ethnic group in the United States today, yet they represent only about 8 percent of the population.[25] But as Table 1–6 demonstrates, Hispanic youths account for almost a quarter of all under-eighteen arrests for murder and non-negligent manslaughter. Hispanics are also disproportionately represented among adults arrested for these homicide crimes. In recent years, roughly 16 percent of adults arrested for murder or non-negligent manslaughter have been Hispanic.[26] Still, the over-representation of Hispanics is clearly greatest among juveniles.

Hispanics, like Blacks, are undoubtedly the victims of discrimination in the criminal justice system, and so these figures must also be interpreted with caution. Like Blacks, Hispanics are probably somewhat more likely than Whites to be arrested for homicide crimes they commit. Yet, even allowing for such discrimination, there can be little doubt that, like Black youngsters, Hispanic youths account for a disproportionate share of homicides committed by persons under the age of eighteen.

It should be noted, however, that the overrepresentation of Hispanic youths is not limited solely to homicide crimes. Like Blacks, Hispanics also

Table 1–6
Number and Percentage of Murder and Non-Negligent Manslaughter Arrests (under Age 18) by Ethnic Origin 1982–1986[27]

Year		Hispanic	Non-Hispanic
1982	Number	317	1,052
	Percent	23.2	76.8
1983	Number	244	790
	Percent	23.6	76.4
1984	Number	161	701
	Percent	18.7	81.3
1985	Number	246	898
	Percent	21.5	78.5
1986	Number	270	967
	Percent	21.8	78.2

account for a disproportionate share of the under-eighteen arrests for all major violent crimes, including rape, robbery, and aggravated assault.[28] Similarly, Hispanics account for a disproportionate share of adult arrests for these same crimes.[29]

Victim–Offender Relationship

Juvenile homicides may also be categorized statistically according to the relationship between perpetrator and victim. While much of the research to date dealing with juvenile homicide has focused on youths who kill a parent or another close family member, the fact is that only a rather small percentage of juvenile killers kill their parents or stepparents, and only a slightly larger percentage kill other family members.

In 1984, the most recent year for which United States juvenile homicide arrest data have been analyzed with regard to victim–offender relationships, data regarding these relationships were available on 787 cases.[30] As Table 1–7 indicates, only 8 percent of these youths killed parents or stepparents, and only 9 percent killed other family members. The vast majority of these youngsters killed either acquaintances or strangers.

Further analysis of these same data also demonstrate two clear and statistically significant associations: (1) between victim–offender relationship and whether the homicide was incidental to a theft offense (such as larceny, burglary, or robbery) and (2) between victim–offender relationship and whether the homicide was committed individually or by a group. Table 1–8 demonstrates the first association: in this sample intrafamilial homicides were almost never incidental to a theft offense while 6 percent of the acquaintance homicides and 58 percent of the stranger homicides occurred in the course of a theft offense.

As Table 1–9 demonstrates, when the victim was an acquaintance or stranger, the majority (53 percent) of these juvenile homicides were perpe-

Table 1–7
Number and Percentage of Juvenile Homicides by Victim–Offender Relationship 1984[31]

Relationship	Number	Percentage
Parent/stepparent	65	8.26
Other family member	74	9.40
Acquaintance	387	49.17
Stranger	261	33.17

Table 1–8
Victim–Offender Relationship and Homicide Incident to Theft[32]

| | Type of Homicide | |
Relationship	Incident to Theft	Not Incident to Theft
Parent/stepparent	1 (1.5%)	64 (98.5%)
Other family member	1 (1.4%)	73 (98.6%)
Acquaintance	14 (6.2%)	363 (93.8%)
Stranger	151 (57.9%)	110 (42.1%)

Note: X^2 = 281.47, df = 3, p < .001

Table 1–9
Victim–Offender Relationship and Number of Homicide Perpetrators[33]

| | Number of Perpetrators | |
Relationship of Victim to Identified Juvenile Perpetrator	Single Individual	Two or More Individuals
Parent/stepparent	53 (81.5%)	12 (18.5%)
Other family member	65 (87.8%)	9 (12.2%)
Acquaintance	224 (57.9%)	163 (42.1%)
Stranger	82 (31.4%)	179 (68.6%)

Note: X^2 = 109.80, df = 3, p < .001

trated by multiple offenders acting in concert. But when the victim was a family member, less than 20 percent of the homicides were committed by more than a single perpetrator.

These victim–offender data also suggest a third significant association, that between the gender of the juvenile killer and the relationship to the homicide victim. As Table 1–10 illustrates, the victims of female perpetrators were almost always family members or acquaintances, while the victims of male perpetrators were more likely to be acquaintances or strangers.

Finally, among the cases covered by these victim–offender relationship data, younger juveniles were somewhat more likely than older juveniles to have killed family members. Also Whites were somewhat more likely than non-Whites to have killed family members. Yet neither age nor race showed a statistically significant association with the relationship between victim and offender.[35]

Interestingly, however, other data appear to suggest that there are certain significant differences between victims killed by juveniles and those killed by

Table 1–10
Victim–Offender Relationship and Gender of Juvenile

Relationship	Sex of Offender	
	Male	Female
Parent/stepparent or other family member	95 (13.8%)	44 (44.0%)
Acquaintance	338 (49.2%)	49 (49.0%)
Stranger	254 (40.0%)	7 (7.0%)

Note: $X^2 = 68.65$, df = 2, p < .001

older perpetrators. For example, an analysis of homicide arrest data from New York City for the years 1973–1980 found that homicide perpetrators under the age of sixteen "disproportionately killed victims that can be considered 'soft targets,' children twelve and under and adults aged sixty and over."[36]

Circumstances of the Homicide

One final set of issues that are addressed to some extent by the available aggregate data on juvenile homicide relates to the circumstances under which these killings occur. For example, to varying degrees, these data help specify: (1) the relationship between juvenile homicides and other crimes (theft crimes generally and robbery specifically); (2) the extent to which these homicides are perpetrated by groups as opposed to individual killers; and (3) the extent to which weapons such as guns and knives are used to accomplish these homicides.

Homicide, Theft and Robbery

As illustrated in Table 1–8 above, a substantial percentage of nonfamilial juvenile homicides are committed incident to (i.e., in the course of accomplishing) some sort of theft crime. Indeed, the data reviewed there suggest that the majority (57.9 percent) of "stranger" homicides committed by juveniles (killings of persons unknown to the youthful perpetrators) were committed incident to some crime of theft.[37]

While there are a variety of theft crimes (e.g., simple larceny, robbery, burglary, etc.), robbery (the use of force or threat of force against a person to steal from him/her) is, for obvious reasons, the theft offense most likely to eventuate in homicide.[38] Interestingly, the degree to which robberies committed by juveniles eventuate in homicides appears to be almost a direct function of age.

Additional analysis of the New York City arrest data mentioned earlier found that the likelihood that a robbery would result in a homicide was strikingly and positively correlated with the age of the youngest perpetrator in the robbery.[39] Where the youngest perpetrator was twelve or thirteen, fewer than two robberies in a thousand eventuated in a homicide. Where the youngest perpetrator was fourteen, the rate was just slightly more than two killings in every one thousand robberies. But by age fifteen, the rate of killings per thousand robberies almost doubled. By age sixteen and seventeen the rate virtually tripled; and by age nineteen, the likelihood that a robbery victim would be killed was roughly seven times higher than it was when the youngest perpetrator was fourteen or younger.

These findings are, of course, entirely consistent with the earlier mentioned findings (displayed in Table 1–3) that, based upon national arrest data, the overall incidence of juvenile homicide seems to vary directly and positively as a function of age—that is, that among juveniles, as age levels rise, so does the annual number of arrests for murder and non-negligent manslaughter.[40]

Individual versus Group Killings

One of the major problems with aggregate arrest statistics is that these data fail to specify whether or not those arrested acted alone or in concert with other criminal perpetrators. For example, a gang-perpetrated killing may result in several arrests for homicide, but aggregate arrest statistics, by themselves, provide no means of determining that. This is especially troublesome when it comes to juvenile crime, since there is good reason to believe that a substantial proportion of such crime is perpetrated by two or more youths acting in concert.[41]

How many juvenile killings are committed by individual perpetrators as opposed to multiple perpetrators acting in concert? As noted earlier, available data specifying victim–offender relationship (displayed in Table 1–9) indicate that multiple-perpetrator juvenile homicides are rather rare when the homicide victim is related to a perpetrator; constitute a substantial portion (42.1 percent) of juvenile acquaintance homicides; and make up the majority (68.6 percent) of juvenile stranger homicides.[42]

Analyses of the above-mentioned juvenile arrest data from New York City provide further insights into the question of individual versus multiple-perpetrator juvenile homicides. The New York City data indicate that whether a homicide is committed individually or by a group is clearly correlated with the age of the offenders—younger perpetrators being more likely to act in concert with others.[43] From ages fourteen through sixteen, nearly half the homicides were committed by groups of juveniles; by age seventeen, group-perpetrated homicides fell to about 30 percent; and by age eighteen, only about a quarter of the killings were group perpetrated.[44]

Other data, covering all of New York State, paint a similar picture.[45] In 1987, for example, all homicides in New York State known to have been committed by youngsters under the age of twelve were committed by a single perpetrator. Among killings committed by juveniles in the thirteen to fifteen age range, 60 percent were perpetrated by multiple offenders. And among killings committed by youths sixteen to nineteen years of age, just under 50 percent were perpetrated by multiple offenders.

Weapons Used

National data regarding all arrests for murder and non-negligent manslaughter consistently indicate that firearms are used to perpetrate the majority of homicides. According to these data, firearms were used in 58 percent of homicides in 1983, 59 percent in 1984, 59 percent in 1985, 59 percent in 1986, and 59 percent in 1987.[46] It appears that a slightly lower percentage, though still a majority, of juvenile homicides are perpetrated with firearms.[47] Interestingly, though not surprisingly, gun use in juvenile homicides is lower in younger age groups and seems to increase steadily with increasing age.[48]

2
Review of the Research

Although juveniles represent only a small fraction of all homicide perpetrators, their homicidal acts are of major concern to society. Juveniles who kill challenge long-standing and widely held conceptions of childhood and adolescence and create a serious dilemma for the criminal and juvenile justice systems. The social and legal dilemmas posed by these youngsters are reflected perhaps most acutely in the continuing debate over how they should be dealt with in our system of justice: whether youngsters who kill should be tried as juveniles or as adults, and whether they should be subject to the same criminal penalties as adult killers, including capital punishment.

Not surprisingly, this debate has generated more heat than light. Ultimately, deciding how society and law should deal with homicidal youth will require answers to a number of difficult questions: Who are these youngsters who kill? Why do they kill? To what extent, if any, do they pose a continuing threat to society? And, what, if anything, can be done to rehabilitate them and reduce the magnitude of that threat?

Courts and other legal authorities are already asking—and "answering"—these questions on an ad hoc, case-by-case basis. A substantial proportion of juvenile homicide defendants are being tried as adults; many of those convicted are receiving lengthy prison sentences; and at least some juvenile killers are being sentenced to die. But a more general and systematic social and legal response to the problem has proven elusive, largely because solid empirical data on juvenile homicide are sorely lacking. A lot has been said, written, and published about juveniles who kill; but, to date, precious little has been learned.

The professional and scientific literature on children and adolescents who kill is surprisingly sparse—both in quantity and in quality. Most publications on the subject share a number of common but significant methodological shortcomings. To begin with, much if not most of this body of literature deals with juveniles who kill family members, primarily parents. As noted in chapter 1, however, juveniles who kill parents or other family members represent only a small proportion—less than 20 percent—of homicidal youth. Moreover, the little empirical research that has been directed at juveniles who kill outside the family suggests some clear differences between them and their counterparts who kill family members. These potentially important differences have undoubtedly been obscured by the fact that juvenile homicide researchers have focused to such an extent on intrafamilial homicides. While their conclusions may well be valid with regard to juveniles who kill within the family, many cannot be readily generalized to the much larger—and, in many ways, apparently different—group of juveniles who kill acquaintances and strangers.

Research on juvenile homicide has also generally been limited by problems with the samples of study. First, with few exceptions, samples have been extremely small. The bulk of empirical data on juvenile homicide comes from anecdotal case studies—reports on extremely small samples of homicidal youngsters: commonly fewer than ten, often under four, and sometimes just a single case.

The ability to generalize from these rather small samples has been further limited by selection bias. In nearly all studies, subjects have been selected on the basis of their availability to the investigators. Most of the investigators have been psychologists and psychiatrists; thus, almost all subjects have been juveniles who not only killed within the family but were referred for psychological/psychiatric evaluation/treatment. Typically, the author has been the mental health professional who evaluated and/or treated the homicidal juvenile subjects.

Moreover, for the most part, those few studies that did involve greater sample sizes and more sound sampling procedures have been plagued with methodological limitations, flaws that significantly limit any generalizations that might be drawn from their results. Virtually none of these studies have employed control or even comparison groups, and most researchers have relied upon their own, sometimes idiosyncratic, interests and theories in deciding what data to collect, how to collect it, and how to report it.

As a result of these shortcomings, it is difficult to draw reliable generalizations from these studies. Still, some data, limited though they may be, are better than no data. And despite these difficulties, it is possible at least to summarize current data and to suggest promising avenues for further research.

The vast bulk of the literature to date on juveniles who kill is directed at describing the characteristics of these youngsters and their families, their prehomicidal behavior and adjustment, and the types of homicides they commit.

Individual Characteristics

Who are the juveniles who kill? Are they emotionally disturbed, mentally ill, mentally retarded, learning disabled, neurologically impaired, or simply "normal" youngsters who commit extremely abnormal acts?

Emotional Disturbance/Mental Illness

Most of the data on juveniles who kill have been gathered in clinical settings by mental health professionals evaluating and/or treating these juveniles, a fact that is hardly surprising. Killings committed by children and adolescents are so rare and often so apparently inexplicable that there is a natural tendency to question the mental health and emotional well-being of any youngster who kills.[1] Undoubtedly, for that very reason if no other, the vast majority of youngsters charged with homicide are referred, at some point in the legal process, for psychological and/or psychiatric evaluations.

Nor is it any surprise that, like most people referred for psychological and/or psychiatric evaluations, most juveniles who kill wind up with one diagnostic label or another being applied to them. What is perhaps surprising, however, is that while there is tremendous variation in psychiatric diagnoses of juveniles who kill, the overall trend is clearly toward the less serious end of the diagnostic spectrum.

To begin with, although some juvenile killers are psychotic, it seems clear that most are not. As one clinician put it, "The behavior [may have been] 'psychotic' but the youths were not."[2] As Table 2–1 illustrates, in most of the reports specifying diagnoses, only a small fraction of the juvenile killers studied were said to be psychotic.

Even the small number of juveniles diagnosed as psychotic in these samples probably represents an exaggeration of the true incidence of psychosis among juveniles who kill. Not only are these primarily clinical samples but even among clinical samples of juveniles who kill, there appears to be a tendency on the part of some clinicians to overdiagnose psychosis. Cornell, for example, cites the example of one clinical report on three juveniles who killed.[3] All three youths (ages fifteen to seventeen), who committed brutal and senseless killings, were diagnosed as schizophrenic, despite their failure to exhibit any psychotic symptoms either before or after the killings. Cornell also observes that in some reports, clinicians appear to have erroneously diagnosed juvenile killers as psychotic based largely if not entirely upon the youth's claim of amnesia for the crime.[4] By itself, amnesia is not indicative of psychosis.[5] Indeed, claimed amnesia for the events surrounding a violent crime may well be symptomatic of malingering.[6]

In two studies, virtually all of the juvenile killers reportedly demonstrated

Table 2–1
Number and Percentage of Juvenile Killers Determined to Be Psychotic[7]

Authors and Date of Study	Number of Juveniles	Number Psychotic	Percentage Psychotic
Bender (1959)[8]	33	5	15.15
Stearns (1959)[9]	5	0	0.00
Marten (1965)[10]	2	0	0.00
Smith (1965)[11]	8	0	0.00
Hellsten & Katila (1965)[12]	5	0	0.00
Scherl & Mack (1966)[13]	3	1	33.33
Malmquist (1971)[14]	20	3	15.00
Walsh-Brennan (1974)[15]	11	0	0.00
Sendi & Blomgren (1975)[16]	10	6	60.00
King (1975)[17]	9	1	11.11
Tanay (1976)[18]	3	0	0.00
Sorrells (1977)[19]	14	0	0.00
Rosner et al. (1978)[20]	45	10	22.22
Russell (1979)[21]	24	2	8.33
Petti & Davidman (1981)[22]	9	0	0.00
Russell (1986)[23]	2	0	0.00
Cornell et al. (1987)[24]	72	5	6.94

psychotic symptoms, but the authors did not report formal diagnoses of psychosis.[25] In still another more recent study in which formal diagnoses were not reported, Lewis and her colleagues found that among fourteen juvenile killers, seven were psychotic, four had histories consistent with severe mood disorder, and three had experienced periodic episodes of paranoid ideation.[26] Seven of these subjects suffered from mental disorders manifested initially in early or middle childhood. While these findings obviously conflict with the trend observed in other studies, it must be noted that all fourteen of these subjects were persons on death row awaiting execution for crimes they committed while they were juveniles. As is discussed in greater detail in chapter 9, only a tiny fraction of juvenile killers are sentenced to die, and they generally do not seem representative of the more general population of juveniles who kill.

For the most part, juvenile killers studied by researchers to date have fallen into the diagnostic category of personality disorder, sometimes referred to as character disorder. Personality (or character) disorders are characterized by inflexible, maladaptive "patterns of perceiving, relating to, and thinking about the environment and oneself."[27] Smith, for example, reports that all eight juvenile killers he studied suffered from what he called episodic dyscontrol, a personality or character disorder characterized by a lack of control over aggressive impulses, resulting in episodic explosive outbursts.[28] None of these eight youngsters were found to be psychotic.

Among the forty-five youthful male homicide perpetrators studied by Rosner and his colleagues, "the largest number of adolescents (22) was classed within the diagnostic category of Personality Disorders."[29] Similarly, Russell found that twenty-one out of twenty-four juvenile killers had been diagnosed as character disorders.[30] And Sorrells found that among fourteen juvenile killers diagnosed, eight suffered personality disorders, while one was diagnosed as neurotic, one as unsocialized aggressive reaction, one as a multiple personality, and three as adjustment reactions.[31] In Sendi and Blomgren's study, although six of ten juveniles who killed were said to be suffering from schizophrenia, the remaining four all were diagnosed as personality disorders.[32]

Unfortunately, although personality disorders can be classified according to type (e.g., antisocial, paranoid, avoidant, dependent, etc.),[33] only one of the studies reported to date named the specific types of personality disorders suffered by the youths in their sample. Of the eight personality disordered youths in Sorrells' study, two were described as explosive personalities, two as passive-dependent personalities, and the remaining four as passive-aggressive, overcontrolled, immature, and schizoid personalities.[34]

In still other studies of homicidal juveniles, the majority have suffered no diagnosable mental disorder at all. Fiddes, for instance, found that among the thirty-seven juvenile killers she studied, only seventeen could be described as "psychologically abnormal."[35] According to Fiddes, most of the homicidal youths in her study were "chronic 'bad lads' rather than overtly psychologically disturbed ones."[36]

Similarly, Walsh-Brennan reported that only three of the eleven homicidal youngsters he studied suffered any mental disorder, and these three were found to suffer only "mild anxiety reactions."[37] More recently, Brandstadter-Palmer reported that among the twelve juvenile first degree murder defendants she studied, none had any history of mental illness.[38]

The conclusion that most juveniles who kill do not suffer from major mental disorders is supported as well by studies that, though not reporting actual diagnoses, have specified the prior mental health treatment history of the subjects. For instance, in her pioneering study of juveniles who killed, Bender reported that among thirty-three subjects she examined, none of whom were psychotic at the time of the killing, only fifteen had any prior history of psychiatric/psychological treatment.[39] Similarly, Corder and his colleagues reported that only three of the ten adolescents in their parricide sample had any prior psychiatric history.[40] And, more recently, Cornell and his associates reported that among their sample of seventy-two juvenile killers, only sixteen had prior outpatient psychiatric treatment and only eleven had previously received psychiatric treatment on an inpatient basis.[41]

Mental Retardation

Hays and his colleagues found that a sample of twenty-five juveniles who killed had significantly lower IQs than a similar sample of thirty-nine juvenile status offenders.[42] The homicidal youths had a mean full scale IQ of 80, while the status offenders had a mean full scale IQ of 87.1. In terms of mean IQs, both groups were below average in intelligence, but well above the IQ cut-off for mental retardation. These findings are consistent with IQ data reported in other studies of juveniles who killed. Petti and Davidman, for example, found that among the nine homicidal youngsters they studied, "full scale IQs ranged from 73 to 106 with a mean and median of 89."[43] Similarly, Solway and colleagues report that among eighteen juvenile killers in their study, the mean full scale IQ was 82 and the range was 59 to 107.[44] Finally, Lewis and associates, who recently tested fourteen death row inmates convicted of murders committed while juveniles, found that while only one of these convicts was mentally retarded (full scale IQ = 64), only two of the fourteen had IQs above 90.[45]

These studies suggest that juveniles who kill tend to be below normal in intellect, although generally not mentally retarded. Other studies report finding generally normal or above normal intelligence among samples of juveniles who killed. In Bender's early study, for example, she found that only two out of thirty-three juvenile killers she examined were mentally retarded; the vast majority had IQs in the normal or above normal range.[46] In another early study, Patterson found that among six juvenile killers he studied, one was mentally retarded (IQ = 67), one dull (IQ = 80), and the remaining four average or above average (IQs ranging from 103 to 120).[47] Later, King reported that among the nine juvenile killers in his sample, IQ measurements fell into the 92 to 104 range.[48] Finally, in a much more recent study, Brandstadter-Palmer found that among the twelve juvenile homicide defendants she studied, IQs ranged from 75 to 125 with a mean of 100.[49] Seven of these twelve youngsters had IQs above 100.

Learning Disabilities

Just as the research finds a variety of intellectual levels among juvenile killers, so too does it find significant variation in terms of these youngsters' academic achievement. Many of the juvenile killers described in case studies were reported to have been experiencing significant academic problems at the time they killed, despite their generally average or better intellectual capacities.[50] Other general reports have also emphasized the correlation between cognitive and language deficits and juvenile homicide.[51]

In their 1988 study of juvenile killers on death row, Lewis and her co-workers found that ten out of fourteen had major learning problems, that only three were reading at grade level, and that three had never even learned to read until they were incarcerated on death row.[52] For the most part, these findings are supported by other studies of broader groups of juveniles who kill.

In the earliest studies, Patterson found that three of six juvenile killers had learning problems,[53] and Bender found that seventeen of thirty-three homicidal juveniles had significant problems with reading.[54] More recently, Sendi and Blomgren reported poor academic performance among five of ten juvenile killers,[55] and King reported that every one of the nine homicidal youths in his sample "was most severely retarded in reading and drastically stunted in language skills."[56] Brandstadter-Palmer found that among those old enough to quit school, all but one of the juvenile murder defendants in her study had done so at some point between grades seven and eleven.[57]

Neurological Impairment

In the general population of juveniles, mental retardation and learning difficulties may or may not be associated with or caused by neurological impairment. Although this appears true for juvenile killers as well, it has long been acknowledged that juveniles who kill often do suffer from neurological defects. For example, three decades ago Bender reported that among fifteen juvenile killers tested, ten had abnormal electroencephalogram (EEG) tracings.[58] Later, Woods reported two cases in which homicidal youths were found to exhibit a particular EEG dysrhythmia—"6- and 10-per-second positive spiking"—which he claimed was associated with juvenile homicidal behavior.[59] And in the early 1970s, Kido reported that five of eleven juveniles charged with murder were found to have abnormal EEG patterns.[60]

More recently, Lewis and her colleagues have documented a similarly striking prevalence of neurological impairment in two groups of juvenile killers, one general in nature and the other consisting solely of those sentenced to death. Among the more general group, Lewis et al. obtained neurological information on eight of twenty-four homicidal youths:

> [T]hree had histories of grand mal seizures and abnormal EEGs, one was macrocephalic and had an abnormal EEG, and three others had demonstrable lapses of fully conscious contact with reality . . . and a variety of psychomotor epileptic symptoms. . . . Of note, six had received severe head injuries in childhood . . . resulting in loss of consciousness.[61]

Among the death row group, the findings were even more striking. Lewis and her associates found that all fourteen of these subjects had histories and/or symptoms consistent with brain damage.[62] In fact, eight had experienced head injuries "severe enough to result in hospitalization and/or indention of the cranium"[63] and nine had "serious" documented neurological abnormalities, including focal brain injury, abnormal head circumference, abnormal reflexes, seizure disorders, and abnormal EEG findings.

On the other hand, results of other studies have been more equivocal. Numerous case studies have documented juvenile killers with no apparent neurological impairment.[64] Similarly, several more systematic investigations have found very little in the way of neurological impairment in groups of juvenile killers. For example, Petti and Davidman found evidence of brain damage in only one of eleven homicidal school-age children;[65] Walsh-Brennan reported that none of ten juvenile killers he studied suffered epileptic symptoms;[66] and Sendi and Blomgren reported that only 20 percent of the juvenile killers they studied demonstrated abnormal EEGs.[67]

It should also be noted that whether or not a given juvenile killer suffers from neurological dysfunction may not be ascertainable from published clinical accounts of his or her case. Restifo and Lewis, for example, discovered that the same case—that of a paperboy in his early teens who beat, stabbed, and strangled a female customer for no apparent reason—was reported three different times by three different clinicians.[68] In the first clinician's report, the boy was described as having been born after an especially difficult labor, having suffered a malformation of the head, having suffered anoxia from carbon monoxide at age five, and later having been knocked unconscious when struck between the eyes with a baseball—all suggesting at least the possibility of neurological damage and/or dysfunction.[69] Yet neither the second nor the third report made any mention of such trauma.[70]

Family Characteristics

The research and clinical literature on juveniles who kill frequently describes the families of these youths as broken, disturbed, neglectful, and abusive. Most of these studies deal with juveniles who killed family members, primarily parents, and who were also referred for psychological/psychiatric evaluation and/or treatment; so there is undoubtedly some selection bias at work here, as noted earlier. Still, it seems clear that many juveniles who kill do come from broken families in which one or both parents are disturbed, neglectful, and/or abusive

Broken Families

Although many youngsters now grow up in homes broken by parental separation and/or divorce, the percentage of such youths seems much greater among those who kill—at least among juvenile killers who are the subjects of published research and case studies. Moreover, this trend has been observed consistently for nearly half a century. For example, as early as 1942, Patterson reported that five out of six juvenile killers he studied came from broken homes marked by serious marital disturbances.[71]

Four decades later, Petti and Davidman found broken homes among seven of nine homicidal youths they studied.[72] Similarly, Rosner et al. reported that thirty-three of the forty-five juvenile killers in their study were from broken homes.[73] Among the ten homicidal youths described by McCarthy, nine had been deserted by at least one parent.[74] Sorrells found that only eight out of thirty-one homicidal juveniles in his sample "were living with both natural parents at the time of the homicide."[75] And, most recently, Brandstadter-Palmer found that among the twelve juvenile murder defendants in her study, only one was living in an intact family.[76]

These results have been consistently supported by a number of case studies in which the homicidal youngsters described lived in families broken by divorce or parental separation.[77] Two multi-subject studies with findings contrary to this trend are those reported by King and Fiddes. Of the nine homicidal youths in King's sample, "most homes were intact at the time of the homicide."[78] Fiddes reported that twenty-two of the thirty-seven homicidal youngsters she studied were from intact families; even so, more than 40 percent came from broken homes.[79]

Parental Psychopathology

Much of the research and clinical literature on juveniles who kill suggest that many of these youngsters have parents who are alcoholic and/or mentally ill. Most recently, in their study of fourteen juvenile killers sentenced to die, Lewis et al. found that nine of these youngsters had at least one parent who was an alcoholic, was mentally ill, and/or had been hospitalized for psychiatric treatment.[80]

Earlier studies of more general groups of homicidal juveniles have reached similar results. For example, among the parents of nine juvenile killers studied by Petti and Davidman, six mothers and three fathers had histories of psychiatric treatment.[81] Among the thirty homicidal youths studied by Corder et al., nineteen had at least one parent who suffered from alcoholism or another mental illness.[82] Among thirty-one homicidal juveniles studied by Sorrells, five had alcoholic fathers, five had alcoholic mothers, nine had fathers who were described as "emotionally erratic," and "ten had mothers who were probably disturbed."[83] And among the parents of twenty-one homicidally aggressive children studied by Lewis et al. in an earlier investigation, 52 percent of the fathers and 33 percent of the mothers were alcoholic, 33 percent of the fathers were "known to the courts or police," and 43 percent of the mothers had been hospitalized for psychiatric treatment.[84] Parental psychopathology such as alcoholism and mental illness has also been detailed in many other case reports of juveniles who killed.[85]

Abuse and Neglect

Probably the single most consistent finding in the research on juvenile homicide to date is that children and adolescents who kill, especially those who kill family members, have generally witnessed and/or been directly victimized by domestic violence.

The most common form of domestic violence witnessed by juveniles who kill appears to be spouse abuse—the use of physical violence by one parent against another. For example, Lewis and her colleagues, who studied twenty-one homicidal children, reported that "in 62 percent of the households of homicidal children, the fathers had been physically abusive to the mothers, compared with only 13 percent of nonhomicidal children."[86] Describing the home lives of the nine homicidal youngsters in his sample, King reported that "Family situations were full of turmoil. Usually there were brutal fights between the parents."[87] These findings are supported by many case studies in which children and adolescents who killed have been described as growing up in families marked by spouse abuse.[88]

The results of at least one study, however, seem to indicate that witnessing the abuse of one parent by another is more likely to be associated with parricide than with other forms of juvenile homicide. Corder and his co-workers compared three matched samples of juveniles who killed, ten who killed parents, ten who killed relatives or close acquaintances, and ten who killed strangers.[89] In the parental homicide or parricide group, five of ten juvenile killers had come from families in which there was chronic physical abuse of the mother by the father. In both the stranger homicide group and the relative/acquaintance group, none of the ten juvenile perpetrators had come from homes in which the father physically abused the mother.

The notion that witnessing spouse abuse in the family is more likely to be associated with parricide also receives support from the clinical literature on juvenile homicide. Several case studies have described juveniles who killed their fathers after witnessing incidents of spouse abuse.[90] Indeed, there are several reports of cases in which juveniles have apparently killed an abusive parent after the other parent consciously or unconsciously encouraged the youngster to do so.[91]

Although witnessing spouse abuse is common among juveniles who kill, being personally victimized by child abuse seems even more common. The literature is replete with statistical and anecdotal evidence regarding the extremely high incidence of child abuse victimization among juveniles who kill. For example, among the fourteen juvenile death row inmates studied by

Lewis and her colleagues, twelve had been "brutally" abused physically.[92] Earlier, looking at a more general sample of homicidally aggressive children, Lewis et al. found that 55 percent of the twenty-one children they studied had been physically abused.[93]

Similarly high rates of child abuse victimization have also been observed in other multi-subject studies of juvenile killers. For example, Sendi and Blomgren reported that among ten juveniles who committed homicide, six had been subjected to what these authors called "parental brutality."[94] Among a control group of ten nonhomicidal youngsters hospitalized for psychiatric treatment, they found only one juvenile who had been subjected to such abuse by parents. King reported that most of the nine homicidal juveniles he studied had been physically abused by their parents: "The children were subject to beatings. The sample youth most often was singled out for abuse."[95]

Like witnessing spouse abuse, being victimized by child abuse may well be more associated with parricide than with any other kind of juvenile homicide. Among the juvenile killers studied by Corder et al., 70 percent of those who killed parents had been victims of physical child abuse, but only 30 percent of those who killed family members or acquaintances and 20 percent of those who killed strangers had been so victimized.[96] The correlation between child abuse and juvenile homicidal behavior has also been repeatedly and strikingly documented in a host of published case studies.[97]

While most of the child abuse reported in the literature on juvenile homicide is physical abuse, several accounts also suggest that many juveniles who kill have also been abused sexually. For example, in the recent death row study by Lewis and associates, five of fourteen juveniles who killed had previously been sodomized by older family members.[98] Earlier, Sendi and Blomgren found that while four of ten adolescent killers had been "seduced" by a parent, none of the ten youngsters in a control group had experienced such abuse.[99]

The findings of Corder and colleagues suggest that sexual victimization by a parent may also be more likely found in cases where the child-victim has killed his/her parent. Corder et al. found evidence of "sexual overstimulation by parent" among four of ten youths who killed parents, but none of ten who killed relatives and acquaintances, and none of ten who killed strangers.[100]

Prehomicidal Behavior and Adjustment

As noted earlier, available data suggest that most juveniles who kill are not seriously disturbed psychologically. Still, the data also suggest that many if not most of these juveniles have exhibited some form of noticeably deviant behavior prior to committing homicide. The most common forms of such behavior found among juveniles who kill are antisocial conduct, substance abuse, truancy, running away from home, enuresis, and problems relating to peers.

Antisocial Conduct

Among those studied to date, many if not most juveniles who kill have prehomicidal histories of antisocial behavior, reflected in records of arrests and criminal convictions. For example, among the thirty-seven juvenile killers studied by Fiddes, twenty-nine had prior criminal convictions: twelve had two or three convictions and the rest between four and eight convictions.[101] Looking at arrests rather than convictions, Rosner and his colleagues found that thirty-one of forty-five juvenile killers studied had been arrested at some time prior to the homicide.[102] Indeed, the mean number of arrests among this group of homicidal youths was 3.75. Sorrells reported that among thirty-one homicidal youths he studied twenty-five had committed prior offenses, six had one or two prior offenses, and nineteen had between three and twenty-six.[103] Sixteen of these youths had previously committed personal injury offenses and thirteen had been incarcerated.

More recently, Cornell et al. reported that among the seventy-two juvenile killers they studied, thirty-one had no prior arrests, fifteen had one prior arrest, twelve had two prior arrests, and fourteen had three or more prior arrests.[104] They also found that youths in this homicidal group had significantly less serious prior criminal records than did those in a comparison group of nonhomicidal youths charged with only larceny offenses.[105] At about the same time, Rowley reported that among the sixty-eight juvenile killers in his sample for whom criminal records were available, just a little more than one quarter (26.5 percent) had no prior court contacts (delinquency or status offense charges), 20.6 percent had one prior contact, 33.8 percent had two to four prior contacts, and 19.1 percent had five or more court contacts.[106] And Brandstadter-Palmer found that among the twelve juvenile murder defendants in her sample three had multiple previous arrests including felonies, one had a prior arrest for "night prowling," another had an earlier arrest for aggravated assault, and seven had no histories of arrest.[107]

Some studies have explored prehomicidal antisocial behavior more generally. McCarthy, for example, reported that nine of the ten juvenile killers in his study had extensive histories of fighting and other antisocial behavior prior to killing.[108] Other studies, however, have found little or no incidence of prior antisocial behavior among juveniles who killed. For example, Malmquist reported that none of the twenty homicidal youths in his study had engaged in prior crimes of personal violence.[109] Walsh-Brennan reported that only two of the eleven juvenile killers he studied had even minor prior criminal records.[110] And Patterson reported finding very little in the way of prior delinquency of any kind among the six juvenile killers he studied.[111]

Still other researchers have found major differences in the incidence of prior antisocial behavior depending upon the nature of the youthful homicide perpetrator or the relationship between the perpetrator and homicide victim. Zenoff and Zients divided their youthful homicidal subjects into three sub-types: sexual-identity conflict killers (relatively normal youngsters with sexual identity problems that seemed related to the homicide); nonempathic killers (essentially self-centered, impulsive youngsters with cognitive deficits); and innocent killers (juveniles who killed accidentally or in self-defense).[112] Of the six juvenile killers in the sexual-identity conflict group, none had prior court records for violent offenses and only two had referrals for property offenses. Only one of the innocent killers had any history of assaultive behavior. But all seven youthful killers in the nonempathic group had histories of both assaultive behavior and numerous property offenses.

Corder and associates, who divided their homicidal subjects on the basis of victim–offender relationship, found histories of aggressive behavior in all ten juveniles who killed strangers, in six of ten who killed acquaintances or relatives, but in only three of ten who killed parents. Similarly, Corder and colleagues found that nine of ten youngsters who killed strangers, five of ten who killed acquaintances or relatives, and one of ten who killed parents had previously been jailed or otherwise institutionalized for criminal acts.[113]

Substance Abuse

Criminological research in general indicates that there is a significant if not causal relationship between substance abuse and criminal activity, especially violent crime. Surprisingly few studies of juvenile killers have examined this relationship, but those that have provide rather striking results. In the earliest published investigation exploring the relationship between substance abuse and juvenile homicide, Malmquist found that five of twenty juvenile killers had been abusing barbiturates, amphetamines, psychotomimetics, marijuana, and/or psychedelic drugs prior to committing homicide.[114] After discussing these findings, Malmquist casually predicted that "[t]he impact of drugs on a homicidal act ... is a situation that will be seen with increasing frequency."[115]

Malmquist's prediction seems to have been borne out in two more recent studies. In one, five years later, Corder and co-workers reported that while almost none of the thirty adolescent killers they studied had been intoxicated at the time of their homicidal acts, six of these youngsters did have histories of alcohol and/or drug abuse.[116] Interestingly, however, five of these six substance abusers had killed strangers, none had killed acquaintances or nonparental relatives, and only one had killed a parent. Somewhat earlier, Sorrells had reported that eight of the thirty-one homicidal youths in his study had been under the influence of alcohol and/or other mind-altering drugs at the time of the homicide.[117]

More recently, Cornell and associates reported that thirty-eight of the seventy-two homicidal youths they studied had killed while intoxicated.[118] Moreover, they reported finding no significant difference in "intoxication status" among three groups: youths who killed family members, those who killed "familiar persons," and those who killed strangers.[119]

Cornell and his colleagues also reported finding no significant differences in frequency of drug and alcohol abuse (none, occasional, and regular/heavy) between their group of seventy-two juveniles who killed and a comparison group of thirty-five juveniles who committed nonviolent larcenies.[120] Still, among the youths in the homicide group, twenty-four were regular or heavy alcohol users, and twenty-nine were regular or heavy drug users. Only nineteen of the homicidal youths did not use alcohol and only fifteen did not use drugs. Similarly noteworthy data have also been reported by Brandstadter-Palmer, who recently found that two thirds of the dozen juvenile murder defendants in her sample had histories of substance abuse.[121]

Truancy and Running Away

Truancy and running away from home, two often-related phenomena, are frequently reported behaviors among juveniles who kill. Truancy was emphasized in a number of early reports on juveniles who killed.[122] More recently, while not examining truancy per se, Cornell et al. reported that thirty-five of the seventy-two homicidal juveniles in their study had either dropped out or been expelled from high school.[123] By the same token, however, sixty-six of one hundred juveniles in their "nonviolent larceny" comparison group had dropped out or been expelled from school.[124] Rowley's recent data are strikingly similar: though all were below the legal age for dropping out of school, 43.1 percent of the youths in his homicidal sample and 62.7 percent of those in his nonhomicidal/violent felony sample were not attending school at the time of their offenses.[125]

Not surprisingly, in this context, running away from home has been reported almost exclusively as a behavior engaged in by juveniles who eventually killed one of their parents.[126]

Enuresis

Violence researchers have long regarded childhood enuresis—"the repeated involuntary or intentional voiding of urine during the day or at night into bed or clothes, after an age at which continence is expected"[127]—as one of the more powerful predictors of later violence. Specifically, a great deal of scholarly, clinical, and empirical attention has been devoted to the so-called triad of enuresis, fire setting, and cruelty to animals, symptoms that often seem to appear conjointly among children who later engage in violent behavior.[128] Neither fire setting nor cruelty to animals has received much attention in the literature on juveniles who kill, but the same cannot be said about enuresis.

For nearly three decades, clinicians and researchers have been fascinated with the apparent correlation between enuresis and juvenile homicide. In a 1961 article entitled "Enuresis in Murderous Aggressive Children and Adolescents," Michaels set the theoretical stage for much of the later interest in this relationship.[129] "[P]ersistently enuretic" individuals, Michaels suggested, "cannot hold their tensions, are impatient, and are impelled to act. They feel the urgency of the moment psychologically, as at an earlier date they could not hold their urine."[130]

In several studies, substantial proportions of the juvenile killers studied were suffering or had suffered from enuresis. Five of the eight homicidally aggressive boys described by Easson and Steinhilber were or had been enuretic.[131] Both "murderous" six-year-olds described by Tooley were fire setters and one was enuretic.[132] Bernstein has described a homicidal eight-year-old boy who was enuretic.[133] One of two girls who killed, described by Russell, was a sixteen-year-old who was encopretic and had been enuretic until the age of fourteen.[134]

In addition to these reports, Lewis et al. found that more than a third of the twenty-one homicidally aggressive children in their sample were enuretic, as compared to 21 percent of a nonhomicidal comparison group who had also been committed to a child psychiatry inpatient service.[135] Sendi and Blomgren reported finding histories of enuresis among three of ten homicidal adolescents, three of ten adolescents who threatened homicide, and two of ten adolescents who neither committed nor threatened homicide but who were hospitalized for psychiatric treatment.[136]

Problems Relating to Peers

Finally, a number of clinicians and researchers have pointed to the problems that juvenile killers have had relating to their peers. Marten, for example, described two sixteen-year-old killers, each of whom was regarded as "good" and "obedient" by adults but had essentially no peer relations.[137] Similarly, Zenoff and Zients described their six teenage "sexual-identity conflict" murderers as able "to relate meaningfully to other people" but demonstrating traits of "passivity and compliance" which "lead their peers to reject them."[138] More recently, Rowley reported that 55.7 percent of the juvenile killers in his sample were described by state youth officials as having "abnormal" peer relations.[139] Interestingly, however, Rowley reported essentially the same finding for the juveniles in his nonhomicidal/violent felony sample: 61.9 percent were described as having "abnormal" peer relations.[140]

The findings of Corder and co-workers suggest that juveniles who commit parricide may be more likely than other juvenile killers to have demonstrated difficulties relating to their peers. Corder and his colleagues found an absence of peer relations among seven of ten juveniles who killed their parents, three who killed a relative or close acquaintance, and three who killed a stranger.[141]

Types of Homicides

As noted earlier, several researchers have specifically attempted to categorize and compare juveniles who kill on the basis of the type of homicide committed.[142] Others, while not specifying types of homicide per se, provide data that can be categorized in a similar fashion. Specifically, these data make it possible to categorize these juvenile homicides with regard to the following factors: victim–offender relationship; means of homicide; motivation for the killing; and the presence or absence of accomplices.

Victim–Offender Relationship

As indicated in chapter 1, most juvenile killers kill acquaintances or strangers, not members of their own families. Many studies fail to specify the relationship of the juvenile killer to his/her victim, but this pattern in victim–offender relationship is reflected in at least some studies. For example, among the seventy-two juvenile killers studied by Cornell and his colleagues, twenty-three killed strangers, thirty-four killed acquaintances or friends, and fifteen killed family members.[143]

Six of ten juvenile killers in Sendi and Blomgren's investigation killed acquaintances or strangers while four killed family members.[144] Six of the twenty-nine homicidal youths studied by Cormier and Markus killed parents while the other twenty-three killed strangers or acquaintances.[145] Nine of the sixteen juvenile killers described by Russell killed family members (three matricides, three patricides, two sororicides, and one fratricide) while seven killed persons unrelated to them.[146] Eight of eighteen juvenile homicides reported by Solway et al. involved victims within the family.[147] And twenty-four of thirty-seven juvenile killers studied by Fiddes killed persons they did not know.[148]

In many other studies and reports, however, most of the juvenile killers have killed members of their own families. For example, Patterson's early report described six cases, four of which involved juveniles killing either a parent or (in one case) a foster parent.[149] In Hellsten and Katila's sample of six homicidal youths, four killed parents.[150] All three homicides described by Duncan and Duncan involved juveniles killing their parents.[151] Similarly, all three cases described by Scherl and Mack[152] and all three discussed by Tanay[153] were parricides. Numerous other reports and case studies have also emphasized or been devoted exclusively to homicides within the family.[154]

Means of Homicide

In many published accounts of juvenile homicide, the means of homicide is either not reported or referred to only in passing. In other studies and reports, however, the ways in which the homicides were perpetrated are described explicitly or aggregated according to type of weapon, if any.

Most of the killings described in the published literature on juvenile homicide were perpetrated with guns, knives, or the killer's bare hands, although occasionally other objects have reportedly been used. Perhaps the most consistent and striking finding with regard to means of homicide is the extent to which juveniles who kill do so with guns. For example, Cornell et al. recently reported that one third of the seventy-two juveniles they studied had killed with guns.[155] Similarly, one third of the eighteen juvenile homicides studied by Solway and colleagues were accomplished with guns.[156] Among the ten juvenile homicides reported by Sendi and Blomgren, six were committed with guns.[157] And all four of the juvenile killers described in detail by Malmquist killed with guns.[158]

There is reason to believe, however, that choice of weapon may be related to victim–offender relationship or to the degree of planning in killings committed by juveniles. Cornell et al. found significant differences in weapon use among juveniles who killed, depending upon victim–offender relationship: "Family members were most often murdered by an adolescent with a gun, while familiar persons were most often murdered with a knife, and strangers were most often murdered without the use of a weapon."[159]

Earlier, Solway and colleagues reported that all eight intrafamilial killings in their sample of eighteen juvenile homicides were impulsive and that seven of these eight were committed with knives.[160] All four (out of eighteen) killings described as planned homicides were carried out with guns. The remaining six killings were all incidental to the commission of other crimes and were accomplished with guns, knives, and other instruments.

Motivation

Many juvenile homicides appear motiveless or at least to have what Stearns called "obscure motivation."[161] In Sorrells's study of thirty-one homicidal youths, for instance, eight victims were killed "with no apparent motive."[162]

In other cases, however, the juvenile killer's motive seemed reasonably apparent, though not always understandable.

For example, many if not most of the parricides described in the literature seem rooted in the juvenile's desire for revenge against and/or escape from a parent who is (or at least is perceived by the youth to be) abusive. Examples include: a fourteen-year-old boy who shot and killed his "sadistic, sexually abusive father";[163] three brothers who "formed a conspiracy to kill their father in revenge for his brutality to the family";[164] a seventeen-year-old boy who had been "restricted almost consistently to his room for three to four years prior to shooting his mother";[165] and "an adolescent who murdered an abusive father after years of being physically abused and witnessing the abuse of other family members."[166]

Some parricides also appear motivated not only by a desire for revenge or personal escape from an abusive situation but also by some desire to protect and/or please a parent. For example, Patterson described a fourteen-year-old boy who shot and killed his father who had abused the boy's mother.[167] Malmquist told of a fifteen-year-old boy who shot and killed his stepfather after the boy's mother, who had just been abused by the stepfather, handed the boy a pistol and said, "I know you're big enough to protect me now."[168] And Hellsten and Katila described the case of a fourteen-year-old boy who "conspired with his mother's lover to kill his father and assisted in the killing by striking his father a blow on the head."[169]

Killings of other family members generally seem less clearly motivated. Examples from the literature include a fifteen-year-old who beat, choked, stabbed to death, and sexually mutilated a cousin who "nagg[ed] him about his dirty shirt";[170] a fifteen-year-old boy who accidentally saw his thirteen-year-old sister undressed, impulsively tried to rape her, and later shot her to death while she was sleeping;[171] an eleven-year-old who shot and killed his sister "in a quarrel over a few pennies";[172] a fourteen-year-old boy who deliberately shot and killed his sister apparently because "he was jealous of her for the father's affection";[173] and a paranoid youth who "stabbed his younger brother with a knife, believing that he was carrying out a religious commandment to kill the Antichrist."[174]

Killings outside the family also appear to have various motivations. Killings of acquaintances seem most commonly to be related to some immediate interpersonal conflict or to be incidental to the commission of other crimes, such as burglary or rape.[175] Killings of strangers generally seem to occur in the course of committing other crimes, such as burglary, robbery, and rape, but often have no apparent motive.[176]

3
Intrafamilial Homicides

Intrafamilial homicide is neither rare nor historically unique. Members of the nuclear family have been killing each other from times immemorial.[1]

As noted in the preceding chapters, while much of the literature on juveniles who kill is devoted to youngsters who kill their parents or other family members, it appears that the vast majority of juvenile killers kill outside their own families. The best available data suggest that less than 20 percent of the victims of juvenile homicides are members of the immediate family of the youthful perpetrator. These data also indicate that among intrafamilial homicides, the percentage of parental victims is slightly lower than the percentage of other family member victims.[2] To put it another way, juveniles who kill within the family are somewhat more likely to kill relatives other than parents.

If not for the overemphasis placed upon intrafamilial homicides in the juvenile homicide literature, these figures would not be surprising. In recent years it appears that in the United States, in cases where the relationship between victim and perpetrator is known, fewer than a quarter of all homicides have been intrafamilial.[3]

Though relatively infrequent, intrafamilial homicides committed by juveniles are especially intriguing and troubling. In many ways, taking the life of one's own kin (whether mother, father, brother, or sister)—especially when done by a child or adolescent—seems the most dreadful of crimes. Yet in just as many ways, if not more, intrafamilial homicides—especially those in which juveniles kill their parents—are perhaps the most understandable of all killings

Parricide

Parricide, the killing of one's parent, may take one of three forms: patricide, matricide, or both. The true incidence of parricide is unknown, but one recent estimate suggests that about 2 percent of all homicides in the United States are parricides.[4] FBI data consistently suggest that among those arrested for murder or non-negligent homicide, less than 1 percent have killed their fathers and a slightly lower percentage have killed their mothers.[5] Unfortunately, these data are for arrestees of all ages, so there is no way to say with any certainty how many parricides are committed by juveniles. Also undetermined is how many of those arrested for murder have killed both mother and father.

What little systematic research there is on the subject of parricide suggests that both matricide and patricide "are virtually always carried out by sons."[6] But, as is discussed in some detail below, there are a number of recent cases in which daughters have killed mothers and/or fathers.

Those few professionals who have researched and written about juvenile parricide emphasize a common theme: youngsters who kill a parent have generally been severely victimized by that parent. For example, Sadoff concludes that "a bizarre neurotic relationship exists between the victim and his assassin in which the parent-victim mistreats the child excessively and pushes him to the point of explosive violence."[7]

Similarly, Tanay emphasizes that parricide may be adaptive and often "has a large element of self-preservation."[8] As Tanay views parricide, it is generally a reaction to parental cruelty and abuse, "a last resort effort to protect the psychic integrity of the perpetrator threatened with psychic disintegration" by the behavior of a sadistic parent.[9] Elsewhere, Tanay has described many parricides as "family integrating experience[s]."[10] In defense of these conclusions, Tanay observed that:

> The statement that a parent killing may be adaptive has a blasphemous quality. In a number of cases such a conclusion has forced itself upon me, not only by the history that preceded the killing but also by the consequences which the slaying had upon the life of the perpetrator and the entire family.[11]

More recently, echoing both Sadoff and Tanay, Mones and Morris have concluded that parricide is most often a response to long-standing child abuse. As Mones has written, "[T]he child who kills his/her abusive parent is taking that action which is most likely (in the child's perception) to prevent him/herself from being further abused. The act is one of self-preservation."[12] Mones also emphasizes that youths who kill their parents tend to "fall into a rather unique category of delinquency."[13] These youths, he notes, rarely have any history of delinquency and "do not present the characteristics of either the classic status offender or the classic violently aggressive delinquent."[14]

Similarly, Morris concludes that most youngsters who kill their parents are "abused children [who] killed because they believed, after repeated beatings and threats, that they were in mortal danger."[15]

Patricide

In recent years, the subject of patricide has been brought into the public spotlight by several widely publicized and very different cases—the cases of Deborah and Richard Jahnke, Jr., in Wyoming, Cheryl Pierson in New York, and Sociz Junatov and Robert Lee Moody in California. All of these cases appear to validate the theories and observations of Tanay, Sadoff, and Mones.

For years, Richard Jahnke, Sr., epitomized Tanay's description of the typical victim of parricide: He "was a sadistic person who tortured the entire family [who] lived in dread of [him], incapable of normal family life."[16] Specifically, Mr. Jahnke repeatedly and brutally beat his wife and children (Deborah and Richard, Jr.) and sexually abused his daughter, sometimes in the presence of her brother.[17] Although Richard, Jr., sought help from both his mother and the authorities, nothing was ever done to stop his father's abuse.[18]

Finally, in November 1982, after being abused by his father for some fourteen years, sixteen-year-old Richard Jahnke, Jr.—with the help of his eighteen-year-old sister Deborah—ambushed Richard Jahnke, Sr., in his driveway and shot and killed him with one of his own guns.[19] Richard and Deborah were convicted and sentenced to terms in prison; however, their cases received nationwide publicity and eventually both youngsters had their sentences commuted by the Governor of Wyoming.[20]

More recently, the nation's attention was captured by an unusual case of parricide on Long Island in New York. By her own admission, sixteen-year-old Cheryl Pierson, a popular high school cheerleader, promised to give a seventeen-year-old classmate, Sean Pica, $1,000 if Pica would kill her father.[21] Although it seemed "like a game" to Cheryl, Sean bought a rifle and then ambushed James Pierson outside his home at six o'clock in the morning, fired five shots into Mr. Pierson, and killed him.[22]

Sean Pica pleaded guilty to manslaughter and was sentenced to eight to twenty-four years in prison after the prosecutor told the judge that Pica was a "cold blooded murderer" who had killed Mr. Pierson "out of sheer greed."[23] Cheryl Pierson, on the other hand, pleaded guilty to the same offense, and received a sentence that allowed her to be released from jail after serving only 106 days.[24]

Why? When Cheryl was about twelve, during what turned out to be her mother's fatal illness, her father began sexually abusing her. Cheryl's mother died and the sexual abuse, including intercourse, continued on a regular basis, coupled with occasional physical abuse as well.[25] At the time Cheryl sought a hired killer, her younger sister was just about to turn twelve years old, and Cheryl feared that her father would begin abusing her, too.[26]

Eighteen-year-old Sociz "Johnny" Junatov was charged with attempted murder after trying twice to kill his father.[27] First, a drifter—hired by Johnny for $3,000—shot the father twice in the stomach but failed to kill him. Then, the drifter's girlfriend was enlisted to kill the father. Dressed in a nurse's uniform, she entered the father's hospital room and injected him with a syringe full of battery acid. When that attempt failed, Johnny was arrested when an undercover police officer, acting on a tip, received a $5,000 offer from Johnny to kill his father.

Johnny freely admitted his role in the conspiracy to have his father killed, but claimed—during a trial in which he was acquitted—that he believed he had to kill his father or be killed by him. He said that when he was twelve his father abused him by tightening a dog leash around his neck. He also said his father forced him to quit school at age fourteen to work in the family restaurant eighteen hours a day. Finally, Johnny said that when he resisted and tried to run away, his father stripped and beat him in front of neighbors and then kept him in chains in order to keep him from running away again.[28]

Another eighteen-year-old California youth, Robert Lee Moody, responded to years of abuse by trying to kill his father. Unlike Johnny Junatov, he succeeded. After fatally wounding his father with three shotgun blasts, he was convicted but given a four-year suspended prison sentence (with five years probation and an order to spend two years abroad working as a Christian missionary) by a judge who called Robert's dead father the "scum of the earth."[29]

During the four-day bench trial, the judge heard evidence that Robert's father had terrorized his family for years. According to the evidence, he had encouraged Robert to take illegal drugs and watch pornographic movies, raped two of Robert's sisters, fondled another of Robert's sisters, and forced Robert's mother to become a prostitute to help pay for a boat he wanted. The judge also heard evidence that the shooting took place a few hours after Robert had witnessed his father beating his mother.

Although the scenario of abuse followed by homicide is a common one among patricide cases, not all juveniles who kill their fathers elicit the kind of sympathy Cheryl Pierson, Johnny Junatov, and Robert Moody did. Mones, for example, describes the case of a girl who, after years of being sexually abused by her father, shot and killed him. Despite evidence of the sexual abuse, she was sentenced to serve from five to twenty years in an adult prison.[30] Morris also describes several cases of patricide in which juvenile killers have received lengthy prison sentences and notes that in patricide prosecutions, the insanity defense has rarely been used and has rarely resulted in acquittal.[31]

In addition to the Jahnke, Pierson, Junatov, and Moody cases and others described in the media in recent years, a number of patricides have been described in case studies in the clinical literature. Virtually all of these cases have involved juveniles killing physically, psychologically, and/or sexually abusive fathers or stepfathers. For example, Hellsten and Katila described a thirteen-and-a-half-year-old boy who shot and killed his sleeping father, an alcohol abuser who had regularly abused the boy and the boy's mother.[32] Prior to the killing, the boy had stolen money from the father but had demonstrated no other behavior problems. Upon examination, after the killing, he showed no remorse, seemed to be of above normal intelligence, and demonstrated no signs of serious psychopathology or neurological dysfunction.

Similarly, Russell summarized three cases in which adolescent boys killed their fathers: "[T]he three murdered fathers were violent, hard-drinking men, abusive and unfaithful to their wives. They held rejecting, hypercritical and belittling attitudes towards their sons and frequently called attention to the mother-son relationship."[33] As for the three juvenile killers: "They had always been well behaved, compliant boys, good students, and inclined towards intellectual defenses."[34]

Earlier, Patterson described a similar case of a fourteen-year-old boy who shot and killed his father, who "was alcoholic, sadistic toward the family, unfaithful, inclined to steal, and had over a considerable period of time indulged in incestuous relations with a sibling of the [boy]."[35] This boy, who had fantasized killing his father for several months before doing it, had an IQ of 120, did good academic work, had only a minor record of previous delinquency (shoplifting), and did not appear seriously disturbed.

More recently, Benedek and Cornell described the case of seventeen-year-old "Fred," who shot and killed his father in their living room during an episode in which the father was beating Fred's sister.[36] Fred and other family members described the father as a brutal and tyrannical alcoholic who, for years, had physically abused Fred, his sister, their younger siblings, their late mother, and their stepmother. Indeed, Fred's mother's suicide, four years earlier, had been precipitated by abuse inflicted upon her by her husband, Fred's father. Fred, who had been forced at times by his father to "punish" his younger siblings, had achieved above average grades in school, graduated from high school a year before the killing, and had no psychiatric or criminal history.

While all of the juveniles in these cases were adolescents, even younger children sometimes kill their abusive fathers. Indeed, in one recent Detroit case, a three-year-old boy shot and killed his father as the father was beating the boy's mother. The boy's mother described the killing as an accident, but the boy reportedly told authorities: "I killed him. Now he's dead. If he would have hit my mother, I would have shot him again."[37]

At the time of the killing, the father was intoxicated. After arguing with the boy's mother, he fetched a pistol and set it on a nearby table as he assaulted her. According to two other adults and three children who were also in the room, the three-year-old grabbed the gun, aimed it at his father, and fired. Gunpowder residue tests established that the three-year-old had, in fact, done the shooting.

As noted in chapter 1, while juveniles who kill outside the family often do so in concert with others, killing in the family is generally an individual act. Indeed, it appears that less than 20 percent of intrafamilial juvenile homicides are committed by more than a single perpetrator.[38]

While it appears that most patricides, indeed most parricides, fit this pattern, at least one theorist has suggested that juveniles who kill parents are often consciously or unconsciously prompted, if not encouraged, to do so by others in the family, particularly other parents.

Referring to children who kill in what he called a "family conspiracy," Sargent speculated that "sometimes the child who kills is acting as the unwitting lethal agent of an adult (usually a parent) who unconsciously prompts the child so that he can vicariously enjoy the benefits of the act."[39] Sargent cited several cases, including one in which an eight-year-old boy shot and killed his abusive father after the boy's mother repeatedly expressed the wish that the father would die. The clinical literature on juvenile homicide includes descriptions of several cases which might be described as "family conspiracy" patricides.

In some of these apparently "conspiratorial" patricides, the parental encouragement is subtle. Russell, for example, described the case of Peter, a "studious," "quiet," "good boy" of fourteen, who "blew his sleeping stepfather's head off one night with a shotgun his mother [an abused wife] had bought for him."[40] In other clinical reports, the "conspiracy" is much more obvious. Malmquist, for example, describes what may well be the most blatant case of this type reported in the clinical literature. In this case, a fifteen-year-old boy had often seen his father beat his mother while the father was intoxicated.[41] Finally, after one such beating, the father had gone out to fetch a piece of wood to use on the mother. While the father was gone briefly, the mother sat down next to the boy, told him "I know you're big enough to protect me now," and handed the boy a pistol, which he promptly used to shoot and kill his father.[42]

Hellsten and Katila provide other clear-cut examples of parental or surrogate parental encouragement. In one case, a fourteen-year-old boy responded to his mother's direct request and actually assisted her in strangling his father.[43] Interestingly, unlike what appear to be the typical family dynamics in patricide cases generally, here the slain father "was a mild and inoffensive farmer of regular ways of life who took care of his family," while the mother was "hard-natured, energetic, ordering, quarrelsome and aggressive, a 'veritable home tyrant' [who] always instigated the children to act against their father and his relatives."[44] While this woman was later suspected of being schizophrenic, the son who joined her in the killing was a boy of better than average intellect, who had done reasonably well at school, and seemed well adjusted both before and after the killing.

Hellsten and Katila also relate the details of a case in which a fourteen-

and-a-half-year-old boy helped his mother's lover kill the boy's father.[45] The boy was first approached by the mother's lover. After the boy agreed to the lover's plan for killing his father, the boy consulted his mother, who said she was not in favor of it but would not forbid it. After sharing some liquor, the boy and his mother's lover beat and stabbed the father to death. Again, the family dynamics were atypical for patricide. The father, though "didactic and narrow-minded," was not abusive or alcoholic.[46] The mother, however, was an alcohol abuser who "led an irregular life" and was often unfaithful to her husband.[47] Until the killing, the boy had been a generally well behaved youngster of better than average intellect who did well in school. After spending two years in an institution, during which he "behaved faultlessly," he was released and almost completed college before being expelled for substance abuse. After serving in the military, he worked for a while as a teacher but continued to be a substance abuser and ended up spending another year and a half in a penal institution (where his behavior again was "faultless") before the authors lost track of him.[48]

Two more recent cases from outside the clinical literature also illustrate the dynamics of "family conspiracy" patricides. In 1981, a sixteen-year-old Indiana youth told police he tripped while carrying a gun and accidentally killed his father. Four years later, when his mother was tried for murder in the killing, it was revealed that the boy had killed his father at his mother's request. Testimony at the trial indicated that his mother started asking him to kill his father several months before the shooting. Initially he refused, but finally agreed after his mother threatened to kill herself if he did not kill his father. The boy then shot his father as he lay sleeping on a sofa.[49]

In 1985, a seventeen-year-old upstate New York youth was charged as an accessory to the murder of his stepfather, who had repeatedly abused the boy and the boy's mother. Prior to the killing, the boy's mother told him that she would give $50 to have her husband killed. The boy, who was of borderline intelligence, passed this "offer" on to a friend who told a second friend. The second friend, who was nineteen, immediately agreed to do the killing for the amount "offered." That night, the nineteen-year-old showed up at the family's home, got the stepfather's loaded rifle, and then—with the seventeen-year-old by his side—ambushed, shot, and killed the stepfather. The boy, his mother, and the nineteen-year-old shooter all pleaded guilty to homicide charges.[50]

Even where there is no "conspiracy," explicit or implicit, between parent and child, the killing of one parent to protect the other parent is not an uncommon scenario in juvenile patricide. The case of the three-year-old in Detroit described earlier is one example. A more recent case in the Los Angeles area illustrates the same dynamics with an older child.

In the Los Angeles case, an unidentified fifteen-year-old boy shot and killed his stepfather as the stepfather was beating the boy's mother. The stepfather, who reportedly had abused his wife for fourteen years, was slamming her against the metal security door outside the family's home when his fifteen-year-old stepson grabbed a gun from the man's bedroom and shot him once through the door. Wounded, the stepfather released his wife, but the boy chased him into the driveway and fired three or four more shots, killing him.[51]

Some "family conspiracies" are not between parent and child but between or among siblings. When juveniles conspire with siblings to kill their fathers, the family dynamics generally seem to fit the typical patricidal pattern of paternal abuse. The case of Richard and Deborah Jahnke is, of course, one example.[52] Duncan and Duncan provide another: "Three brothers, aged fifteen, thirteen, and ten formed a conspiracy to kill their father in revenge for his brutality to the family. The family of thirteen children lived in a tar paper dwelling on a 40-acre farm. The home was the picture of squalor and poverty. The authorities had received many reports of the father's extreme cruelty."[53]

Matricide

Like patricides, matricides generally appear to involve killings of abusive parents. But in cases of matricide, in contrast to patricide, the more severe abuse inflicted by the parent-victim upon the juvenile-perpetrator is frequently psychological or sexual rather than physical. Two recent cases of matricide illustrate these dynamics.

In June 1988, a seventeen-year-old New York high school senior beat his mother to death with a baseball bat at about three o'clock in the morning on the very day he was scheduled to speak as class valedictorian at his high school graduation.[54]

Since he had been an infant, this boy's mother had responded to his obvious intellectual gifts by relentlessly pushing him to achieve. And achieve he did: First in his class throughout school and number one in his high school graduating class of 250, he had been admitted to one of the nation's leading universities with a full scholarship. The killing—which occurred just two months before he was scheduled to leave for college—climaxed several months in which his mother (a widow with no other children and few interests in life other than her son) selected the college he would attend, constantly berated his girlfriend, abused him psychologically, threatened him, and occasionally struck him.[55] On the night of the homicide, the boy's mother had abused him verbally and physically, threatened to kill him, and backed him into a corner in his bedroom. In response, he picked up a baseball bat and beat her to death.[56]

In October 1987, another seventeen-year-old New York youth shot and killed his mother who he claimed had been physically, sexually, and psychologically abusing him for years.[57] As far back as he could recall, his mother—

who had several children but had never married—had beaten him and his siblings on a regular basis with sticks, belts, and extension cords, ostensibly as a form of discipline. Also, for as long as he could remember, his mother had called him vile names and repeatedly told him that if she could turn back the hands of time, she would never have given birth to him. Finally, according to the youth, his mother had been sexually abusing him since he was seven years old. What started out with her fondling his genitals in the bathtub, progressed to making him masturbate her, and ultimately led to sexual intercourse between mother and son. By his account, the last episode of sexual abuse took place just minutes before he picked up a rifle and shot his mother five times.[58]

Published clinical accounts of matricide are relatively rare, but clinical interest in matricide dates back at least half a century. The pioneer work appears to be that of Wertham, who—half a century ago—reviewed the sparse literature on matricide, reported one case study and concluded that the perpetrators of matricide were generally young, intelligent males who had no prior history of delinquency but had excessively close attachments to their mothers.[59] According to Wertham, the motive in most of these killings was the fusion of unconscious hatred and sexual desire for the mother.

This psychodynamic formulation, though obviously speculative and difficult to generalize, does receive support from some of the above-described cases, as well as from a number of published clinical accounts of matricide. For example, Scherl and Mack have reported three cases of matricide—two committed by teenage boys and one by a teenage girl—all sharing a common pattern of "severe early maternal restrictiveness . . . deprivation, provocation, and harshness"; an "unusually intense and conflict-laden" mother–child relationship; and extremely violent killing.[60]

In the single case Scherl and Mack described in detail, fourteen-year-old Richard shot and killed his mother as she lay sleeping.[61] Several hours earlier the mother had directed—as she often did—Richard's father to beat Richard with a belt. For years, Richard had been physically and psychologically abused by both his father and mother. His father had beaten both him and his mother, but clearly the worst abuse was that inflicted by his mother. She would often kick and slap Richard and call him names like "fucking bastard," lock him in his room, and force him to kneel for hours at a time.[62] A number of times she exposed her breasts and genitals to him. Two months before the homicide, Richard found her and her lover together in bed.

Psychological and medical evaluations revealed that while Richard had a history of running away and minor delinquency, he had an above-normal IQ, manifested no organic pathology, and suffered no major mental illness. He was diagnosed as suffering a personality disorder.

Why did Richard kill his mother? Scherl and Mack conclude—apparently with good reason—that this was largely a victim-precipitated homicide. In their words: "[H]er repeated gross seductions and brutal treatment of him, her highly eroticized, humiliating demands of the boy for absolute submission, unmitigated by tenderness, forced him into a position where to be free of her he felt he had no alternative but to kill her."[63]

Undoubtedly many, perhaps most, matricides fit this general pattern, but clearly others do not. For example, some matricides seem more the result of the juvenile perpetrator's psychological problems than any significant provocation on the part of the victim. Consider, for example, these three fairly recent cases:

A sixteen-year-old boy shot his mother three times in the back after they argued about whether he had misplaced a knitting needle. Evidence showed that the youth had been drinking whiskey and sniffing gasoline fumes shortly before he killed his mother as she sat watching television.[64]

A fifteen-year-old boy and a fourteen-year-old friend robbed, beat, and stabbed to death the fifteen-year-old's mother. Interviewed after the killing, others who knew the boy said he and his mother got along well, but that he was a "bully" who was "always smarting off."[65] Another friend of the boy's said that the robbery and killing were motivated by boredom: "All we want is something to do, somewhere to go."[66]

Fifteen-year-old "Bob," recently described in the clinical literature by Benedek and Cornell, stabbed his mother to death and afterward was found in the basement of his home, reading a Bible and chanting: "Kill the Devil."[67] Upon evaluation after the killing, Bob described his strong belief in witchcraft and said that he had received special messages from rock music lyrics, directed to him and suggesting that he kill his mother. Bob's mother was described as having abused him, and there was evidence that he had twice run away from home before the killing. For two months prior to the killing he had become increasingly withdrawn, seclusive, and apathetic—avoiding friends, often skipping school, talking about witchcraft and demonic possession, refusing to eat, and complaining that his mother was poisoning his food.

Recently, a number of reported juvenile matricides have apparently been drug related. For example, Hamill has briefly described four cases in New York City which he attributes to the effects of the street drug "crack."[68] A seventeen-year-old boy was charged with choking his mother to death after she confronted him about his "addiction to telephone party lines," a fad among New York teens.[69] Another New York boy was charged with stabbing his mother to death when she refused to give him $200—money he owed to a crack dealer. A fifteen-year-old girl from the suburbs stabbed her mother to death after the mother made a comment about the girl's poor grades. Finally, fifteen-year-old Andrea Williams and her eighteen-year-old boyfriend killed Andrea's mother with a knife and a machete because she objected to their relationship.

Although there appear to be no published accounts of cases in which matricides have been subtly or blatantly encouraged by fathers, there are reports of matricides committed jointly by siblings. As seems to be the case in patricides committed jointly by siblings, when juvenile siblings conspire to kill their mothers, the family dynamics appear likely to fit the common matricidal pattern of maternal abuse described earlier.

The dynamics in these matricidal conspiracies are illustrated by a recent case in which two Georgia sisters, seventeen and fourteen, admitted shooting and killing their mother but told police they did so "because their mother physically and emotionally abused them, and their mother's boyfriend sexually abused them."[70] The killing reportedly took place while the mother was attempting to spank one of the girls.[71]

Similar, though somewhat different, dynamics are illustrated by the case of two brothers fourteen and twelve, who together beat their stepmother to death. Though apparently not overtly abusive, this woman clearly neglected and rejected her stepsons, both of whom were considerably below normal in intellectual development. According to Hellsten and Katila, "The stepmother mistreated the boys; she was severe and loveless and took poor care of them so that they actually went hungry frequently. . . . It seemed as if neither had received normal love and tenderness to speak of in this home."[72]

Finally, it is worth noting that like the Cheryl Pierson patricide case described earlier,[73] at least some juvenile matricides involve accomplices from outside the family. One such case is that of fifteen-year-old Andrea Williams, mentioned above. Andrea and her eighteen-year-old boyfriend, apparently under the influence of drugs, hacked Andrea's mother to death with a combat knife and a machete, reportedly because the mother objected to their relationship. The two teens "left her on the apartment floor, then partied and smoked drugs and had sex . . . for nine days."[74]

Another recent example of juvenile matricide perpetrated by a teenager acting with an accomplice is that of a sixteen-year-old Connecticut girl who conspired with her nineteen-year-old boyfriend to kill her mother.[75] The boyfriend strangled the girl's mother with a stocking and then, accompanied by two other youngsters, twenty and seventeen, dumped the mother's body near a highway in Massachusetts. After the killing and recovery of the body, police confiscated a note the boyfriend had written to the sixteen-year-old girl before the killing: "To my Dreamgirl . . . I will do the deed. I promise you."[76]

Although the motive in this case was unclear, in an earlier case a sixteen-year-old California boy conspired with two other young men, twenty-three and eighteen, to kill his mother because "She was always either beating me up or my brother up."[77] Torran Lee Meier, Richard Parker, and Matthew Jay allegedly strangled Torran's mother, placed her body into a car alongside Torran's eight-year-old brother, doused the car with gasoline, set it afire, and pushed it over a 60-foot cliff. Amazingly, the brother survived.

Torran's maternal grandmother said Torran was driven to kill by his mother who made his life "a living hell" through years of physical and psychological abuse.[78] Evidence introduced at the youth's trial indicated that his thirty-four year old mother frequently called him a "faggot," humiliated him and questioned his manhood in front of others, provocatively exposed herself to him alone and in the presence of others, and criticized and belittled anything he did or tried to do.

A jury found that this pattern of abuse led to an "emotional breakdown" that prevented Torran from acting with malice or premeditation.[79] Torran was convicted of a lesser charge and committed to the custody of the state youth authority until his twenty-fifth birthday. His adult accomplices were each sentenced to serve from fifteen years to life in prison.

Patricide-Matricides and Familicides

In addition to simple patricides and matricides, there are occasional cases in which juveniles kill both their parents. There are even cases in which juveniles kill not only their parents but their siblings as well.

"Something is very terribly wrong. You just don't do ... that without something being wrong with you."[80] So said Sheriff Don Collins of a sixteen-year-old Kansas boy who shot and killed his parents while they slept and then repeatedly shot and killed his eight-year-old brother as the brother tried to aid his wounded mother.[81]

Sheriff Collins was probably correct in his assessment. In many ways, the dynamics of mass killings of family members by juveniles are similar to those in simple parricides. Juveniles who kill both parents and/or destroy their entire nuclear families are often abused youngsters, but many if not most of these young mass family killers are also psychologically disturbed, often seriously mentally ill.

In some instances, the extreme manner in which these multiple killings are committed suggests that the juvenile perpetrator must have been psychologically disturbed. Consider, for example, the seventeen-year-old who killed his father, stepmother (who was three months pregnant), and two half-brothers, one six years old and the other just eight months old. Both parents were shot, the older boy was strangled, and the infant was beaten to death. The bodies of all four were found when the seventeen-year-old boy fled after an aunt demanded that he let her into the family home. At that time, the victims had all been dead for at least four days. After the killing, there were unverified reports that the boy's father "kept a tight rein on his son, forced him to work long hours ... and was very protective ..."[82]

Consider also the case of a sixteen-year-old Minnesota boy who was arrested for the ax-murders of his mother, father, nine-year-old brother and fourteen-year-old sister. Not surprisingly, he was committed to a psychiatric hospital for evaluation prior to trial.[83] Finally, consider the recent case of a fourteen-year-old New York youth who shot and killed his parents and seriously wounded his seventeen-year-old sister. When taken into custody after the killings, which were apparently spurred by an argument over his school attendance, the fourteen-year-old was wearing military fatigues. When booked on murder charges, he identified himself as "Rambo."[84]

In other multiple intrafamilial killings, evidence other than, or in addition to, the manner of death makes it clear that the juvenile perpetrator is seriously disturbed. Consider, for example, the cases of Ginger Turnmire, John Justice, Patrick DeGelleke, and Wyley Gates.

Ginger Turnmire was fifteen years old when, in April 1986, she shot and killed her mother and father as they returned home from a church picnic.[85] That same day, she calmly told friends what she had done but later testified in court that a long-haired and bearded motorcycle gang leader, known to her only as "Papa Smurf," had done the killings after searching the house for drugs. At a pretrial hearing, a judge determined that Ginger should be tried as an adult, after psychiatric testimony indicated that Ginger suffered from severe identity and behavioral problems but not serious mental illness. In her own testimony, she conceded that she was addicted to Valium.

Judge James Beckner said that a major factor in his decision was the failure of previous efforts to treat Ginger. In the words of the judge: "All efforts of treatment have failed. Responses by Miss Turnmire have been negative."[86] Ginger was subsequently convicted of first-degree murder and sentenced to life in prison.

John Justice was a seventeen-year-old high school honor student when, in September 1985, within a period of about two hours, he stabbed his mother, brother, and father to death and then rammed his father's car into another car, killing the driver of that vehicle. At John's trial on murder charges, psychiatrists testified that John hated his mother and that he was upset over his parents' refusal to help pay for his planned college expenses. The state's psychiatrist testified that John was afflicted with a personality disorder, but the psychiatrist called by the defense testified that John suffered from an undiagnosed psychosis. The jury found John Justice not guilty by reason of insanity in the killings of his father and brother, but guilty of killing his mother and the driver of the car.[87]

Patrick DeGelleke was fifteen years old when he set his adoptive parents' home on fire as they slept. His mother died in the fire; his father died eleven days later from burn complications. For years prior to the killing, Patrick had demonstrated behavioral and emotional problems and had been in counseling. At school he had trouble concentrating and often stared off into space for hours. After his parents took him to court, alleging that he was involved in truancy and theft and that they could no longer control him, he feared that they were going to send him away. According to a psychologist, his parents' petition to the court "threw Patrick into a psychotic rage . . . during which he lost his sense of reality and set the fire."[88]

Seventeen-year-old Wyley Gates, a high school honor student who ranked second in his class, was charged with murder after four people—his father, brother, cousin, and the woman who lived with his father—were all found shot to death in the Gates's family home.[89] According to the police, Wyley confessed to the killings, and there was evidence that he and two class-mates had plotted the murders.

At trial on murder and conspiracy charges, Wyley's attorney sought to suppress the youth's confession on the grounds that the police had denied him the presence of an attorney. His attorney also presented the testimony of two psychiatrists and a psychologist, who testified that Wyley was psychotic. Indeed, one psychiatrist, a nationally recognized authority on juvenile vio-lence, testified that Wyley suffered from paranoid schizophrenia, experienced auditory hallucinations just before the killings, and tried hard to convince her that he was "perfectly normal."[90] A jury concluded that Wyley's confession should be suppressed, but convicted him of conspiracy to commit murder.

Occasionally familicides are committed by juveniles acting in concert with siblings. One recent case of this sort is that of a nineteen- and sixteen-year-old brother and sister from Oklahoma, charged together in the slayings of their father, stepmother, and two-year-old half-sister.[91] The brother told authorities that he shot and killed his father with a high-powered rifle be-cause the father was beating his sister. He said he then shot his mother as she came at him with a baseball bat. Finally, he turned the gun on his half-sister, who had witnessed the other two killings. Prosecutors said that both teen-agers participated in the crime. Specifically, they alleged that the sixteen-year-old helped her brother move the three bodies to a nearby trash dump and then fled with him to Texas.

Fratricide and Sororicide

In some instances, juveniles kill their siblings. Sometimes, as in the John Jus-tice case, a sibling is killed along with a parent or parents. But in other cases, a juvenile kills only his or her brother or sister. While it may be tempting to assume that these killings generally result from some extreme form of sibling rivalry, the cases described in both clinical and media accounts defy such a simplistic explanation.

Tooley, for example, described two six-year-olds who made "murderous attacks" on younger siblings.[92] Two factors stood out in both cases: abuse and neglect. Six-year-old Mary had been left to baby-sit for her younger brother since she was four and he was two. Mary, who later reported that she had been sexually abused by one of her mother's boyfriends, tried to pour Clorox down her baby sister's throat and had succeeded in setting her bed covers on fire. Six-year-old Jay, "neglected by a childish, self-centered mother and beaten by an immature and brutal young father," twice set fire to his younger sister's dress before drowning her.[93]

Other very young children seem to have killed siblings accidentally or at least without any real intention to kill. For example, in her pioneering clinical reports on children who killed, Bender described numerous cases in which young children killed siblings in what appeared to be accidents, including six "evidently unintentional deaths" resulting from fires set by the victim's siblings ranging in age from five to twelve years.[94]

Other more recent sibling homicides charged to young children provide similar examples. For instance, an eight-year-old New York City boy was recently charged with homicide in the death of his eleven-year-old sister, who died in a fire he set while playing with a cigarette lighter. At the time of the fire, the boy was already under psychiatric care because he refused to stop playing with matches.[95] Earlier, a four-year-old New York City girl had removed both of her twin three-week-old brothers from their cribs and had dropped each of them, fatally fracturing their skulls.[96]

In the clinical literature, Petti and Wells described their evaluation and treatment of a twelve-year-old boy who "accidentally" killed his twin brother.[97] This youngster, when teased by his brother and a friend with a squirt gun, responded with a loaded gun. He pointed the gun at the other boys and threatened to shoot them. The gun went off, both boys were shot, and the twin brother was killed. The boy who killed his brother demonstrated no evidence of behavior problems prior to the shooting, and had no history of psychiatric/psychological treatment.

Older juveniles who kill siblings present a more varied picture of dynamics and motivation. For example, a thirteen-year-old Colorado girl who shot and killed her eight-year-old sister seemed to have been driven by hatred for her mother as well as by fairly serious psychopathology. Psychiatrists testified that she had a long-standing and intense hatred of her mother. The girl was confined to a state psychiatric hospital following the killing, and her attorney argued that she was possessed by the devil and asked the court to order that she be exorcised.[98]

The case of a sixteen-year-old Chicago youth presents an even clearer picture of psychopathology underlying the killing of a sibling. This youth quarreled with his eight-year-old brother over a bicycle, pulled the younger boy off the bike by the throat, and then knocked him down a flight of stairs with a Karate-style kick to his chest, killing him. The sixteen-year-old, who had been released from a mental institution just a month earlier, had a five-year history of psychiatric hospitalizations and had set fire to his family's home on three separate occasions.[99]

In the case of a fifteen-year-old Nebraska boy who shot and killed his twelve-year-old sister, child abuse seems to have played at least some role. In court, the boy's attorney presented testimony as to the severe abuse the boy had suffered during the first five years of his life.[100] The attorney then argued that, "This is the hand he was dealt. None of it was his fault. He never had a chance."[101]

More recently, a fifteen-year-old Massachusetts girl reportedly confessed to a friend that she poisoned two foster children—one two years old and the other fifteen months old—who were living in the home of her adoptive parents. The girl, who was found with a bottle labeled "poison" just days after the toddlers' deaths, had a history of suicide attempts and was later admitted to a state mental hospital for children.[102]

In still another case, that of sixteen-year-old Thomas C., described in the clinical literature by Leong, both abuse and psychopathology appear to have been key factors in a sororicide. Thomas, who was "clinically depressed," shot and killed his depressed fourteen-year-old sister Jody at her request.[103] Thomas and Jody had been locked out of the family home as punishment and forced to live above the garage. Despondent, Jody asked Thomas to help her commit suicide, which he did. Psychiatric evaluation revealed that Thomas had been physically abused by his mother, had been "shuttled back and forth" between his divorced parents during a custody dispute, had both a personal and family history of depression, was treated with antidepressant medications a year before the killing, and had previously attempted suicide with the help of his sister, Jody.[104]

Finally, in the case of a seventeen-year-old West Virginia boy who shot and killed his sixteen-year-old sister, no motive was discerned. What was known about this boy, however, was that three years earlier he had kidnapped a five-year-old girl, slit her throat, and abandoned her body in the attic of his family's home in Ohio. He was convicted of kidnapping and aggravated murder in that incident and served eighteen months in an Ohio detention center.[105]

Clinical reports of sibling homicides committed by juveniles, though very few in number, also present diverse dynamics and motives. Interestingly, all three reported cases of this sort involved adolescent or preadolescent boys who killed their sisters. Patterson described an "ordinary" eleven-year-old boy who shot and killed his sister in a quarrel over a few pennies.[106] The boy was of average intelligence, was apparently normal psychologically, and had no prior record of delinquency. Although the boy was not neglected or abused by his parents, it was clear that they showed greater attention to the sister and unknowingly created a "competition for affection and recognition" between brother and sister.[107]

Later, Woods described "Tom," a fifteen-year-old farm youth who accidentally observed his thirteen-year-old sister undressing, impulsively tried to rape her, and then, several hours later, shot her to death as she lay sleeping.[108] Tom later explained the crime: "I had to kill her or my mother would have found out that I had done something bad."[109]

Though "bright normal" in intelligence, not psychotic, not suffering any neurological impairment, and posing no behavior problems at home or at school, Tom was described as a passive, compliant boy whose relationships with others were "superficial and dependent."[110] Following the killing, it was learned through sodium amytal ("truth serum") interviews that, unknown to his parents, Tom had for several years molested his sister and been preoccupied with fantasies of rape and murder, generally directed toward his sister.

Finally, Schmideberg described "Danny, who, at the age of thirteen, after careful preparation, killed his sister in cold blood."[111] Danny, who came from a "respectable middle class family living in a respectable neighborhood" had at times been truant and had done some stealing but generally "was regarded as a normal boy of good reputation."[112] With no apparent motive—"except that he was jealous of her for the father's affection"[113]—Danny practiced shooting a rifle for two weeks and then shot and killed his sister, stole $150 of his parents' money, and ran away. Though he later turned himself in to the police, Danny never showed any remorse. Later he explained that he had done what he did at age thirteen because he knew he would be treated more leniently than he would have been a short while later at the age of fourteen.

4

Homicides Committed in the Course of Other Crimes

M
any, perhaps most, nonfamilial juvenile homicides are committed during the course of another crime such as robbery, burglary, or rape. Some researchers have lumped these other-crime-related homicides together for purposes of analysis and comparison with other sorts of juvenile homicides.[1] In some cases, this makes sense. Indeed, some juvenile killings involve all three crimes: robbery or burglary, rape, and homicide. It seems clear, however, that the dynamics of killings committed by juveniles in the course of economic crimes like robbery and burglary are often much different from those of killings committed in the course of sex crimes such as rape or sexual abuse. Thus, this chapter will examine sexual homicides and theft-related homicides separately.

Theft-Related Juvenile Homicides

Regardless of the age of the perpetrator, many homicides are committed incidental to theft crimes. As Table 4–1 illustrates, annually, from 1983 to 1987, between 9 and 10 percent of cleared homicides in the United States— that is, those resulting in arrests—have occurred in the course of or in furtherance of a robbery (the forcible taking of the money or property of another).[2] A substantial percentage of these homicides have also occurred in the course of other theft offenses such as burglary (breaking and entering for purposes of theft) or simple larceny.[3]

Among homicides perpetrated by juveniles, it appears that an even greater percentage are committed incident to theft offenses. For example, twelve of the twenty-nine juvenile homicides described by Cormier and Markus were committed in the course of robberies, burglaries, and purse snatchings.[5] More recently, Rowley, Ewing, and Singer analyzed FBI supplementary homicide data and found that 22.49 percent of juvenile homicides in one recent year were committed "incident to theft."[6] Rowley et al. also found that while juvenile killings of family members were almost never theft

Table 4-1
Percentage Distribution of Homicides Committed in the Course of or in
Furtherance of Robberies 1983–1987[4]

	Year				
	1983	1984	1985	1986	1987
Total homicide arrests	18,673	17,260	17,545	19,257	17,859
Percent incident to robbery	10.6	9.3	9.2	9.5	9.4

related, and juvenile killings of acquaintances were rarely theft related, nearly 60 percent of juvenile homicides committed against strangers were theft related.[7]

While such killings are often described as "motivated" by robbery or theft, this terminology is usually a rather gross oversimplification if not a misnomer. Very rarely does one need to kill another person to steal from or rob that person. By far the vast majority of burglaries, larcenies, and even armed robberies are completed successfully without killing anyone. Only a minute percentage of theft crimes result in a homicide.

For example, in 1987, according to FBI estimates, there were in the United States 517,704 robberies,[8] 3.2 million burglaries,[9] and nearly 7.5 million larcenies,[10] but fewer than 21,000 murders and non-negligent manslaughters.[11] Similarly, FBI data for the same year indicate that while there were 25,779 juvenile arrests for robbery, 122,399 juvenile arrests for burglary, and 282,329 juvenile arrests for larceny, there were only 1,454 juvenile arrests for murder and non-negligent manslaughter.[12] FBI data for preceding years paint a very similar picture of the homicide to theft crime ratio for both adults and juveniles.[13]

Why then, and under what circumstances, do juveniles kill during the course of a robbery, burglary, or other larceny? To begin with, it appears that theft-related homicides committed by juveniles may be characterized as either unintentional or intentional.

Unintentional Theft-Related Homicides

Many, perhaps even most, homicides committed by juveniles in the course of robberies, burglaries, and other theft crimes appear to be unintentional if not accidental. A juvenile committing a robbery or burglary panics and overreacts when, for example, a burglary victim unexpectedly appears and confronts the juvenile burglar or when a robbery victim resists or attempts forcefully to thwart the robbery. In one such case, for example, a twelve-year-old California youth entered the home of his elderly next-door neighbor, planning to steal something. Unexpectedly confronted by the eighty-year-old man, the boy panicked, pulled a kitchen knife from his pocket, and stabbed the man once in the chest.[14]

In another case of such overreaction, sixteen-year-old "Donald" killed a vagrant while robbing the man. According to Cornell and Benedek, Donald admitted that he and a friend were in the habit of robbing street people when in need of money. In this instance, the robbery victim resisted by calling Donald and his accomplice names and spitting at them. In response, Donald hit the man in the head with a brick, killing him. Later, Donald claimed, plausibly, that he never intended to kill the man but hit him only to "get even" for the name-calling and spitting.[15]

Other such killings undoubtedly result from the accidental overuse of force, as when the perpetrator means only to instill fear in the victim, but misjudges the level of force used. For example, Hellsten and Katila described the case of a fourteen-year-old boy who, short of money, stole a pistol and later pulled it on a cab driver in an armed robbery. Although the boy planned only to scare the driver into giving him her money, the gun discharged and the driver was shot and killed.[16]

Still other "accidental" theft-related homicides seem to occur when a juvenile uses force that proves to be excessive for an especially vulnerable victim—for example, an elderly person who is frail and/or in poor health. In a typical and all-too-common case of this sort, Anthony M., a twelve-year-old New York City youth grabbed an eighty-three-year-old woman's handbag with such force that the woman was spun around, knocked to the sidewalk, and dragged a short distance.[17] While recovering from surgery for a broken hip, she developed congestive heart failure and died two days later from a myocardial infarction. At trial, the judge found that Anthony "created a substantial and unjustifiable risk when he selected [the elderly woman] as his victim, that he was heedless of the peril created by his violence, and that his criminal act set in motion the sequence of events that led inexorably to her death."[18] Thus, the judge concluded that Anthony "committed acts that if done by an adult would constitute the crimes of attempted robbery in the first degree, assault in the first degree, and manslaughter" and committed Anthony to a state institution for delinquents.[19]

Intentional Theft-Related Homicides

When juveniles intentionally kill the victims of theft crimes they are in the course of perpetrating or have just perpetrated, the motivation for such killings is rarely accomplishment of the theft. Indeed, in many, perhaps most, such cases, the theft itself has been accomplished before the killing. Instead, such crimes seem motivated by (1) sexual impulses; (2) abuse of and/or involvement in the sale of drugs; and/or (3) a peculiar kind of peer influence or pressure which occasionally seems to occur when two or more perpetrators jointly commit a theft crime.

Sexually-Related Killings Incidental to Theft Crimes

As is described in more detail later in the section on sexual homicides, some juveniles who kill theft victims do so after raping or otherwise sexually abusing them. In such cases it often appears that the juvenile perpetrators intend only to rob or burglarize; but when confronted by a vulnerable female victim they impulsively decide to exploit their advantage over the victim, rape her, and then kill her to avoid being identified and prosecuted for rape. In one such case, for example, a seventeen-year-old Florida youth robbed a convenience store to get money to run away from home. After robbing the clerk at gunpoint, the youth drove the woman to a wooded area, forced her from the car, and impulsively raped her. Then, to avoid being identified, he shot and killed her.[20]

In another case, two New York State boys, both seventeen years old, broke into a home late at night intending to steal money they thought was hidden there. Unexpectedly confronted by one of the occupants, a sixty-seven-year-old woman, one of the youths beat, sodomized, and killed the woman while the other watched.[21]

Drug-Related Homicides Incidental to Theft Crimes

As was noted in chapter 2, there appears to be a significant if not causal relationship between substance abuse and criminal activity, especially violent crime. Although few researchers have specifically examined this relationship in the context of juvenile homicide, those data that have been reported clearly suggest a link between substance abuse and juvenile homicide.[22] Malmquist, for example, reported that five of twenty juvenile killers in his sample had used barbiturates, amphetamines, psychotomimetics, marijuana, and/or psychedelic drugs prior to committing homicide.[23] Similarly, Sorrells reported that eight of the thirty-one homicidal youths in his study were under the influence of alcohol and/or other mind-altering drugs at the time they killed.[24]

The extent to which these data may be generalized to theft-related killings is unknown. It is worth noting, however, that among the thirty-seven juvenile killers included in Cornell, Benedek, and Benedek's study—all of whom had killed "during the course of another crime, such as robbery or rape"[25]—twenty-seven (72.9 percent) were intoxicated on alcohol and/or other drugs at the time they killed.[26]

The case of Ralph Deer, Jr., a seventeen-year-old Louisiana youth, is fairly typical of those in which intoxicated juveniles kill during the course of a theft crime.[27] After ingesting six tabs of LSD and drinking three cups of grain alcohol mixed with Kool-Aid, Ralph (accompanied by another juvenile) entered a convenience store intending to rob the cashier. Ralph pointed a loaded and cocked shotgun at the cashier, who handed over $11. As Ralph turned, the gun discharged, shooting and killing the cashier. Although Ralph pleaded insanity, based upon his drug and alcohol intoxication, he was convicted of first-degree murder and sentenced to life in prison when the jury deadlocked over the question of whether he should be sentenced to die.

In other drug-related homicides incidental to theft crimes, drug intoxication appears to interact with the juvenile killer's already-disturbed psychological makeup. For example, Heath Wilkins, a seventeen-year-old Missouri youth, and a friend, "both tripping on LSD,"[28] entered a liquor store planning to commit a robbery. After robbing the female clerk, Heath killed her out of fear that she could identify him.

While drugs were clearly implicated in this case, so too, it seems, were Heath Wilkins' background and psychological makeup. He was abandoned by his father, a mental patient, at age three and left with his mother, a drug abuser, who frequently beat him. By the time Heath reached kindergarten he was smoking marijuana and by age seven he was setting fires and committing house burglaries. From the age of ten until just months before the murder, Heath was a ward of the state and spent his time living in detention facilities, mental institutions, and foster homes. At the time of the killing, he was living in an outdoor children's park.[29]

One of the psychological examiners appointed to evaluate Heath after the killing concluded that:

> [Heath's] capacity to manage and control affect is tenuous and inconsistent, leaving him subject to impulsive actions. . . . He is intolerant of intense affects such as anxiety, depression or anger, in that such feelings are overwhelming, interfere with his ability to think clearly, and give rise to impulsive actions. He is vulnerable to massive infusions of intense rage which leads to spasms of destructive action. His rage co-mingles with a profound depressive experience generated by an excruciating sense of lonely alienation whereby he experiences both himself and other people as being lifeless and empty . . .[30]

Theft-related homicides not only occur while their juvenile perpetrators are under the influence of drugs; many such killings occur in the course of theft crimes motivated by a desire to obtain money to buy drugs.[31] Moreover, at least some juvenile homicides occur as a result of what are essentially economic disputes—what might be called "turf wars"—over drug sales. In these cases, juveniles kill fellow drug dealers to insure their own market or that of their drug-dealing employers.

For example, police in Dallas recently reported that "[t]eenagers armed with semiautomatic weapons have become the new front-line soldiers in the city's drug wars."[32] According to narcotics officers there, teenagers are not only selling cocaine and manufacturing crack, but also committing assaults and even murders to protect the drug dealers who employ them."[33]

One such case is that of John Charles Smith, a fifteen-year-old New York youth, who moved to Dallas at the suggestion of several Jamaican drug dealers who had told him that he could make easy money in Dallas.[34] Smith received an eighteen-year prison sentence after being convicted of three drug-related, execution-style killings. Smith shot the three victims a total of twenty-seven times—including three shots through the soles of one victim's feet and ten shots fired at another victim as he tried to telephone for aid. When interviewed after sentencing, Smith said he expected to receive $5,000 from the dealers he worked for when he is released from prison. Similar cases involving the use of juveniles as "enforcers" in drug trafficking have been reported in New York and New England.[35]

Peer-Influenced Theft-Related Homicides

Two Pennsylvania men, one sixteen years old and the other twenty-two, broke into an apartment, intending to burglarize it.[36] Unexpectedly confronted by the occupant of the apartment, the older burglar beheaded him with a kitchen knife. The two then left the man's head and body lying on the floor of the apartment near a wall on which they had scrawled in blood the word "redrum"—murder spelled backward. The idea apparently came from the Stephen King horror movie, *The Shining.*[37]

In Minnesota, two sixteen-year-old boys broke into the home of an eighty-six-year-old neighbor—a man who used to holler at the boys when they used his yard as a shortcut.[38] After stealing a jar of pennies from the home, the boys attacked the man with a hunting knife, left him for dead, and set fire to his house in an apparent effort to cover up the killing. The victim, who died from a stab wound to the heart, was later found with multiple stab wounds and a slit throat. A local pastor who knew both boys said: "One was in constant trouble. . . . The other one . . . was never a discipline problem."[39]

Finally, in New Hampshire, two sixteen-year-old boys, both intoxicated on drugs and alcohol, broke into the home of an elderly neighbor, intending to burglarize it. Confronted by the woman's dog, one boy slit the animal's throat, killing it. Then, confronted by the woman herself, one boy attacked her and stabbed her. When the other boy tried to flee, the attacker demanded that the fleeing youth remain and help kill the woman because she had seen both their faces. Together, the boys stabbed the woman more than thirty times in the stomach, neck, and face. After the killing, the youths stole a large sum of money and numerous groceries from the woman's home and attached grocery store. Within hours, witnesses said, the boys were partying with friends, bragging about the killing, and congratulating each other.[40]

One of these youths, the woman's first attacker, had a lengthy history of criminal violence. The second youth, described by psychologists as immature, passive, and dependent, had a history of burglaries and drug possession, but no record of any previous violence.[41]

These three cases and numerous other similar cases[42] have a number of points in common. First, all started out as theft offenses, robberies or burglaries. Second, all eventuated not only in killings, but in especially brutal and heinous killings, well beyond anything needed to complete the underlying theft crime. Third, all involved two youngsters acting together. Fourth, all appear to have involved some disparity between the backgrounds of the actors—disparities suggesting that one may have been the leader and the other the follower.

In the first case, one was sixteen and the other was twenty-two years old. In the second, one was a known troublemaker while the other had no history of being a discipline problem. And in the third, one had a history of violent criminality while the other, a generally passive-dependent youth, did not.

Taken together, these commonalities suggest a pattern of homicidal violence in which one actor, probably the older and/or more violent one, initiates the violence against the victim and then induces the other actor, the younger and/or less violent one, to join in the violence against the victim. The atrocious nature of these crimes further suggests that the joint involvement of the perpetrators works to create a situation in which the juveniles are unable to stop with simply killing the victim, but instead go on to inflict gratuitous and especially heinous violence. Specifically, it may be that the violence of one perpetrator feeds upon—or is somehow stimulated by—that of the other and thereby escalates to the point of atrocity. As detailed later in this chapter, a similar pattern of peer-stimulated homicide also seems to occur in some sexual killings.

Sexual Homicides

In their recent book on the subject, Ressler, Burgess, and Douglas define a sexual homicide as one in which there is evidence or observations indicating that the killing was sexual in nature.[43] According to Ressler and his colleagues:

> These include: victim attire or lack of attire; exposure of sexual parts of the victim's body; sexual positioning of the victim's body; insertion of foreign objects into the victim's body cavities; evidence of sexual intercourse (oral, anal, vaginal); and evidence of substitute sexual activity, interest, or sadistic fantasy.[44]

With that definition in mind, it appears that at least some homicides committed by juveniles are sexual homicides. The actual percentage of juvenile killings that are sexual in nature is unknown and difficult to estimate for several reasons. First, most crime statistics do not differentiate sexual and nonsexual homicides. Second, even in obvious cases of rape-homicide, the crime most often reported is homicide, not rape.[45] Third, those investigating homicides "may not recognize the underlying sexual dynamics of what appear to be either ordinary or motiveless murders."[46]

The difficulty in determining whether a given homicide is sexual in nature is well illustrated in the cases presented in Stearns's early work, "Murder by Adolescents with Obscure Motivation."[47] Stearns described five adolescent boys, all of whom killed females under conditions suggesting the possibility of, but not clearly establishing the presence of, some kind of sexual motivation.

The first boy, a fifteen-year-old, was giving a "scantily clad" fourteen-year-old girl a ride on his bike, with her astride the handlebars facing him, when he stopped, pulled out a gun, and shot her four times.[48] The second youth, age thirteen, entered the home of a forty-one-year-old woman "clad in white shorts and a halter only," knocked her unconscious with a milk bottle, put a laundry bag over her head, strangled her, and then plunged a knife into her abdomen.[49] The third youngster, eighteen years old, was leaving the home of a dressmaker, who had just mended his jacket, when he seized the woman, strangled her, and then tied a pair of cloth panties around her neck. He then hit her in the head several times with a rolling pin, plunged a butcher knife into her heart, and tied her feet together with a piece of cloth. The fourth, also eighteen, went to a home where his girlfriend was baby-sitting, greeted her at the door with a bayonet, and then used it to stab her forty-six times. The final youth, a boy thirteen, who had lured a thirteen-year-old girl into the woods and then plunged a knife into her back, told police he "wanted to see her breasts."[50]

On the other hand, what appear to be juvenile sexual homicides may not be. In a recent New York City case, for example, a sixteen-year-old boy stabbed his mother to death after she refused to give him $200 to pay off a debt he owed to a drug dealer.[51] The boy then opened his mother's shirt, disrobed her body from the waist down, and telephoned the police. When the police arrived, the youth told them that he had come home and found his mother dead. Upon further questioning, he admitted that he had killed her and then arranged the body to make it appear that she had been sexually assaulted.

While, as these cases illustrate, it is often difficult to say with any degree of certainty whether a juvenile homicide is sexual in nature or sexually motivated, data on juvenile perpetration of other sex crimes make it clear that a fair number of juveniles do act out their sexual impulses in criminally deviant ways. For example, in 1987, youths under the age of eighteen accounted for roughly 16 percent of all forcible rapes reported by the FBI in its annual compilation of crime statistics.[52] During the same year, according to FBI data, about 16 percent of all other sex crimes (crimes other than forcible rape or prostitution) were committed by persons less than eighteen years of age.[53]

Additionally, both the clinical literature and mass media reports of juvenile homicides include at least some incidents of clearly sexual homicides committed by youths under the age of eighteen. While difficult to categorize or classify with precision, the reported juvenile sex killings seem to fall into four (sometimes overlapping) categories: (1) sexual homicides committed by juveniles who are clearly seriously disturbed psychologically; (2) killings apparently committed in efforts to cover up or avoid being identified with rape or other sex crimes; (3) group rapes that eventuate in homicide; and (4) individual and group robberies that lead to impulsive rape and homicide.

Psychologically Disturbed Perpetrators

Not surprisingly, a number of the sex-related killings described in the clinical literature on juvenile homicide were committed by youngsters who were obviously very disturbed psychologically. Woods, for example, described "Steve," a fifteen-year-old boy who killed his middle-aged cousin after she nagged him about his dirty shirt.[54] Steve hit the woman's head repeatedly with a pipe, then choked her, and finally used a knife to mutilate her genitals. After the killing, he revealed that for the two previous years he had been peeping into women's windows, had been engaging in fantasies of rape and murder, and twice had actually attacked women. Describing one of these attacks, he said:

> It's like the devil inside saying go ahead and grab her, stab her, choke her, kill her. . . . Like a magnet pulling you. . . . I feel hot and excited and the sex feelings are very strong. I had to hit her with a rock over and over. I wanted to choke her to death and then rape her.[55]

Following the killing of his cousin, Steve was committed to an inpatient psychiatric facility and was diagnosed as suffering from chronic schizophrenia.

In one of the earliest clinical reports of a sexual homicide committed by a juvenile, Patterson described a fourteen-year-old boy who ax-murdered a neighbor boy and then mutilated his genitals with a knife.[56] The perpetrator was mentally retarded and three years behind in school. According to Patterson, "[i]t was never felt that this case was satisfactorily understood," so "for the protection of society he was committed as feebleminded."[57]

In perhaps the most unusual case described in the clinical literature, Ressler, Burgess, and Douglas profiled one teenager who raped twelve women, five of whom he also killed, within a period of four years.[58] After committing the first of these rapes when he was fourteen years old, this youth was committed to a state psychiatric facility for eighteen months and remained under psychiatric care on probation thereafter. Psychiatric diagnoses included adjustment reaction, character disorder, and multiple personality. It was not until his sixth rape that he began killing his victims. Ultimately he was convicted and sentenced to life imprisonment.

More recent cases may be classified as sexual homicides committed by psychologically disturbed juveniles, either because the killer's mental state is so clearly disturbed at the time of the offense or because the nature of the crime itself bespeaks clear psychopathology in the perpetrator. A recent New Jersey case illustrates sexual homicide committed by a youngster whose mental state was seriously disturbed at the time of the crime. A fifteen-year-old boy was ordered to stand trial as an adult after he was charged with raping, sodomizing, and beating a thirteen-year-old neighbor girl he barely knew.[59] After assaulting the girl, the boy allegedly dragged the girl facedown for several hundred feet, threw her into a creek where she drowned, and then attended a birthday party for a girl he had been dating. Examined by psychologists and psychiatrists, the boy said he had been responding to voices which "commanded him to do things"[60]

In a Texas case, the brutal and bizarre manner of the rape/killing suggested that its perpetrator, seventeen-year-old Jay Pinkerton, must have been seriously disturbed. Jay, who was executed in 1986, broke into a woman's home and stabbed her more than thirty times.[61] The evidence showed that Jay "cut open the deceased's abdomen and ejaculated into it before slitting her throat."[62] Autopsy evidence further indicated that after killing the victim, he penetrated her vagina with "a cylindrical object, approximately five or six inches in length [which] could have been a penis."[63]

In some instances, the psychological disturbance suffered by a juvenile who commits a sexually related homicide is clearly drug and/or alcohol induced. A clear example is the case of sixteen-year-old "Charlie" described recently by Benedek and Cornell.[64] Charlie looked into the window of the home of an elderly woman and "thought I might have sex with her if I went in."[65] In his words, "I went in and said, 'Are you going to give me what I want.' And she said, 'No, get out of my house.' And then I took a stick and I hit her."[66] The woman's partially nude body was later found in her home; she had a fractured skull and wounds on her legs, arms, and vaginal area.

Upon examination by a mental health professional, Charlie stated that he had spent the afternoon of the killing drinking beer and smoking marijuana and was intoxicated when he sexually abused and killed this woman. In his words, "I remember I had a buzz on. A pretty strong buzz."[67] Further evaluation revealed that Charlie had been abusing alcohol since the fourth grade.

Killings Committed to Avoid Identification and Prosecution for Rape or Other Sex Crimes

It is often difficult to determine why a juvenile perpetrator, having committed a rape or other sexual offense, then kills the victim. In many cases, however, it appears that at least part of the motivation for such a slaying lies in the perpetrator's concern that if the victim is left alive, she will identify him and he will be prosecuted. In such cases, the killings frequently appear to be the result of impulsive afterthoughts about avoiding detection and arrest.

Perhaps the classic example from the clinical literature is the case of "Tom," described by Woods and recounted in chapter 3. Fifteen-year-old Tom attempted to rape his thirteen-year-old sister, shot her to death several hours later, and explained to the authorities: "I had to kill her or my mother would have found out that I had done something bad."[68]

Three other more recent cases of this sort include one in which a sixteen-year-old Missouri boy sodomized and then strangled an eleven-year-old boy; a second in which a thirteen-year-old Illinois boy sexually abused and then killed an infant; and a third in which a thirteen-year-old boy from New Mexico sexually molested and then suffocated a five-year-old girl.

In the Missouri case, which took the police almost two and a half years to solve, the teenager dumped the eleven-year-old's body beside a set of railroad tracks. He was not apprehended until years later, and then only after police received an anonymous tip linking him to the crime.[69] In the Illinois case, the youth, who was baby-sitting, attempted to have sex with an eleven-month-old baby and then tried to stop her from crying by holding her head under water and beating her.[70] Finally, in the New Mexico case, the teenage boy, who was also baby-sitting, got drunk, sexually penetrated the child, and then suffocated her.[71] Although this boy had an extensive history of drug and alcohol abuse, psychological examination revealed that he suffered no serious psychopathology.

Group Rapes Eventuating in Homicide

While there are no definitive data, it appears that most adults who commit sexual homicides do so individually.[72] Among juveniles, however, sexual homicides seem much more likely to be committed by two or more youths acting in concert. Generally there is nothing to indicate that these youths are seriously disturbed psychologically, but their crimes are among the most vicious and senseless of all juvenile homicides. Often what begins as an impulsive act of sexual violence gets out of hand, the youths are apparently spurred on by each other's violence, and the result is a particularly vicious killing. In many such instances, the dynamics seem strikingly similar to those in the peer-influenced theft-related homicides described earlier in this chapter.

Kramer recently presented an especially vivid account of one such sexual homicide, perpetrated by fourteen-year-old Wayne, twelve-year-old Billy, and sixteen-year-old Frankie in New York City.[73] These boys spotted a fifty-year-old woman sleeping on a bench in the park one night. As Frankie explained,

> [W]e saw this lady sleeping on the bench. Billy said, "Let's drag her behind the house." I smacked her . . .Billy put his hand over her mouth . . . then we all dragged her behind the [boat] house. . . We started taking her clothes off [and] feeling on her body. . . . She was fighting us back so I smacked her and Billy smacked her twice and Wayne smacked her once. Then she stopped fighting.[74]

Then, according to Frankie, the boys took turns holding the woman down, raping and sodomizing her. Afterward, when she tried to get up, the boys beat her to death with a golf club, sticks, and their hands.

In recent years, a number of other sexual homicides have been committed by two or more juveniles acting together. Victims in these killings ranged from young children to a sixty-five-year-old man.

In one widely publicized Vermont case, two teens, fifteen-year-old James Savage and sixteen-year-old Louis Hamlin, dragged two twelve-year-old girls off a path and into the woods, where they forced them to disrobe, tied them up, tortured, raped, and stabbed them both, and then killed one of them.[75] For two weeks prior to the killing the boys had egged each other on with talk of finding and raping "some girls."[76] On the day of the killing, they had been hunting squirrels with BB guns when they saw the two victims and impulsively decided to ambush them.

Questioned after arrest, Savage claimed that there had been no advance plan to kill the girls, "only to rape them, tie them up and flee."[77] Once the attack began, however, the two seemed to lose control. Savage started to choke one of them and told the other to look away or he would shoot her. Then Hamlin told her, "Now you're going to know what it feels like to be shot five times—to be killed—to be slaughtered like a pig."[78] The violence escalated until ultimately the youths shot the girls with a BB gun and stabbed them.

More recently, three teens in Ohio threw a large piece of concrete from an overpass onto a car traveling on an interstate highway below.[79] The car, which carried two young women, was damaged, and the driver pulled over to the side of the road, where the youths offered the two women a ride to a nearby pay telephone. The women accepted the ride and were later raped and bludgeoned to death by at least two of the youths, a nineteen-year-old and a seventeen-year-old. An eighteen-year-old, who was also charged, confessed to taking part in the concrete-throwing, but said he left when the others revealed their plan to rape the women. Interestingly, before the rapes and killings, one of the women actually used the telephone to call the police and her mother. One of the youthful killers also took the phone briefly to explain to the mother the location of the women's car.

In a somewhat similar occurrence, just a month later in Illinois, four young men—including an adult, a fourteen-year-old, a sixteen-year-old, and a seventeen-year-old—commandeered a car driven by a female medical student driving home from a late-night study session.[80] The youths raped the woman, stabbed her more than forty times, and then crushed her head with a slab of concrete before fleeing.

Still more recently, two groups of youths, acting separately, sexually abused and killed a six-year-old boy and sixty-five-year-old man. In the first case, three Louisiana boys, sixteen, fourteen, and thirteen, all with lengthy criminal records, kidnapped a six-year-old boy who lived in the same apartment building one of them lived in. The teenagers then beat and sexually abused the boy before drowning him in a swimming pool half a mile from his home.[81] In the latter case, two adults, twenty-two and twenty-three, and a sixteen-year-old boy were charged with sexually abusing and beating to death a sixty-five-year-old man whose half-naked body was dumped behind an automobile dealership in Wyoming.[82]

Robberies Resulting in Impulsive Rape and Homicide

As mentioned earlier, economically motivated crimes committed by juveniles often escalate into assaults and even homicides. A common pattern in such cases is one in which a juvenile perpetrator, in the process of robbing a female, impulsively rapes and then kills the robbery victim. Thus, what begins as an economically motivated crime results in a homicide that may be termed sexual. Crimes of this sort are committed individually and by groups of juveniles acting in concert, but most such crimes seem to be group endeavors.

The case of Paul Magill, a seventeen-year-old Florida youth, referred to briefly earlier in this chapter, illustrates the apparently less common, individually perpetrated robbery resulting in impulsive rape and homicide.[83] Paul, who had a history of arrests for indecent exposure, "testified that he robbed [a] convenience store because he was angry with his mother and needed money to run away from home."[84]

After robbing the clerk at gunpoint, he realized that she would call the police once he left the store, so he decided to take her with him and abandon her far from a telephone. Paul drove the woman to a wooded area, forced her from the car, and then decided to rape her. While returning to the car after raping the clerk, he realized that she would be able to identify him as the robber and rapist. To prevent that, he shot her twice, killing her, dragged her body into some bushes, and then drove away.

In another case, also mentioned briefly earlier in this chapter, two teenage boys walked away from a juvenile reformatory in New York State intending only to burglarize a house, but ended up sodomizing and murdering an elderly woman who lived there.[85] Terry Lossico and David Hollis, both seventeen-year-olds with histories of juvenile delinquency, walked to a nearby home in which they thought there was a large amount of cash. Upon entering the home through an unlocked window, the youths encountered an elderly man who suffered from multiple sclerosis. When they hit the man with a stick, they awakened the man's wife, a sixty-seven-year-old woman.

According to Lossico, she started turning on lights and yelling at the intruders. In Lossico's words, "She was making no sense, really. I grabbed her and pulled her out into the hallway and threw her on the floor. Then I hit her with a stick. I hit her in the back of the head about three times. She was down on the floor and I kicked her in the mouth."[86] After this beating, as the woman lay dying, Lossico sodomized her while Hollis stood by and watched.

In at least some of these group-perpetrated robberies-turned- rape/killings, it appears that more immature, less assertive, and sometimes disturbed youths impulsively become involved in the rape and killing of the victim as a result of another youngster's example, direction, or leadership. An example is the case of David Buchanan, a Kentucky teenager, who planned a robbery which resulted in the rape and murder of a twenty-year-old female gas station attendant.[87]

Sixteen-year-old David approached two other youths with his plan and they agreed to help him rob the gas station. David told Troy Johnson to wait in the car while he and Kevin Stanford robbed the gas station. While David tried to locate and then open the safe, Kevin took the attendant into a restroom and raped her. When he could not open the safe, David joined Kevin in the restroom and the two youths then took turns raping and sodomizing the young woman. A short while later, Kevin kidnapped the woman and drove off with her in her car. Ultimately, David and Troy caught up with them and then stood by and watched while Kevin shot and killed the woman.

Less than a year before this incident, a psychologist, who evaluated David after his arrest on burglary charges, had reported that:

> [David] presents as a quiet, rather withdrawn and at least moderately depressed sixteen year old black youth. . . . His thinking . . . is extremely simplistic and very concrete. Impulse controls even under minimal stress are felt to be very poor. He is not seen as sophisticated but rather as a very dependent, immature, probably pretty severely emotionally disturbed, and very easily confused youth. . . . He will be easily led by other more sophisticated delinquents or youths. He has very limited interpersonal skills and is likely to be seen by other youths as a pawn to be used.[88]

5
Senseless Homicides

I t might be argued that all juvenile homicides are senseless, almost by definition. Such killings rarely serve any sensible purpose. Still, many juvenile killers kill for reasons that seem understandable, even if not sensible. For example, as noted in earlier chapters, some abused children kill their abusive parents, youthful robbers and rapists sometimes kill their victims to prevent the victims from identifying them, and some juvenile killings result from the unintended use of excessive force aimed at obtaining victim compliance with robbery or rape.

In addition to these sorts of killings, there are, however, many juvenile homicides that can only be described as senseless. While it is obvious that senseless killings are extremely deviant acts, it does not necessarily follow that youths who commit such acts are seriously disturbed or otherwise significantly abnormal. Indeed, in many cases, senseless, even brutal and bizarre, killings are committed by relatively normal juveniles acting on impulse—often in conjunction with or under the influence of other juveniles. Some of these youths are disturbed, some even appear to be sociopathic, but very few show signs of gross psychological or psychiatric disturbance; most have functioned at home, at school, and in the community prior to the killing. As noted in chapter 2, very few juveniles who kill are psychotic.

Included in the present discussion of senseless juvenile homicides is a group of killings which have been diversely categorized as (1) "thrill" killings; (2) "hate" killings; (3) "revenge" killings; (4) "cult-related" killings; (5) "romantic" murder-suicides; and (6) killings committed by mentally disturbed juveniles.

"Thrill" Killings

Perhaps the prototypical impulsive homicide committed by a relatively normal juvenile is the "thrill" or "dare" killing of a total stranger selected at random. Such killings are generally but not always committed by two or more youths acting together and also vary in their degree of intentionality. Some are clearly deliberate and premeditated while others seem reckless or even accidental.

In one recent case, for example, two fourteen-year-old California youths were convicted of murder.[1] One loaded a .22 caliber rifle, handed it to the other, and dared him to fire the gun out the window at a truck driver in a parking lot two stories below. The second youth fired the rifle, shooting and killing the truck driver. Earlier that same day, the first youth had randomly fired the rifle into a bus, wounding a thirteen-year-old girl.

The youth who accepted the dare and shot the driver was described by family and friends as a religious, caring, and sensitive boy who just happened to be "in the wrong place at the wrong time and with the wrong person" and "accidentally" killed someone.[2] According to the evidence, however, the boy accepted the gun, spent two minutes aiming it, and then killed the driver "just for the sport of it."[3]

In a similar—though perhaps less intentional—impulsive and random killing, a pair of seventeen-year-old boys dropped a 187-pound boulder from a highway overpass onto oncoming traffic.[4] The boulder struck a car and crushed to death a three-year-old child who was asleep in the front seat.

So-called thrill killings are also occasionally committed by juveniles acting alone. Recently, for example, fifteen-year-old Rod Matthews of Massachusetts was convicted of second-degree murder for killing a fourteen-year-old neighbor.[5] Matthews, who was fourteen at the time of the killing, lured his victim into the woods, stalked him from behind, and then beat the boy to death with a baseball bat.

Matthews later described for two friends how he had plotted the killing. He also took the two to see the victim's bludgeoned body as it lay in the woods, reportedly telling one friend he had committed the homicide because he "wanted to know what it was like to kill somebody."[6] In convicting Matthews, the jury rejected his claim that he was insane and that the crime was caused by the side effects of Ritalin—a prescription drug Matthews took for hyperactivity.

In another, perhaps less deliberate, "thrill" killing involving only one youth, a fourteen-year-old New Mexico boy randomly fired a .22 caliber rifle out a second-story window into a backyard in which a group of children were playing.[7] This youth was charged with first-degree murder when one of the shots he fired struck and killed a nine-year-old boy. Although the shooter was described as a boy frequently in trouble, subsequent psychological evaluation found insufficient evidence to indicate that the killing resulted from a mental disorder.

Other slayings that might be classified as "thrill" killings are much less deliberate. An all-too-common scenario is that in which two or more youngsters engage in one or another version of a fatal game of Russian roulette. In one recent case, for example, fifteen-year-old Stephen was in his bedroom showing two thirteen-year-old friends his collection of weapons: a sawed-off shotgun, Chuka sticks, and a gravity knife. Stephen then escorted his two friends to his parents' bedroom, where he took out his father's shotgun. He then took five shotgun shells from a shelf.[8]

Knowing that three of these shells were "live" and two were "dummies," Stephen randomly loaded four of the shells into the gun's magazine. He then pumped the shotgun and—without knowing whether the shell he chambered was live or a dummy—pointed the gun directly at one thirteen-year-old and said, "Let's play Polish roulette. Who is first?"[9] Stephen then pulled the trigger. The live round tore through the thirteen-year-old's chest, lung, and shoulder, killing him. Stephen was convicted of "depraved indifference murder."[10]

"Bias" Killings

In a number of other cases of random and impulsive killings committed by juveniles, victims apparently have been targeted for lethal violence on the basis of their membership in a minority group. Such so-called hate or bias crimes have included the killings of homeless people, homosexuals, and members of racial minorities.

Homeless People

In recent years, homeless people have become a common target of juvenile violence, sometimes homicidal violence. In one case, for example, two sixteen-year-old California youths were walking in a Burbank park when they decided "to rid the park of bums."[11] With no provocation, they attacked two homeless men, killing one with karate kicks and beating the other into a coma. In a similar incident in Florida, four high school classmates beat to death a Native American transient who was living on a concrete ledge under an expressway.[12] The boys told the police that they had attacked vagrants in the past and had enjoyed it. And in still another such incident, two seventeen-year-olds and a sixteen-year-old from Massachusetts were charged with beating, stabbing, and mutilating a seventy-three-year-old homeless man in his sleeping place in a downtown alleyway.[13]

Whether any of these youths harbored actual bias against their homeless victims or simply found them convenient and vulnerable targets is not entirely clear. In either case, however, it appears that the victims' mere status as homeless vagrants caused them to be targeted for death.

Homosexuals

Homosexuals have also become a target for juvenile violence, including homicidal violence. While some juvenile killings of homosexuals are arguably classifiable as "revenge" killings (see below), in other instances homosexuals have been slain by juveniles apparently just because of their sexual orientation. For example, a twenty-nine year old homosexual man from Georgia was recently beaten, shot in the head, and run over by two teenage boys, ages seventeen and fourteen, who then "went around town bragging about it."[14] No motive for the killing was established, but one investigating officer said the police had received information "that these boys just don't like gays."[15]

Racial Minorities

Not surprisingly, members of racial and ethnic minorities have also been singled out for attack, sometimes lethal attack, by juveniles. Perhaps the most widely known case of this sort in modern times is New York City's so-called Howard Beach incident.[16] In the Howard Beach incident, about a dozen White youngsters, mostly teenagers, confronted three Black men outside a pizzeria in the predominantly White Howard Beach neighborhood. The White youths, yelling racial epithets and armed with baseball bats and other weapons, chased the three Black men through the streets. The band of youths chased one Black man into the path of an oncoming car, which struck and killed him. The youths caught a second Black man and severely beat him. The third Black man escaped injury.

Three of the White youths—two who were eighteen and one seventeen years old—were convicted of manslaughter. Several others were convicted of riot charges and the rest were acquitted. At sentencing, one youth apologized to the dead man's mother for "your senseless loss." At an appellate argument in the case, lawyers for the youths convicted of manslaughter conceded that the attack and killing had been—contrary to the youths' prior assertions— "racially motivated."[17]

In another much more intentional killing, two California youths, seventeen and nineteen years old, shot and killed two Mexican laborers.[18] According to authorities, the youths committed the killings because they "didn't like Mexicans."[19] Police reports indicated that the two youths—whom they characterized as "aspiring Rambos"—had searched for Mexican targets, killed the laborers with eleven shots from a semiautomatic assault rifle, and then "boasted about the crime to friends and acquaintances."[20]

In a similar though undoubtedly less premeditated incident, four New Jersey youths, apparently part of a much larger self-proclaimed group of "Dotbusters," beat a thirty-year-old Indian man to death on a city street.[21] The so-called Dotbusters—"self-named for the red bindi mark applied to the foreheads of many married Indian women"—are said to have been responsible for numerous violent attacks against immigrants from both India and Pakistan.[22] The youths in this particular case, aged fifteen to seventeen, denied any racial motive in their brutal attack on their Indian victim, insisting they attacked the man because he was bald. Charged with murder, they were convicted only of assault.

"Revenge" Killings

Among the most brutal and senseless of homicides committed by juveniles are those attributed to revenge. In many cases, it appears that such killings result from the youthful perpetrator's desire to avenge some sort of sexual abuse previously committed against him or her by the homicide victim. In Oregon, for example, a seventeen-year-old boy—one of two boys who were sexually abused by a Boy Scout leader—shot and killed the Scout leader in front of the man's home just a week after a court had sentenced him to serve only fifteen days in jail for the abuse.[23] In a similar case, a seventeen-year-old California boy admitted killing a child pornographer and dumping his body into an abandoned mine shaft after the two fought over nude pictures the man had taken of the boy.[24]

In a Texas case of this sort, two seventeen-year-olds and a twenty-year-old lured another twenty year old into the woods and then shot him in the face and body with four different guns, killing him.[25] After one of the seventeen-year-olds was convicted of murder, his father and a psychologist who examined him testified that the killing occurred because the victim had earlier tried to engage the boy in homosexual relations.

In an Oregon case, a seventeen-year-old youth responded to being fired from his brief job at an ice cream store by returning to the store, forcing the manager who had fired him to kneel in an ice cream freezer, and then shooting the man in the base of his skull.[26]

In another senseless and bizarre juvenile killing motivated by a desire for revenge, three male prostitutes, aged nineteen, eighteen, and fifteen, killed a forty-one-year-old college professor who had charged them with forging his signature on a $900 check.[27] When the professor refused to drop the charges, the teens threatened him with countercharges of child molestation. The professor dropped the charges, but within days the three youths broke into his home and attacked him after he came home unexpectedly, taking them by surprise. The youths knocked the man unconscious and then bound, gagged, blindfolded, and suffocated him on his living room couch. Before leaving the scene, they also put out a cigarette on the man's abdomen, covered his head with a tote bag, spattered food on the walls, and scrawled "redrum" (murder spelled backward) on a wall. All three youths were runaways with clearly troubled backgrounds, but none had been identified as mentally ill.

Occasionally the use of deadly force by juveniles appears to be a form of revenge for teasing or scapegoating. Two recent Midwestern cases illustrate this kind of response. In the first, a fourteen-year-old Illinois boy, described as a "lonely outcast," was charged with attempted murder after stabbing three classmates who relentlessly teased him about his clothes.[28] More recently, a twelve-year-old Missouri boy, who was constantly teased by classmates about his obesity, pulled a gun from his gym bag during a seventh-grade history class, shot and killed a classmate, and then used the gun to kill himself. The boy, an honor student described by his junior high school principal as "a quiet, reserved . . . good student," had warned another student a week earlier "not to come to school because he was going to shoot everyone."[29]

In a somewhat similar case in California, a seventeen-year-old boy shot and killed a classmate who exposed the youth's homosexuality on the night of his high school graduation.[30] The youth had concealed his homosexuality since his early teens, fearing that his family would disapprove. After his father confronted him with rumors that he was a homosexual, the youth stopped his classmate on the street, hoping to scare him into recanting his story. When the schoolmate responded by calling him a "faggot," he shot and killed him. A jury later convicted the youth of second-degree murder.

Sometimes what appear to be revenge killings may not be so simply explained. For example, a seventeen-year-old California youth recently fatally stabbed a fifty-two-year-old male homosexual neighbor.[31] In his own defense, the youth claimed that the victim had made sexual overtures to him and at the time of the killing was trying to force his way into the youth's home. The prosecutor described the youth's account of the killing as "willful misrepresentations" and the boy was convicted of manslaughter.[32]

Interestingly, in this case it was suggested that the real motive for the youth's killing of a homosexual may have been his earlier victimization, not by the man he killed but by a group of his own peers. Two months before the killing, the youth was held down by four of his football teammates while another teammate used a broomstick to prod him in the buttocks. The broomstick slipped and was jammed into the youth's scrotum, causing a painful injury which required medical care including stitches. While the youth's family and teachers minimized the significance of this trauma, others aware of the incident characterized it as "tantamount to homosexual rape." They suggested that it could have been "an underlying motive" for the later killing of the homosexual who may or may not have made advances to the youth.[33]

In an even more obscure purported case of "revenge" killing, a fourteen-year-old New York youth strangled a two-year-old boy. The fourteen-year-old explained that he killed the toddler because the boy and his mother had recently moved into his home and the two-year-old's mother was "annoying" his own mother.[34] Despite the teenager's assertions, it seems far from clear that this killing was really motivated by vengeance. Like a number of other obscure juvenile killings attributed to "revenge," it may well be that this youth simply seized upon revenge as an after-the-fact explanation for an otherwise inexplicable act.

"Cult-Related" Killings

Only relatively recently have law enforcement authorities, criminologists, and others begun to recognize that an increasing number of senseless and/or bizarre killings are somehow related to the occult. From various reports it appears that some homicides, including some senseless killings committed by juveniles, are motivated by or otherwise related to the perpetrator's involvement in a cult or in cultlike rituals.

The clearest of cult-related killings involve juvenile perpetrators who are actually members of cults. Other cult-related killings are committed by youths who, while perhaps not formally members of any cult, fancy themselves as cultists. Finally, a number of such killings seem to occur in the course of acting out fantasy games that border on cult rituals.

Killings Committed By Juveniles in Cults

Several recent cases illustrate the wide variety of dynamics in killings perpetrated by juveniles who are actually involved in cults. In Florida, two brothers, aged eighteen and sixteen, both members of the violent, neo-Nazi cult called the "skinheads," beat and stabbed to death a Black man.[35] After the killing, the boys' father described how he had watched them "change from happy children . . . to sullen, depressed teenagers who hung swastikas on their bedroom walls."[36] The father explained that his older son had joined the skinheads two years earlier and that his younger son had followed the older boy into the youth cult, known for its Nazi symbolism and hatred of Blacks and homosexuals.

In a Nebraska case, Dennis Ryan, a sixteen-year-old boy, was convicted, along with his father, of murder in the cult-related torture killing of James Thimm.[37] Michael Ryan, the boy's father, was the self-imposed leader of a survivalist cult headquartered on a farm in southeastern Nebraska. Prior to discovery of the killing, the group—which consisted of twenty adults and children, including Michael Ryan, Dennis Ryan, and James Thimm—had been stealing machinery and cattle and stockpiling guns and ammunition in preparation for "Armageddon." The farm where they lived together was an armed and heavily guarded encampment.

The elder Ryan claimed he would speak to God and gave orders in the name of "Yahweh." He ran the group like an army and assigned ranks to his armed followers, including his son Dennis, who was fifteen years old at the time of the killing of Thimm. While the others held lower military ranks, Michael Ryan was "king" and Dennis Ryan was "prince." The "prince" had authority over the other followers and relayed messages to them from the "king."

At some point, Michael Ryan decided that Thimm was to be demoted to the rank of "slave." As a result, for the month prior to his death, Thimm was kept chained to a post at night but allowed to work around the farm during the day. A month or so before Thimm's death, the younger Ryan shot him in the face. Thimm recovered from the wound without medical attention, but the day before his death, Michael Ryan, Dennis Ryan, and three other followers took turns torturing Thimm. Each man inserted a greased shovel handle into Thimm's rectum and then administered fifteen lashes with a bullwhip and a livestock whip. The next day, just before Thimm died, the same group, including Dennis Ryan, again inflicted fifteen lashes each and were each directed by Michael Ryan to shoot one of Thimm's fingers.

Prior to his trial, Dennis Ryan was given a complete psychological evaluation, including a battery of psychological tests. The evaluation revealed that Dennis was average or above average in intelligence and showed "pretty good reality contact," but had the overall maturity of a twelve- or thirteen-year-old.[38] The evaluation further revealed that Dennis "strongly and uncritically" accepted his father's "religion."[39]

More recently, in New York and Missouri, groups of allegedly devil worshipping teenagers have ganged up on and brutally killed their peers. In the New York case, seventeen-year-old Richard Kasso and an eighteen-year-old companion were charged with killing a seventeen-year-old peer during a "satanic ritual."[40] Richard, who for three years had belonged to the "Knights of the Black Circle,"[41] a "loose satanic cult" of more than twenty teenagers, confessed that he stabbed the victim repeatedly while his companion held him down.[42]

Richard told authorities that the assault was initially prompted by the victim's theft of drugs belonging to him. But he also told the police that as the assailants were leaving the scene of the stabbing, the victim cried out and a crow cawed. Richard said he interpreted these sounds as an order from the devil to kill the victim. According to his signed statement, Richard then went back, stabbed the youth in the face, and cut his eyes out.[43]

According to Richard Kasso's parents, he had been a "gifted pupil and athlete" until he reached the seventh grade, at which time he "became insubordinate at school" and took part in a burglary.[44] In the three years leading up to the killing, Richard had abused and sold drugs, threatened his sisters, threatened and attempted suicide, and been arrested for digging up a grave to obtain bones for a satanic ritual.[45] Just one day after he was arraigned on murder charges, Richard committed suicide—using a bedsheet to hang himself in his jail cell.

In the Missouri case, three teenagers, all members of a self-styled satanic cult, beat another teenage boy to death with baseball bats, tied a 200-pound boulder to his body, and dumped it into a well.[46] The boys, all aged seventeen, admitted that the killing was, in effect, a human sacrifice to Satan. For months prior to the killing all three boys had been fascinated with satanism and satanic rituals. Together they planned the killing and made several aborted efforts to kill the victim before finally doing so.

Jim, who struck the first of some seventy blows to the victim, had been an honor student and altar boy until age eleven. Thereafter, he had a history of drug abuse, temper outbursts, academic problems, and extreme cruelty to animals. According to one report, Jim's friends recalled watching him "drive screws through a Barbie doll's head, then burn the plastic face and wish out loud that it was human."[47] Despite such obvious signs of deviance, Jim's only psychiatric history consisted of a few sessions with his parents at a local mental health center.[48]

Ron, a second youth involved in the killing, came from a troubled family background. His drug-addicted father was a drifter who had held thirty jobs in four years. Like Jim, Ron was also a drug abuser. He too had been to the local mental health center for family counseling. Ron told a psychotherapist that he was obsessed with morbid and violent fantasies of hurting others, was interested in satanic worship, and feared that he was possessed by demons.[49] The psychotherapist, who assured Ron's mother that this was simply a normal phase of adolescence, would later tell the court that he did not find Ron's fantasies, interests, and fears "atypical" among adolescents.[50]

At his trial for murder, a psychiatrist testified that when Ron took part in the killing, he lacked the capacity to differentiate reality and fantasy.[51] The psychiatrist added that Ron had simply followed along when his friends suggested making a human sacrifice to Satan.[52]

Pete, the third participant in the killing, claimed to be an abused child who often heard voices in his head telling him to do evil acts. At trial, the same psychiatrist who testified for Ron told the jury that when Pete took part in the killing, he was suffering from a psychosis induced by drugs, "heavy metal" music, and the influence of Jim.[53] The jury rejected both Ron's and Pete's claims of insanity and convicted them of murder. Jim pleaded guilty to murder. All three boys were sentenced to life in prison without parole.

In another case of juvenile homicide growing out of a youth's involvement with a self-styled satanic cult, a sixteen-year-old Oklahoma boy killed a convenience store clerk and then, several months later, shot and killed his mother and stepfather as they slept.[54] Sean Sellers, described by others as an exceptionally bright student, initially became interested in satanism when, as a preteen, he started reading books on the subject and playing the fantasy game Dungeons and Dragons. Within a few years, he was carrying out satanic rituals, both alone and with others, including one solitary ritual in which he used his own blood to write: "I renounce God, I will serve only Satan . . . Hail Satan."[55]

Within the year prior to the first killing, Sean had dropped off the high school honor roll, lost interest in sports, adopted a "scruffy, semi-Rambo" appearance,[56] and was conducting satanic worship services in an abandoned farmhouse with eight or so other youths who had joined his self-styled cult. These sessions culminated in an incident in which Sean and one of his fellow Satan worshippers conducted a "sacrificial ritual." The boys stole a .357 Magnum and drove to a convenience store, looking for a clerk there who had once refused to sell them beer. Finding the clerk in the store, Sean shot and killed him.

Following this murder, Sean became romantically involved with a teenage girl. When his parents forbade him to see the girl, he ran away. After his parents found him and brought him back home, he killed them. On the night of the killing, Sean returned home from the pizza parlor where he was working part-time. He dressed in black ritual attire, lit candles, conducted a satanic service, and went to sleep. Some time later that night he awoke, found a revolver, tiptoed into his parents' room, and shot and killed his mother and stepfather.

Sean Sellers pleaded not guilty by reason of insanity, claiming that he had no recall of any of the killings. The jury rejected that defense, found Sean criminally responsible, and convicted him of capital murder. Sean was then sentenced to die.

In still another case of juveniles forming a self-styled cult and then committing a ritual killing, three Minnesota youths, aged nineteen, seventeen, and thirteen were charged with killing a thirty-year-old drifter.[57] The oldest youth, who pleaded not guilty by reason of insanity, reportedly told the police that he and the two younger youths formed a "vampire cult" after repeatedly watching a movie about a gang of teenage vampires. Then, prior to the killing, he and the two others youths "talked about finding a victim and slashing his wrists to drink his blood."[58]

Finally, and most recently, a fifteen-year-old California boy confessed to his role in a ritualistic killing, the "sacrifice" of a twenty-two-year-old man in a satanic "initiation ritual." The youth told authorities that he and four young adults, all members of a "satanic coven," were present at the victim's purported initiation—a ceremony in which members of the group handcuffed the victim, slashed his throat, and then threw his body in a drainage ditch.[59]

Killings Committed by Juveniles Fascinated
with Satanism

In some cases where juveniles have committed what might be called cult-related homicides or attempted homicides, there is no evidence of actual cult involvement in the sense of belonging to some organized or even self-styled group, but rather only an individual fascination with satanism and satanic rituals.

Such was the case with a fourteen-year-old Illinois boy who was recently charged with attempted murder after he stabbed three classmates who relentlessly teased him about his clothes, decorated with satanic symbols, and his interest in satanism.[60] The boy was described by those who knew him as a "good boy" with a strong religious background who was never known to be in any trouble. The boy's pastor later described him as a lonely outcast whose interest in satanism was a "superficial attempt to find acceptance among classmates who had constantly spurned him."[61]

In Michigan, a fifteen-year-old boy shot and killed his brother and then telephoned the police and threatened to kill his parents, who were due home at any minute, unless the police stopped him.[62] The police arrived and the youth led them to his brother's body in the basement.

Three days after the killing, the boy's parents called police back to the home to show them what they had found hidden in the boy's closet: "a hood, a long black robe, silver chalice, dark blue candle, glass bottle containing red liquid, piece of white parchment paper . . . a paper pentagram . . . a sword, and an upside-down cross."[63] The closet also contained a book, *The Power of Satan,* which gave "step-by-step instructions on how to perform a Satanic ritual."[64] Questioned after the killing, the boy confirmed that he was "into Satanism."[65]

A police detective, consulted for his expertise in cult-related crimes, reviewed the facts and the evidence and gave this analysis of the boy and the killing:

> I think this kid crossed over from the dabbler stage to the self-styled Satanist stage. . . . Here's a kid who's a loner, not doing great in school, into drugs and so on. . . . This wasn't a spur-of-the-moment murder. It was cold and calculated. I believe he felt he was doing his brother a favor by killing him. He was elevating him to a higher level of consciousness. He mentioned those exact words to the police dispatcher.[66]

When a juvenile becomes obsessed with satanism and then kills another person, it seems reasonable if not essential to question the mental health of that juvenile. Undoubtedly, many if not most such youths are subjected to psychological and/or psychiatric examination(s) after they kill. While it appears that most juveniles involved in satanic killings are disturbed, at least to some extent, there is rarely evidence that they are genuinely psychotic. One exception is a case recently reported by Benedek and Cornell. Fifteen-year-old "Bob" stabbed his mother to death and then retreated to the basement of the family home, where he was later found reading the Bible and chanting, "Kill the Devil."[67]

When seen for psychological evaluation, Bob stated a strong interest in witchcraft and said that on the day of the killing he heard special messages directed to him on phonograph records he was playing. These messages, he said, suggested that he kill his mother. Bob also demonstrated little understanding of the charges against him and said that he would be saved by Satan. He was diagnosed as psychotic and found not competent to stand trial.

In some cases, juveniles fascinated with satanism kill others and then kill themselves. One such case involved a fourteen-year-old New Jersey youth who was a paperboy, Boy Scout, and "model son and student" until a month before he stabbed his mother twelve times with his Boy Scout knife, set fire to his books on satanism in the living room while the rest of the family slept nearby, and then went to a neighbor's yard where he committed suicide by slashing his wrists and throat.[68] In the month or so before the killing, the boy had become obsessed with satanic literature and heavy metal music. Just weeks before the killing, he reportedly told a friend that Satan had appeared to him in a vision and had urged him to kill his family and begin preaching satanism.

Juvenile Killings Related to Occult Fantasy Games

Finally, some juvenile killings, which may be described as "cult-related," appear to stem not from any genuine devotion to satanism or the occult but rather from an obsession with fantasy games, such as Dungeons and Dragons, which involve themes of satanic sacrifice, witchcraft, demonology, monsters, and killing.

As early as 1985, two public interest groups asked the Federal Trade Commission (FTC) to consider requiring that warnings precede a television show that was based upon the popular youth fantasy game Dungeons and Dragons. The National Coalition on Television Violence and a parent's group, Bothered About Dungeons and Dragons ("BADD"), told the FTC that this particular fantasy game "has caused a number of suicides and murders."[69]

A psychiatrist who was then president of the National Coalition on Television Violence said in 1988 that more than fifty criminal defendants have been convicted after using what he called the "Dungeons and Dragons defense," an insanity defense based upon involvement with the fantasy game.[70]

He also reported that as of June 1988, "We can link 116 deaths, cases of suicides and homicides, to these antisocial games."[71]

Although the statement that Dungeons and Dragons has caused many murders appears to be an exaggeration, there certainly have been cases in which killings committed by juveniles were at least somehow related to the perpetrator's interest or involvement in fantasy games, including Dungeons and Dragons. In Alabama, for example, three boys—two seventeen-year-olds and a fourteen-year-old—were charged with capital murder in the killing of a convenience store clerk. All three, described by teachers and others as "bright, popular, all-American youths," were frequent players of a fantasy game called "Top Secret."[72]

On the day of the killing, two of the boys agreed to play out their respective roles in the fantasy game and then commit suicide. In playing out their fantasy game roles, they stole guns, drove to the convenience store, shot and killed the clerk, and then took $700 in cash. The third youth alerted the police of the impending suicide. When the two boys were captured by police, they were holding cocked guns to their heads.

In a New York case involving Dungeons and Dragons, a fifteen-year-old boy shot and killed an eleven-year-old boy while playing the game.[73] The fifteen-year-old admitted shooting the eleven-year-old in the head with a .20 gauge shotgun as part of a Dungeons and Dragons fantasy. During the course of the game, he told police, he became convinced that the eleven-year-old "had become evil" and that his own role in the game was to "extinguish evil."[74]

Two other teenagers who had played Dungeons and Dragons with the fifteen-year-old boy testified that the boy had also pointed the gun at them during the course of earlier games. A psychologist who examined the boy testified that although the boy was fifteen years old, he had the maturity of a twelve- to thirteen-year-old. Tried as an adult, he was convicted of murder.

"Romantic" Murder-Suicides

More juveniles kill themselves than kill others. The juvenile suicide rate in the United States, while statistically low, is still more than twice the juvenile homicide rate. More than 5,000 juveniles kill themselves each year.[75] An unknown but undoubtedly small percentage of these suicides are committed as part of what might be called "romantic" murder-suicides—cases in which a romantic relationship between two juveniles ends in the death of both.

In some instances, it appears that these juvenile murder-suicides are the result of an agreement or suicide pact between the juveniles. For example, in one such case, a sixteen-year-old New York girl, a "bright, sensitive" but unhappy child who was under psychiatric care, and her eighteen-year-old boyfriend wrote poetic suicide notes.[76] The girl then stabbed the boy with an 8-inch dagger, slashed her own wrists, and swallowed between 60 and 100 assorted pills.

In a similar but less clear case in Illinois, a teenage couple, who had been dating six months and were planning to become engaged, were found shot to death under circumstances that led authorities to conclude that they had died in a "homicide-suicide."[77] Both youngsters, the eighteen-year-old boy and sixteen-year-old girl, were described by family, friends, and neighbors as normal, active, and happy youths. No motive for the killings was determined.

Whether or not this particular murder-suicide was a joint venture is unclear, but it is clear that at least some juvenile murder-suicides are not. In some instances, frustrated juveniles have killed their erstwhile lovers and then themselves. For example, in a New York case, a fourteen-year-old girl, who was pregnant, broke up with her eighteen-year-old boyfriend. When she would not resume the relationship, he persisted, went to her home, shot her in the head, and then turned the gun on himself.[78]

More recently, in a somewhat similar case, a seventeen-year-old New Hampshire youth quarreled with and then stabbed and seriously injured his father on the day before the boy's scheduled graduation from high school. The boy then went to a local ice cream parlor where he shot and killed two people, including a seventeen-year-old girl who had recently broken up with him, ending their two-year relationship. When police surrounded the store, the boy shot and killed himself.[79]

Killings Committed by Mentally Disturbed Juveniles

Only a very small percentage of juveniles who kill are psychotic or otherwise severely disturbed.[80] Indeed, it even appears that some portion of those relatively few juvenile killers diagnosed as psychotic are, in fact, not psychotic. As was mentioned in chapter 2, homicidal youths who demonstrate no psychotic symptoms are sometimes diagnosed as psychotic, either because they claim amnesia for their crimes or because of the brutal and senseless nature of those crimes.[81] It is also worth noting that a small percentage of youths charged with homicide—mainly those who had prior contacts with the legal and/or mental health system—attempt to feign symptoms of psychosis when examined after killing.[82]

Still, there are numerous cases in which apparently senseless killings are committed by juveniles who are diagnosed as psychotic. These so-called psychotic killings run the gamut of juvenile homicides, but probably the most frequent victims in these cases are members of the juvenile's own family. For example, Patrick DeGelleke and John Justice, whose cases were mentioned in chapter 3, both killed their parents and were later diagnosed as psychotic.

Early one morning, fifteen-year-old Patrick DeGelleke splashed lantern fuel outside the door to the bedroom in which his adoptive parents slept. He then set the room ablaze and killed both parents.[83] Patrick, who had been in counseling of one sort or another for the preceding five years or so, was described in testimony at his murder trial as a quiet, withdrawn youngster who had few friends, was scapegoated by other children, and sometimes erupted into violent and uncontrollable temper tantrums. In school, he had difficulty concentrating, needed continuous supervision, and was often observed "staring into space for hours at a time."[84] Prior to the killing, his adoptive parents had sought intervention from the juvenile court, alleging that Patrick was stealing, skipping school, and becoming uncontrollable.

At Patrick's trial, a psychologist testified that Patrick felt that his parents were planning to have him institutionalized.[85] That, according to the psychologist, recalled past rejections and triggered a psychotic rage in which Patrick lost touch with reality and started the fire."[86] The jury rejected Patrick's insanity defense and convicted him of murder.

John Justice was a "straight-A" honor student, a high school senior with no evidence of prior psychological problems and no history of violent behavior. Yet, within a two-hour span, the seventeen-year-old killed four people: his mother, father, brother, and a neighbor.[87] John stabbed his younger brother to death and then stabbed his mother fourteen times and threw her down a flight of basement stairs. John then left the house by car, picked his father up from work, brought him home, and stabbed him to death. Over the next two hours he drank heavily and tried unsuccessfully to slash his own wrists. Then, in a second suicide attempt, John drove off in the family car at an extremely high rate of speed, smashed the car into the rear end of another car, and killed the driver of that vehicle, a twenty-two-year-old neighbor.

At John's trial on four murder charges, a psychiatrist who examined him testified that John had planned the killings of his family members in advance. Nevertheless, the psychiatrist diagnosed John as psychotic and most likely suffering from schizophrenia. In a highly unusual verdict, the jury found John not guilty by reason of insanity in the killings of his father and brother but guilty of murder in the deaths of his mother and neighbor. After hearing the jury's verdict, John told photographers, "Take all the pictures of me you want, because I'm not living. I'm dead."[88]

Occasionally nonfamilial homicides are also committed by juveniles diagnosed as psychotic. For example, Anthony Broussard and Leslie Torres both committed apparently senseless killings and then introduced evidence at trial that they suffered from psychosis.

Sixteen-year-old Californian Anthony Broussard, whose crimes were dramatized in the movie *River's Edge*, raped and strangled his fourteen-year-old girlfriend, then reportedly laughed and told friends, "I raped and murdered this chick."[89] He also took at least seven and possibly as many as twelve teenagers to look at the body and throw rocks at it over a period of two days before two youths finally reported the killing to the police. Previously, Anthony reportedly had tried to rape two other girls, aged thirteen and fourteen.

Anthony was diagnosed by one psychiatrist as a chronic paranoid schizophrenic with organic brain disease caused by drug abuse. According to this psychiatrist, who testified at Anthony's murder trial, Anthony was devastated when, at the age of eight, he came home one day and found his mother dead. The psychiatrist told the jury that thereafter Anthony's maturation stopped and he developed a pathological fantasy life. Another psychiatrist testified that Anthony appeared to be without feelings or emotion, "as if nothing touched him."[90]

Despite his obvious psychological disturbance, Anthony Broussard pleaded guilty to murder and was sentenced to serve twenty-five years in prison, after the court determined that he was not amenable to treatment in the juvenile justice system. As part of the plea arrangement, the charges relating to the two other girls were dropped.

Seventeen-year-old Leslie Torres, a homeless New York City youth, went on a seven-day "cocaine-inspired rampage" in which he killed five people and left six others wounded in a spree of robberies.[91] When arrested, Leslie told police that he committed numerous killings and robberies to support his $500-a-day addiction to the street drug crack. Testifying at his murder trial, Leslie told jurors that crack caused him to feel like God but that he saw the devil whenever he looked into a mirror.[92] A psychiatrist who examined Leslie testified that the youth suffered from "cocaine-induced psychosis" at the time of the killings.[93] The jury rejected Leslie's insanity defense and convicted him of murder.

Interestingly, while all of these youths—Patrick DeGelleke, John Justice, Anthony Broussard, and Leslie Torres—were diagnosed by at least one psychiatrist or psychologist as psychotic, none of them was fully acquitted by reason of insanity and none presented the classic criteria for such a diagnosis. In these as well as numerous other cases, the diagnosis of "psychosis" may have been stretched somewhat to fit—or at least explain—these horrible killings. As Cornell has observed:

> It seems tenuous to diagnose psychosis because of the impulsivity and rage of the perpetrator at the time of the homicide. There should be some evidence of delusions, hallucinations, formal thought disorder, or grossly bizarre behavior to support a diagnosis of psychosis.[94]

As an example of "a genuine case of psychosis" in a juvenile who killed, Cornell and Benedek described seventeen-year-old "Alan" who stabbed a sixteen-year-old peer to death.[95] When Alan was arrested, he told the police that he had been "under lots of pressure" and that "radio and TV [were] giving me ideas . . . that I had to kill . . . like Baretta."[96]

When examined, Alan admitted killing the other youth and explained that "Jesus died on the cross for me so I wouldn't have to die, but I could kill somebody else so we both could die."[97] Alan also told the examiner that he was "Jesus Christ Superstar," that "music on the radio was directed specifically to him and referred to him as 'the Lord,'" and that a "violent voice . . . told me to kill."[98]

Prior to the killing, Alan had a three-year history of serious mental illness for which he had been hospitalized three times. His most recent hospitalization had taken place after he tried to drown his two younger brothers. After each hospitalization, he had been discharged on psychotropic medications but decompensated when he stopped taking them. The results of psychological testing helped confirm the diagnosis of paranoid schizophrenia.

It may well be that rather than being psychotic, youths such as Patrick DeGelleke, John Justice, Anthony Broussard, and Leslie Torres were instead manifesting what has been called "episodic dyscontrol"[99]—"a syndrome in which an individual with severe ego developmental deficits experiences episodes of severe loss of impulse control."[100] In any event, psychotic or not, it seems clear from the facts that in each of these cases the juvenile killers were significantly psychologically disturbed.

There are other cases in which juvenile killers, though not diagnosed as psychotic, also appear to be seriously psychologically disturbed. The cases of Joseph Aulisio of Pennsylvania, Torran Lee Meier of California, and Brenda Spencer of California are illustrative.

Joseph Aulisio was fifteen years old when he took two children, aged eight and four, into a vacant house, shot them at close range with a shotgun, and then dumped their bodies in an abandoned strip mine.[101] Although Joseph denied committing the crimes, he admitted being at the scene of the killings. The circumstantial evidence was strong, a jury convicted him of murder, and he was sentenced to die in the electric chair. When the jury announced its verdict, Joseph turned to members of his family, raised a clenched fist, and told them, "It's party time."[102] On appeal to the Pennsylvania Supreme Court, his convictions were affirmed, but the death sentence was vacated and a sentence of life in prison was imposed.

At Joseph's trial, a psychologist testified that Joseph, a frequent truant, was learning disabled and had an IQ of 81. The psychologist explained that if Joseph's IQ had been two points lower, he would have fallen into the borderline mentally retarded range of intellectual functioning.[103] Moreover, the psychologist testified that Joseph was an anxious, insecure, angry, and depressed youth, so alienated from others that "he feels lonely even when he's with other people."[104] Other evidence indicated that Joseph had grown up in a chaotic home and had been profoundly affected by his parents' divorce and the earlier death of his infant sister.

Torran Lee Meier, whose case was described briefly in chapter 3, killed his mother and tried to kill his younger brother.[105] Torran and two friends wrestled his mother to the floor and took turns strangling her. They then tried four times to kill Torran's younger brother, ultimately tying him inside a gasoline-soaked car, setting the car ablaze and pushing it over a 60-foot cliff.

Evidence presented at Torran's murder trial indicated that he had been psychologically abused by his mother for years prior to the killing. According to witnesses, Torran was a model youth whose thirty-four-year-old divorced mother constantly berated, belittled, and humiliated him and also went out of her way to be sexually provocative with him—for example, calling him a "faggot" and telling him in front of others that he was "not man enough", doing housework topless in his and others' presence, and swimming nude in front of him.[106]

Expert testimony from a psychiatrist-neurologist indicated that Torran was a youth with brain dysfunction and significantly impaired ability to cope with stress. The physician testified that Torran demonstrated an extremely rare brain wave abnormality and suffered from brain damage, severe allergies, and frequent headaches, all of which impaired his ability to deal with the accumulating stress imposed upon him by his mother. Although this testimony was disputed by experts who testified for the prosecution, the jury accepted Torran's defense that when he killed his mother he was in a state of "diminished capacity" and thus guilty of manslaughter rather than first- or even second-degree murder.

Brenda Spencer was a seventeen-year-old high school senior whose father gave her a semiautomatic rifle for Christmas. A month later, she used the rifle to fire randomly into a crowded elementary school yard across the street from her San Diego home, killing two and injuring nine, including eight schoolchildren.[107] After a six-hour standoff with police, Brenda was captured. Asked why she had done the shooting, she told police, "I don't like Mondays. Mondays always get me down."[108]

Brenda was charged with first-degree murder. After two court-ordered psychiatric examinations, Brenda, who was described as "a quiet tomboy obsessed with guns, violence and fantasies of killing police,"[109] pleaded not guilty by reason of insanity. Later, however, she changed her plea to guilty and was sentenced to two terms of twenty-five years to life imprisonment. A recent report, ten years after the killings, indicated that Brenda has been a "model prisoner" who "has a clean disciplinary record and has adjusted well to [prison]."[110]

6
Gang Killings

The violent gang is not a new phenomenon. Yet its contemporary form re-flects a brand and intensity of violence that differentiate it from earlier gang patterns. The "kill for kicks" homicide is today a source of concern not only in the large city . . . but also in the suburbs and small towns.[1]

This characterization of juvenile gang violence in the United States, pub-lished more than twenty-five years ago, is just as apt today as it was then—perhaps even more so. Major cities, small towns, and suburbs across the country are being terrorized by juvenile gangs,[2] some highly organized and others put together on "the spur of the moment."[3] In cities such as Boston, New York, Chicago, Washington, Detroit, and Los Angeles, gang killings—many of which are drug related—have reached epidemic proportions.[4] Many of these homicides involve gang members killing other gang members, but innocent bystanders are also often killed in what have come to be known as "drive-by" killings[5]—incidents in which gang members drive by a street cor-ner, playground, or other populated public space and spray gunfire, hoping to injure or kill rival gang members.

Solid data regarding juvenile gang involvement in homicides are hard to come by. For example, while there is a large literature on street gangs, much of it is outdated and most of it devotes little if any attention to the specific issue of gang-related killings.[6] In fact, while it is clear that many gang-related homicides are committed by juveniles, there is virtually no mention of such killings anywhere in the clinical or research literature on juvenile homicide.[7]

This chapter is designed to fill at least a portion of that void by reviewing some of the available data on juvenile gangs and gang killings from several major urban areas and by describing a number of specific cases which illus-trate various aspects of the dynamics of these killings.

Although it appears that juvenile gangs exist in communities of all sizes across America,[8] very little is known about these gangs except for those op-erating in the largest metropolitan areas. Gangs in these areas have come under greater scrutiny because they are larger, better organized, and more involved in serious crimes such as homicide. Even in these areas, however,

Table 6–1
Gang-Related Homicides in Los Angeles County 1980–1988[16]

Year	Number of Homicides
1980	351
1981	292
1982	205
1983	216
1984	212
1985	271
1986	328
1987	387
1988	406[a]

[a]Not including "numerous small cities" in Los Angeles County which had not reported as of the date of publication

there is a paucity of gang membership data. For example, while these gangs are often referred to as juvenile or youth gangs, the age makeup of these groups is not entirely clear; some appear to be truly juvenile gangs, others are actually young adult gangs, and still others have memberships ranging from children to middle-aged adults.[9]

Los Angeles is clearly the single area of the United States most heavily infested with juvenile street gangs.[10] Recent reports indicate that Los Angeles County has approximately 600 active street gangs.[11] A Congressional report issued in 1988 estimated that "more than 70,000 gang members live in Los Angeles County alone" and reported that "there were a record 387 gang-related murders in Los Angeles" County in 1987.[12] More recently, the *Los Angeles Times* reported that even this record was broken in 1988. The data published by the *Times,* summarized in Table 6–1, indicate that by the end of 1988, gang homicides in Los Angeles County had "increased fifty percent in three years."[13]

Although the *Times'* statistics for 1988 gang-related homicides were incomplete, the Los Angeles County District Attorney recently reported that 452 people died in gang-related killings in his jurisdiction in 1988.[14] The District Attorney's May 1989 report also stated that "one out of every three homicides in Los Angeles County is gang-related."[15]

In the city of Los Angeles, the overall homicide rate dropped by 11.7 percent in 1988—a year during which there were 734 homicides in the city, the lowest number in ten years.[17] But the number of gang-related homicides rose from 207 in 1987 to 257 in 1988—a 25.3-percent increase.[18] Thus, in 1988, 37.9 percent of all homicides in the City of Los Angeles were gang related. Similarly, during the first three months of 1989, seventy-eight (38.4 percent) of the 203 reported homicides in the city were gang related.[19]

According to Los Angeles police officials, more than half of those killed in gang-related homicides are not gang members but others, including robbery victims and innocent bystanders killed in drive-by shootings aimed at rival gang members.[20] The other victims of these homicides are mainly gang members killed in drive-by shootings or in drug-related "turf wars."[21] In some cases, these drive-by shootings are part of the initiation rites for younger boys who want to become gang members.[22]

Law enforcement authorities in Los Angeles blame the increase in such killings on "heightened narcotics trade and increased use of powerful semi-automatic weapons, particularly among members of black street gangs,"[23] which have been described by the authorities as "the main distributors of crack throughout the Western United States."[24]

Most gang members in the Los Angeles area are Black or Hispanic. It is estimated that of the 70,000 gang members in the county, 45,000 are Chicanos and 25,000 are Blacks.[25] It is also estimated that between 10 and 15 percent of Los Angeles County's Chicano teenagers belong to gangs, many of which date back as far as 1935.[26] For the most part, Los Angeles gang members come from impoverished, drug-infested, high-crime-rate neighborhoods, which lack economic and recreational opportunities and have inordinately high dropout rates.[27]

Other cities, including Boston, New York, and Chicago, have also experienced recent increases in juvenile gangs and gang homicides. In Boston, for example, where official statistics on gang killings are not reported, there were between four and twelve or more gang killings in 1988, depending upon whose statistics are considered.[28] In the first quarter of 1989, two people were killed and more than a dozen injured in Boston gang violence.[29] Although in the past the police have minimized gang activity and involvement in homicides in Boston, recently law enforcement authorities have acknowledged that "youth gangs not only exist in Boston but are becoming larger and more violent."[30] But according to the Boston Police Department, these gangs are not as large or as well organized as those in Los Angeles but are often only small, "loosely organized" groups of "kids from one street getting together and calling themselves by their street name."[31]

As in Los Angeles, gang activity in Boston seems confined largely to the city's poorest neighborhoods, where the school dropout rate is 40 percent.[32] Although there are reportedly only half a dozen "major" juvenile gangs in Boston, there is also a "host of cliques, subsections and 'wannabees,' kids who aspire to be hard-core gang members."[33]

In Chicago, where some 12,000 youths reportedly belong to about 125 gangs,[34] drive-by shootings and other youth gang killings—often committed with automatic and semiautomatic firearms—have become commonplace.[35] There, as in Los Angeles, victims include both rival gang members and innocent bystanders caught in the cross fire.[36] In 1988, Chicago registered its lowest murder rate in twenty years, but gang-related killings increased by 28 percent.[37] In 1987, 47 (6.8 percent) of the 691 homicides in Chicago were classified as gang related; in 1988, 60 (9.1 percent) of Chicago's 658 homicides were gang related.[38]

Police officials in Chicago attribute this increase in gang-related killings to the growing availability of more powerful firearms and to the closing of inner-city hospitals, which increases the likelihood that victims of gang violence will die rather than recover from their wounds.[39]

In Chicago homicides are reported as "gang-related" only when they are "linked to organized gang activity," but in Los Angeles "any killing committed by a gang member is classified as gang-related."[40] It has been estimated that if Chicago used the Los Angeles definition of "gang-related," the number of gang-related killings there would "more than double."[41]

As in Los Angeles, Chicago's youth gang problem is not confined to the city of Chicago, but extends into the suburbs as well. It has been reported, for example, that at least twenty Chicago suburbs are plagued by juvenile gangs and that at least some of these towns and cities have been the scenes of gang-related homicides.[42]

In New York City, youth gangs include both highly organized drug gangs as well as informal bands of youthful marauders who come together solely to attack, rob, rape, and sometimes kill people. New York City drug gangs, whose members range in age from teens to mid-twenties, use violence, including homicide, to further their trafficking in drugs, especially cocaine and crack.[43] Killings committed by members of "young and violent drug gangs"— estimated to number as many as 523 in five years in upper Manhattan alone—appear designed to "eliminate rivals, discourage informers and keep law-abiding residents from complaining . . ."[44] The vast majority of these killings involve territorial fights between rival gangs or disputes with drug customers, but a number of innocent bystanders have also been killed.[45] According to police investigators, "to demonstrate toughness," drug gang members frequently kill in broad daylight on crowded streets, shoot their victims in the head at close range with semiautomatic weapons, and make no effort to keep from being identified.[46]

The other sort of gang violence common in New York City is that committed by so-called wolf packs or posses—"spontaneously organized" gatherings of anywhere from a handful to several dozen teenage (and sometimes younger) boys who commit impromptu, en masse acts of criminal violence, such as the widely publicized 1989 rape and attempted murder of a woman jogger in New York's Central Park.[47] Creation of these "spur-of-the-moment gangs" often seems to occur when older teens decide to "gather a pack" and pressure younger boys to join them.[48] The crimes they commit include larceny, robbery, rape, and homicide. An average of three such incidents occur each day in New York City.[49]

Random, apparently motiveless rampages of the sort committed by these "posses" and "packs" have recently come to be referred to as "wilding"—the word used by youths to describe the gang attack on the woman running in Central Park.[50] Although the name is new, the concept is not. New York law enforcement officials and others have pointed out that what is now called "wilding" has gone on in New York City at least since 1983.[51]

Gang-related homicides committed by juveniles take various forms. Although some statistics on gang homicide—such as those for Los Angeles—include as "gang related" any killing in which a gang member is the perpetrator or victim,[52] for present purposes it seems more appropriate to limit consideration to those killings committed by juvenile gang members in the course of gang activity.

Killings committed by juveniles in the course of gang activity include most of the same sorts of killings discussed in earlier chapters. With the exception of intrafamilial killings, gang-related homicides may be categorized in much the same fashion as nongang juvenile killings—that is, killings committed in the course of other crimes and senseless killings. Juvenile gang killings may be further categorized on the basis of whether the gang is an ongoing, organized group or simply an ad hoc, spontaneous formation. The homicidal acts of these two kinds of gang organizations will be considered separately.

Organized Juvenile Gangs

By far, the majority of juvenile gang-related homicides are committed in the course of the activities of at least loosely organized gangs—groups of juveniles that have some history and to which members are bound by something other than their roles in a single crime or series of crimes. Generally these groups have names, "uniforms" or "colors" (distinctive clothing, jackets, caps, etc.), and/or special signals by which members identify themselves and members of rival gangs.[53]

Killings Committed in the Course of Other Crimes

Occasionally, organized juvenile gangs kill in the course of committing other crimes. Aside from killings related to drug trafficking, however, which are fairly common, killings committed in the course of other crimes seem to comprise a clear minority of juvenile gang homicides. Members of organized juvenile gangs seem much more likely to kill for reasons most would regard as senseless—for example, vengeance, protecting the gang's turf, or just fun.

Drug Trafficking. Juvenile gang killings related to drug trafficking are generally motivated by the youthful perpetrators' desire to protect their economic interests—for example, to prevent their operations from being revealed to authorities, to eliminate or avoid competition, or to enforce collection of money owed for drugs. Several recent gang-related killings illustrate the relationship between drug trafficking and juvenile gang homicide.

In California, for example, three teenagers (including two thirteen-year-old girls) involved in a junior high school drug ring were charged with murdering a fourteen-year-old girl.[54] The victim, who the others believed had reported their drug ring to authorities, had been sexually molested and was found alongside a road with her head wrapped in two garbage bags.

In another California case, two gang members, sixteen and seventeen years old, were charged with murder in the shooting death of a forty-four-year-old man who was attempting to enter the drug business in competition with the gang to which the two youths belonged.[55]

In Detroit, a "teenage drug lord" paid a contract killer to murder one of his competitors.[56] The hired killer broke into the rival drug dealer's home armed with a semiautomatic firearm with armor-piercing bullets. The killer ordered the rival drug dealer and three others to lie on the floor, where he shot and killed them.

Finally, and most recently, in New York City, a nineteen-year-old man was hit and killed by a subway train.[57] According to the police, the man was chased into a subway tunnel by a gang including two boys, sixteen and seventeen years old, one of whom thought the man had stolen $50 worth of drugs from him. The victim attempted to escape his pursuers by jumping onto the tracks, where he was hit and killed. One teen was charged with manslaughter, the other with reckless endangerment.

Robbery and Rape. Although robberies and rapes committed by members of organized juvenile gangs are apparently common, only occasionally do these crimes eventuate in homicide or attempted homicide. And when they do, the homicidal behavior involved often appears both senseless and especially heinous. Two recent Los Angeles area cases illustrate this phenomenon.

In the first, a twenty-six-year-old woman was accosted on the street by a gang of five youths, four of whom were under the age of eighteen. The youths dragged the woman into an alley, took turns raping and sodomizing her, knocked her unconscious, threw her into a dumpster, covered her with a Christmas tree, and then lit both her and the tree on fire.[58] The victim, who survived but lost an arm, a leg, and both breasts, testified that the last thing she heard before being knocked unconscious was one of the youths saying, "We gotta kill her. She knows me."[59] The three oldest youths were convicted of various crimes, including attempted murder, and sentenced to prison for ninety-seven years, sixty-nine years, and thirty-four years, respectively. Their two younger accomplices, ages fourteen and fifteen, were convicted in juvenile court and remanded to the custody of the state youth authority.

In the second and more recent case, three Los Angeles street gang members—two of whom were juveniles—committed two robbery-killings within the space of two hours.[60] In the first killing, the three youths approached a minister and his wife, who had stopped at a phone booth to call for help after a bus carrying their church choir broke down. The youths grabbed the woman's purse, knocked her down, and then robbed, shot, and killed her husband as he stood in the phone booth. The youths then drove to a liquor store and bought beer and cigarettes with the money they had stolen. Two hours later, they returned to the store, approached two men sitting in a car, and demanded money. When the men resisted, one of the youths shot them, killing one and seriously wounding the other. According to a police officer, this second slaying occurred because it was the juvenile perpetrator's "turn to show that he too is a tough guy. He wanted to do a killing."[61]

Senseless Gang-Related Killings

The vast majority of organized gang-related killings appear to be entirely senseless. Most commonly these killings result from indiscriminate efforts by members of one gang to injure or kill members of rival gangs. Victims include both gang members and innocent bystanders.

Innocent Bystanders. Many senseless gang-related killings of innocent bystanders occur as a result of so-called drive-by shootings. For example, in one recent Los Angeles case, five teen gang members, ranging in age from fifteen to eighteen, stole a car and drove by a street corner in an area controlled by members of a rival gang, some of whom stood nearby. Two of the youths fired shotgun blasts from the car. No rival gang members were hit, but the spray of gunfire hit two innocent bystanders, killing an eleven-year-old girl and wounding her aunt with whom she was walking.[62]

In a remarkably similar recent drive-by shooting in Chicago, four gang members, ranging in age from fifteen to seventeen, were arrested and charged with murder and attempted murder after spraying machine-gun fire from a car into a group of people standing in a doorway. A sixteen-year-old girl was hit and killed and three others, including one rival gang member, were wounded. Just an hour before the shooting, the wounded gang member had been seen using hand motions to signal his own gang membership to a passing car apparently driven and occupied by rival gang members.[63]

In other cases, innocent bystanders, particularly children, have been wounded and killed when caught in the cross fire in shoot-outs between rival gangs. In Los Angeles, for example, rival gang members started a gunfight in a neighborhood playground. One of the gunmen, a seventeen-year-old gang member, was charged with murder after a stray bullet hit and killed a nine-year-old boy who was playing in a sandbox.[64]

In still other cases, innocent persons are killed by gang members because they are mistaken for members of rival gangs. In one recent case, for example, a seventeen-year-old Los Angeles youth, who was not a gang member, was confronted, shot, and killed by a fifteen-year-old gang member on a crowded city bus. The victim was killed because the baseball cap he was wearing was blue, the color associated with the "Crips," a Los Angeles gang. The killer was a member of the "Bloods," a rival gang whose "color" was red.[65]

In another case, in Chicago, two gang members, ages fifteen and sixteen, thought that rival gang members were attending a birthday party in a nearby home. The two teens went to the home, knocked on the back door, and then fired into a crowd of twenty people attending the party. Three people were killed and one wounded. Both boys were charged with murder.[66]

More recently, in the Los Angeles area, six teenage gang members—ages thirteen, fourteen, fourteen, fifteen, eighteen, and nineteen—were charged with murder after an eighteen-year-old youth was beaten, kicked, shot, and killed by a group of between eight and twelve youths after he left a party in Sun Valley. Apparently the perpetrators mistakenly believed that the victim was a member of a rival gang. According to a witness, after chasing the victim and catching him, "They kept yelling, 'Where you from? Where you from?' "[67]

Gang Members. Teen gang members also frequently kill one another. Typically these killings are motivated by a desire for vengeance and/or control of territory. A typical vengeance gang killing is the recent "pay-back" stabbing of a seventeen-year-old Santa Monica youth by members of a rival street gang from Venice, California.[68] According to police, the youth was beaten, kicked, and fatally stabbed by five gang members (ranging in age from fifteen to twenty-four) as "payback" or retaliation for an earlier gang attack by Santa Monica gang members on rival gang members from Venice.

A typical gang killing committed in the course of "turf warfare"—that is, as part of a gang's effort to maintain or win control of a neighborhood, park, or other "territory"—is the case in which a seventeen-year-old Los Angeles youth was convicted of murder and attempted murder.[69] The youth and several fellow gang members attacked two members of a rival gang, killing one of them. The attack and killing occurred after graffiti painted on a building by members of the perpetrators' gang was crossed out and replaced with the insignia of the victims' gang. According to a probation report filed in the case, this action "was interpreted as a symbolic challenge to the [perpetrators'] gang."[70]

Ad Hoc or Spontaneous Juvenile Gangs

Although most juvenile gang-related killings are committed by members of organized street gangs, many crimes of violence and at least some homicides are committed by gangs of juveniles formed on the spur of the moment solely for the purpose of committing a single crime or series of crimes. Undoubtedly the best-known instance of this sort is the 1989 gang rape and attempted murder of a twenty-eight-year-old investment banker who was jogging in New York City's Central Park.[71]

Although accounts of this crime vary, it seems clear that a dozen or more boys—most thirteen to fifteen years old—attacked the woman and that as many as eight youths participated in the rape.[72] One of the youths arrested, a fourteen-year-old, said he was one of a dozen teenage boys waiting behind trees when the victim ran past them in the park. According to the youth, "Someone said, '. . . grab her.' . . . Somebody hit her. . . . Somebody dragged her into the bushes."[73] The woman was then stripped, raped, beaten with fists, a brick, and a pipe, and left for dead.

Although the victim survived, there was no doubt that the youths thought they had killed her. In a confession given after the incident, one of the teenage suspects told the police, "I know who did the murder."[74] And another said, "We thought she was dead."[75]

Although the woman was raped, the attack appeared to be senseless and not primarily motivated by sexual desire. Interviewed after the crime, another juvenile suspect in the case was asked why the youths had committed this crime. His response: "It was something to do. It was fun."[76]

Although only a dozen or so youths were involved in the rape and attempted murder, they were apparently just an accidental subset of a much larger spontaneously organized group of youths—perhaps as many as three dozen—who had been "wilding" in Central Park earlier that evening.[77] Earlier this larger group of youths had robbed a homeless man of a sandwich, thrown rocks at a taxicab, chased a man and a woman riding bicycles in the park, and attacked a forty-year-old male jogger.[78] Similar sorts of "wilding" or "wolf-pack" attacks had taken place in the park and elsewhere in New York City for years, although apparently none had ever been so heinous.[79]

Interestingly, though perhaps not surprisingly, the juvenile "wilders" arrested in the Central Park attack bore little resemblance to the typical members of organized street gangs. While members of organized street gangs typically come from impoverished and extremely disadvantaged backgrounds, the New York City "wilders" generally came from working class or middle class homes and were described by their teachers and neighbors as "children of strict parents" and "good students."[80] It does seem significant, however, that three of these youths had prior arrests, including one in connection with a "wolf-pack style robbery."[81]

In other cases that evidence what might be described as "wolf-pack" mentality, youths have actually killed people. For example, in Newark, a fight among teenagers broke out in front of a pizzeria. Ultimately, more than 100 teenagers became involved in the fight between Blacks and Hispanics. When a "good Samaritan" tried to break up the fight, he was attacked by the youths, one of whom beat him to death with a golf club.[82] The seventeen-year-old who allegedly wielded the club was convicted of reckless manslaughter.

More recently, in New York's Spanish Harlem, a forty-one-year-old man was beaten to death by a group of six to eight youths, none of whom had prior criminal records. The victim allegedly stole a $20 bill from a bakery. He was then chased by the group, surrounded, beaten, kicked, and stomped before being pulled away and handcuffed by the police. Rushed to a hospital, he died hours later. Four of his attackers, including a fourteen-year-old boy, were arrested and charged with manslaughter.[83]

Most recently, in what may be the most unusual if not bizarre killing committed by a loosely organized teenage gang, four California teenagers attacked their parents with shotguns and baseball bats, killing one parent and injuring the others. The group consisted of three boys (two fifteen-year-olds and a nineteen-year-old) and one girl (age sixteen).[84] According to authorities, the girl, who led the gang, ordered the attacks on the parents, including the shooting of her own parents. After making plans to steal money, weapons, and a truck and run away, the four systematically attacked their parents. Three parents survived gunshot wounds, but a fourth died after her fifteen-year-old son repeatedly beat her in the head with a baseball bat.

Although there was some evidence that at least some of the four youths had been involved in satanism, police and prosecutors discounted any serious relationship between satanism and the group's homicidal rampage. According to the prosecutor, none of the four youths were "normal everyday kids."[85] Instead, he said, they were all youths from disturbed families who "found each other and agreed to kill their parents."[86]

Finally, in some instances, loosely organized gangs that might be called "wolf-packs" commit repeated crimes over time—and sometimes one of these crimes results in a homicide. For example, in a recent Chicago case, six youths (five of whom were under the age of eighteen) allegedly robbed a thirty-four-year-old man on a subway platform and then killed him with his own hunting knife, which he carried on his belt.[87]

Of the six juveniles, three were charged with murder. Chicago police said the group was suspected of committing as many as fifty "strong-arm" robberies on subway platforms and trains in the span of a few months. One officer said the juveniles committed the robberies in order to obtain money for drugs and video games. He also concluded that the perpetrators did not set out to kill anyone and that the murder victim would not have been killed had he not been armed: "Otherwise he just would have been beaten and gone to work with a swollen lip."[88]

7
Children Who Kill

As indicated in chapter 1, the incidence of juvenile homicide—at least as reflected in arrest rates for murder and non-negligent manslaughter—varies directly and positively as a function of age. As age levels rise, so does the annual number of arrests for intentional homicide.[1] In the past five years, according to FBI data, children under ten years of age have accounted for less than 1 percent of all juvenile arrests for murder and non-negligent manslaughter.[2] Children aged ten to twelve have accounted for only 1.5 percent of such arrests.[3]

Since these data are arrest statistics, they undoubtedly underestimate the true incidence of homicides committed by juveniles twelve years of age and under. Many children who kill, especially very young ones, are never arrested but instead are dealt with legally in some other less formal fashion. Indeed, in most American jurisdictions, there is an irrefutable presumption that youngsters under the age of seven are not responsible for their criminal acts, including homicide.[4]

Still, even taking that bias into account, it seems clear that very few killings are committed by youngsters twelve and younger. Moreover, while the number of arrests of juveniles twelve and under for other serious crimes has been increasing in recent years, the number of arrests in this age group for intentional homicides has been remarkably stable for years.[5]

With the exception of sexually related killings, which are almost unheard of in the twelve-and-under age range, homicides committed by children in this age group run roughly the same gamut as those committed by teenagers. Homicides committed by youngsters in this preteenage group include intrafamilial killings, killings committed in the course of other crimes, and senseless killings.

Intrafamilial Killings

Intrafamilial killings committed by preteens fall into the same categories as those committed by their older juvenile counterparts: that is, patricide, matricide, fratricide, and sororicide.

Patricide

When a preteen kills a parent, the victim is more likely to be the child's father than his or her mother. And when a preteen kills his or her father, the dynamics are likely to be the same as or similar to those in patricides committed by teenage youths. In patricides committed by preteens and by teenagers, spousal and/or child abuse seems to be a common denominator. For example, in two recent patricides committed by youngsters under the age of thirteen, the youthful perpetrators claimed to have been acting in defense of their mothers when they killed their fathers.

In a case mentioned in chapter 3, a three-and-a-half-year-old Michigan boy shot and killed his father.[6] Witnesses confirmed that while the family was having a barbecue, the boy's father, who was intoxicated, became angry with the boy's mother, confronted her with a .25 caliber pistol, laid the gun on a table, and then knocked the woman to the floor and held her down while she screamed. Seeing this, the three-year-old grabbed the gun, aimed it at his father, fired, and killed the man.

The boy confessed to the killing, telling authorities: "I killed him. . . . If he would have hit my mother, I would have shot him again."[7] Although detectives initially disbelieved the boy, gunpowder residue tests confirmed that the three-year-old was the only person present who fired the gun. Concluding that a three-year-old is incapable of forming an intent to kill, the prosecutor declined to press charges against the boy.[8]

In another preteen case of patricide, an eleven-year-old West Virginia girl shot and killed her twenty-nine-year-old stepfather.[9] In a television interview, the girl explained that she killed her stepfather to protect her mother, who was also charged in the killing. The girl said, "I was afraid he was going to get up and kill mommy."[10] Although authorities disputed the girl's version of the killing, they offered no other account. A judge concluded that, based upon the girl's age and level of maturity, she should not be tried as an adult.

Matricide

Juvenile matricide is uncommon, and apparently even more uncommon, if not virtually unheard of, among preteens. There are no reports in the published clinical literature of preteenage youngsters killing their mothers. Indeed, an extensive search of media reports from around the country uncovered only one such case. In that case, a twelve-year-old seventh-grader from suburban Washington, D.C., killed his mother and tried to kill his father, shooting both parents with a .22 caliber hunting rifle.[11]

The boy—who was in a junior high school class for the learning disabled and was described by a neighbor as "real quiet" and "real polite"[12]—reportedly shot his mother once in the head and twice in the side. The shooting took place after the boy and his mother argued over his suspension from school for carrying a small hunting knife. Then, when his father came home from work early, the boy turned the gun on him. The father ran from the house but the boy chased him, firing at him repeatedly until he had shot him three times, critically wounding him.[13]

Fratricide and Sororicide

Not surprisingly—given that parents are generally bigger, stronger, and have more authority than most preteen children—youngsters twelve and under who kill within the family seem most likely to kill siblings. Fratricides and sororicides committed by preteens have been reported in both the clinical literature and numerous media accounts.

In two of the earliest clinical reports on children who kill, Patterson and Bender each described preteens who killed siblings. One of the six youngsters in Patterson's sample, an eleven-year-old boy with average intelligence, above average school achievement, and no prior delinquency, shot and killed his sister "in a quarrel over a few pennies."[14] Later, Bender described two cases in which mentally "defective" five-year-old boys killed younger siblings.[15] One choked his four-week-old sister to death because he was "bothered by her crying."[16] The other boy pushed his three-year-old brother out the window.

More recently, Adelson described a case in which a seven-week-old infant was found dead in her crib by her mother who had left her with her older brother for about ten minutes while the mother visited a neighbor. The infant's seven-year-old brother—a "loner" and "slow learner" with an IQ of 74—told police he had "bopped" the baby "many times" with the leg of a spinning wheel and had bitten her hand because she was crying.[17]

Finally, several clinical and research reports have described cases in which young children have tried to kill their siblings. Tooley, for example, described two "small assassins"—both neglected and abused six-year-olds who acted out homicidally against their siblings.[18] "Mary," who had been repeatedly sexually abused by her mother's boyfriend, set fire to her younger brother and tried to pour Clorox down her infant half-sister's throat. "Jay," who had been frequently beaten by his father, set fire to his sister's dress and held her head under water in a swimming pool.

Describing these two "murderous children,"[19] Tooley observed that "[T]hey saw their weapons as quasi-magical means of making the unwanted and troublesome baby 'disappear.' They did not have a concept of death as involving irreversible stopping of bodily function. But they did have a concept of present and absent."[20] Describing Mary's and Jay's parents, Tooley observed that they had been "startlingly complacent and unconcerned [given] the dangerous extremity of their children's behavior."[21]

Easson and Steinhilber described the case of an eight-year-old who, like Tooley's two "small assassins," had made several "murderous assaults" on a younger sibling.[22] This boy first choked his brother until the younger child was "blue in the face." Next he tried to strangle him with a belt. Finally, he was discovered in the act of trying to drown his brother by holding the younger boy's head under water in a bathtub.

Like the parents of the children reported on by Tooley, this boy's parents were also quite unperturbed by his "murderous assaults." After learning of the first of the above incidents five days after the choking, the boy's mother felt that "It was too late to do or say anything," so she declined to tell the boy's father.[23] After learning of the second incident, the boy's parents did nothing, and his father said he felt that the attempted strangling was just "part of growing up."[24] Only after the attempted drowning did these parents seek psychiatric help for the boy.

Carek and Watson also described a case in which a preteenage child killed a sibling.[25] A ten-year-old boy was left to baby-sit his five younger siblings. When two of the siblings defied him, he threatened them with his father's loaded shotgun. When one of the younger children dropped a toy into the barrel of the gun, the ten-year-old pulled the trigger and killed him. The family initially claimed that the shooting was an accident, but after five months of psychiatric hospitalization, the boy acknowledged that the killing was not accidental.

Most recently, Petti and Davidman described a sample of nine children ranging in age from six to eleven who killed or tried to kill others.[26] Six of these children attempted to kill one or more of their siblings. A seventh child successfully killed his younger brother. Although these researchers did not provide data specific to the seven children who tried to kill or did kill siblings, their account of the nine homicidally aggressive children may be considered overall to be relatively descriptive of these seven sororicidal or fratricidal children. Two of the nine children were living in intact family units; three had been subjected to child abuse; seven were depressed. Three were characterized as borderline psychotic, but none was diagnosed as psychotic. Six had mothers and three had fathers with psychiatric histories. These nine children's IQs ranged from 73 to 106 with both a mean and median of 89.

Other cases of fratricide and sororicide, especially those committed by very young children, often appear to be unintentional if not accidental. Two recent New York City cases illustrate. In the first, a four-year-old girl awoke before her parents and went into the room where her twin three-week-old brothers were sleeping. She lifted them from their cribs and put them in their car seats. When one scratched her, she dropped him to the floor and picked up the other. When he squirmed and cried, she threw him into his crib. Her parents rushed into the room and found both infants dead from skull fractures.[27]

More recently, an eight-year-old New York City boy with "a history of playing with matches" was charged with murder after his eleven-year-old sister died from burns she suffered in a fire which resulted from the boy playing with a cigarette lighter in a closet.[28] Three other family members escaped unharmed, but one of the boy's other sisters was critically injured in the fire. Five years earlier the same boy had started another fire in the home. Since that time he had been receiving psychotherapy. A detective interviewed the eight-year-old after the fire that killed his sister and reported that "He's very sorry this incident took place. At his age, he has a problem. He cannot comprehend the damage a fire can do."[29]

Killings Committed in the Course of Other Crimes

Although preteens often commit crimes, especially theft-related crimes, they are extremely unlikely to kill while committing these offenses. When they do, the killings are often committed by groups of youths and usually seem to have no rational relationship to successful commission of the underlying crime. Indeed, most such cases might better be classified as senseless killings. For example, in a Wisconsin case, an eleven-year-old girl was found guilty of the brutal stabbing and bludgeoning death of a nine-year-old neighbor in an incident triggered when the girl took the younger boy's bicycle. Although two other youths—boys aged twelve and fourteen—were also implicated in the killing, witnesses testified that the eleven-year-old girl "led the attack on the boy with two kitchen knives."[30] All three youths were adjudicated delinquents and committed to juvenile facilities.

More recently, five youths ranging in age from twelve to twenty, all of whom were masked and armed, stormed into the home of a California family, intent on robbery.[31] When one of the would-be robbery victims screamed and startled the young robbers, she was shot and killed "by accident."[32] All five intruders then fled the house empty-handed. Two of the youths, ages twelve and thirteen, were apprehended, confessed, and were convicted of first-degree murder.

Senseless Killings

By far, most killings committed by juveniles may be classified as senseless. Although some of these killings are undoubtedly committed by juveniles who are seriously mentally ill, it appears that the vast majority of senseless killings committed by preteens are not the product of mental illness but rather the culmination of some combination of forces, including immaturity, infantile rage, impulsivity, and, in many cases, fortuity.

Killings Committed by Mentally Disturbed Preteens

In the clinical literature, very few cases have been described in which the young children who killed were psychotic or otherwise seriously mentally ill. Podolsky described one such case and Thom described another. In the case described by Podolsky, an eleven-year-old boy ran around his classroom "making weird noises . . . did not seem to know right from wrong . . . attempted to remove other boys' trousers . . . became increasingly aggressive [and] set several fires."[33] This boy—"who demonstrated some of the early manifestations of childhood schizophrenia"[34]—subsequently killed a playmate.

In the other case reported by Thom,[35] a twelve-year-old newspaper carrier was collecting at the home of a female customer when he asked the woman for a drink of water. When she handed him the water, he hit her over the head with a milk bottle, then pulled a laundry bag over her head, strangled her and knifed her in the abdomen, killing her. When questioned later, the boy readily admitted his guilt and could offer no motive or explanation other than sudden impulse.

According to Thom, this youth was the product of a difficult birth, had suffered anoxia at age five, had been physically abused by his father, was emotionally unstable, and had demonstrated a variety of psychotic symptoms prior to the killing. However, both Stearns and Podolsky, separately reporting on the same case, made no mention of any such problems. Indeed, Podolsky reported that prior to the killing, this boy "had an excellent reputation in the community."[36] Stearns reported that "It was generally said that he was one of the last persons who would be suspected of doing wrong."[37]

Although Thom's report was based upon extensive evaluations of this boy and his parents, Stearns' later report certainly casts doubt upon psychosis as an explanation for this killing. The boy was sentenced to life in prison and was evaluated by Stearns ten years into his sentence. At that point, according to Stearns' psychiatric evaluation, the youngster was well adjusted and his prison behavior had been exemplary. Moreover, as Stearns added, "He has studied hard and hopes to get out sometime, although he once told the writer that, if there was any chance of his ever doing this sort of thing again, he would gladly remain in prison for the rest of his life."[38]

Other Killings Committed by Preteens

Most preteens who commit senseless killings do not appear to be psychotic or otherwise seriously disturbed. Instead, these killings seem to reflect a combination of forces, including immaturity, rage, and lack of impulse control. Moreover, in many such homicides there appears to be a clear element of chance or fortuity. To put it another way, in many of these cases, the juvenile killer and his or her victim were simply in the wrong place at the wrong time.

Children Who Kill Younger Children and Infants. When very young children kill, their victims are most often other children, and usually children younger than themselves. Recently, for example, two four-year-olds, a boy and a girl, beat a five-week-old baby to death in a Connecticut shelter for the homeless, where all three resided.[39] According to police reports, when the baby's mother left her to sterilize a bottle, the two four-year-olds slipped into the room. Minutes later the baby was found lying on the floor, barely breathing and suffering from severe head injuries. An hour later the baby was pronounced dead.

Such cases, though relatively rare, often seem to follow a predictable pattern. Adelson, a coroner, described five such killings, all committed by children eight years old or younger.[40] One of these cases, the killing of an infant boy by his seven-year-old brother, was described earlier in the section of this chapter dealing with intrafamilial killings.

In Adelson's other four cases, three boys and one girl ranging in age from two and a half to eight years old, each killed an infant under the age of eight months. All four infants died from craniocerebral trauma and none showed signs of previous abuse. One infant was struck and dropped to the floor, a second was removed from his bassinet and thrown to the floor, a third was hit with several metal toys, and the fourth was rolled off a bed, bitten, and struck repeatedly with a shoe. Adelson described the four youthful killers as follows: "Three . . . were apparently normal boys. . . . The [girl was] an 8-year old [who had] displayed violently aggressive tendencies . . . but no member of the family had ever considered that her 'difficult' behavior would eventually . . . be responsible for her infant nephew's death."[41]

Overall, Adelson attributed these killings to a combination of forces including not only the young perpetrators' jealousy, rage, and lack of impulse control but also their victims' special vulnerabilities—that is, the frailty and fragility of the infants' heads. As Adelson noted, craniocerebral injuries of the type that killed these infants "occur only in this immature age group."[42]

In some cases in which very young children are killed by other young children, there is good reason to suspect that the juvenile perpetrator is psychologically disturbed and/or an abused child. Three recent cases illustrate. In the first, an eight-year-old Florida boy swung a two-month-old infant by her feet into a piece of furniture.[43] The infant suffered a skull fracture and died. Ten months earlier the same boy had smashed in the windshield of his mother's car after an argument with her. After being charged with murder, the boy was sent to a private facility for the treatment of emotionally disturbed children.

In the second case, two Missouri brothers, four and six years old, attacked a twenty-month-old girl with a shovel, screwdriver, hammer, and brick, reportedly because they thought the girl was "ugly" and because they "didn't like her."[44] After the attack, the four-year-old boy ran to tell his father

and the girl's father, who were playing cards in the kitchen, "She's dead."[45]
Both boys had reputations in the neighborhood for "unruliness," apparently
based in part upon an earlier incident in which the two allegedly broke a car
window to steal juice. At the time of the killing, the boys' father was facing
charges of child abuse as a result of a broken arm suffered earlier by the four-
year-old.

In the third case, two Florida boys, three and five years old, wandered
onto a fifth-floor balcony while their parents were talking in another room.
The five-year-old pushed the three-year-old, who grabbed onto a ledge to
keep from falling. The five-year-old then pried the younger boy's fingers loose
and the boy fell five stories to his death. The five-year-old readily confessed
but later claimed the younger boy told him he wanted to die because his
parents abused him. Psychiatrists and prosecutors, however, concluded that
the five-year-was actually speaking of himself and his own parents, and that
it was the five-year-old himself who was an abused and neglected child. On
that basis, it was decided that the boy should not be charged but rather committed to a residential treatment center for psychotherapy.[46]

Whether or not very young children who kill are emotionally disturbed,
it is clear that their homicidal acts cannot be judged on the same basis as
those of adults, adolescents, or even older children. Most very young children
not only do not have a fully developed sense of the meaning and finality of
death, but they also lack the cognitive and moral development necessary to
fully appreciate the nature and meaning of homicide.[47] Recognizing that, and
unwilling or legally unable to impose punishment upon these children, the
state—not surprisingly—often turns to mental health professionals and facilities to handle them, regardless of whether they are psychologically disturbed.

Impulsive and "Accidental" Killings with Firearms. In a recent letter to the
editor of a big city newspaper, one reader wrote to complain that a story
about children who kill failed to mention one "obvious" fact: "All these children had easy access to guns and ammunition in their own homes."[48]

Easy availability of guns in the home is indeed a major factor in homicides committed by preteens. Some of these firearm killings are clearly intentional but impulsive. Others are less intentional, the result of recklessness or
negligence. Still others present some mix of intent and reckless or negligent
handling of the weapon. What all have in common is that they would not
have occurred but for the young perpetrator's ready access to a loaded gun.

Impulsive killings usually occur when one child becomes involved in an
argument with another child and reaches for a nearby gun to help settle the
dispute. In these killings the perpetrators and victims are generally older children. Several recent cases illustrate this sort of homicide.

In the first, three twelve-year-old boys were lifting weights in one boy's
bedroom.[49] When they left the room, heading for a video arcade, one of the

visiting boys picked up a baseball belonging to the boy in whose room the three had been playing. When the visitor refused to give the ball back, the boy picked up a nearby semiautomatic rifle and shot the visiting boy, who was hit at least fifteen times and suffered twenty-two entrance and exit wounds. Charged with murder, the boy offered no defense and was sentenced to the California Youth Authority for an indeterminate term not to exceed his twenty-fifth birthday. The boy's attorney noted that this youngster had no history of violent behavior, had never been in trouble before, and had never before fired a gun. Explaining how and why the killing occurred, the attorney said, "He was basically taunted into doing it."[50]

In the second case, an eleven-year-old Missouri girl fatally wounded a ten-year-old neighbor boy during a quarrel.[51] The girl and boy had been playing in the girl's yard when an argument erupted. The girl ordered the boy to leave the yard. When he did not leave, she took a .38 caliber revolver from a dresser drawer in her parents' bedroom, shot and killed the boy, and then telephoned the police. According to the homicide detective who responded to the girl's call, "She knew it was a real gun. It's not that they were just playing with it."[52] The detective added, however, that it was not clear whether the girl meant to shoot the boy or merely to scare him.

In the third case, one mentioned in chapter 5, a twelve-year-old seventh-grade honor student from Missouri took his father's loaded .45 caliber pistol to school with him in his gym bag. Later that day, the boy pulled the gun from the bag, threatened his classmates with it, shot and killed a classmate who had teased him, and then shot and killed himself. Just a week earlier, the boy had warned another classmate not to come to school because he intended to "shoot everyone."[53]

Finally, and most recently, a nine-year-old Pennsylvania boy shot and killed a seven-year-old neighbor girl with his father's hunting rifle.[54] The boy, an honor student and Cub Scout, entered his parents' bedroom, took the key to his father's gun cabinet, unlocked the cabinet, removed and loaded the gun, and then went outside where the victim and other children were snow-mobiling. After shooting the girl in the back, the boy removed the spent car-tridge, hid it, and then put the gun back and relocked the cabinet.

The boy claimed that he had been playing "hunter" and accidentally fired the gun. According to the prosecutor, however, the killing was deliberate, perhaps in reaction to the girl's bragging that she was better than the boy at playing video games. In any event, a ballistics expert testified at a pretrial hearing that the rifle could not have been discharged accidentally unless struck with a severe blow forcing the hammer to hit the firing pin.

Clearly unintentional (i.e., reckless, negligent, or accidental) killings with firearms are more likely to be committed by younger children. Typically, in these cases, a child is playing with a gun, intentionally or unintentionally fires the gun, and kills a playmate or someone else who just happens to be in the line of fire. Often these killings take place in the course of child's play: one youthful player finds a gun and turns it on one of his or her peers. That was the case recently in New Jersey, where a four-year-old and an eight-year-old were playing "Cowboys and Indians." The four-year-old found a loaded handgun beneath his grandmother's couch and then used it to shoot and kill his eight-year-old "opponent."[55]

In a similar tragedy in South Carolina, two boys, eight and five years old, wandered into the street and climbed into a truck belonging to a plumber who was working nearby. The boys opened the glove compartment and found a loaded .38 caliber pistol. They removed the pistol and took turns playing with it for about two hours. Then the five-year-old fired the pistol. A five-year-old girl was shot in the head and killed.[56] Although questions were raised about the boy's mental health, and there was "evidence of aggressive behavior by the boy toward other children, before and after the shooting," the death was ruled an accident.[57]

More recently, a six-year-old boy fatally wounded a taxi driver in a hospital parking lot. The boy had been waving his father's loaded pistol out the window of the family car when the gun fired and the taxi driver was shot in the head and killed.[58] Questioned by the police, the boy said, "I was playing with the gun."[59] The father, who said he did not realize his son had taken the gun from a front-seat compartment, was charged with negligence.

8
Girls Who Kill

J ust as young juveniles rarely kill, girls of any age are extremely unlikely to commit homicide. As was indicated in chapter 2, at all age levels under eighteen years, the overwhelming majority of persons arrested for murder or non-negligent manslaughter (i.e., anywhere from 75 to over 90 percent annually, depending upon age) are males.[1] Most years in the United States, boys are twelve times more likely than girls to commit criminal homicide.[2] This gender ratio is not only consistent from year to year but holds true in the over-eighteen age range as well.[3]

Not surprisingly, given this gender ratio, the research and clinical literature on juvenile homicide is based almost exclusively upon the study of male subjects. Many reported studies have excluded girls altogether—some purposely. For example, in explaining why all forty-five juvenile killers in their sample were male, Rosner et al. explained that "Females were excluded from the study because their numbers were so small that their inclusion would have skewed the statistical analysis."[4]

Even where girls have been included in multi-subject reports on juvenile homicide, their numbers have been extremely few: ranging from a low of two out of seventy-two subjects in Cornell and colleagues' recent report[5] to a high of four out of eighteen subjects in Solway and associates' 1981 report.[6] Only one published multi-subject report has dealt exclusively with girls who kill. As Russell, the author of this report, explained: "In an ongoing series of juvenile murderers that has been studied and followed in Massachusetts over the past twenty-five years, there have been fifty cases to date, all but two are boys."[7]

This chapter reviews the clinical and research literature with regard to girls who kill, describes a number of recent cases not covered in this literature, and considers some of the ways in which juvenile killers and their homicides differ as a function of gender.

Clinical and Research Literature

The clinical and research literature on girls who kill is sparse not only in numbers, but also in depth. Only a handful of cases have been described in any real detail.

In his article "Girls Who Kill," Russell, a psychiatrist, described two homicidal girls, one who shot her mother and sister and another who shot a boy she barely knew.[8] In the first of these cases, "Sally" had just turned sixteen when she "put her father's pistol under her pillow one night, and coming to breakfast shot her mother and younger sister . . . dropped the gun, and ran crying hysterically a quarter of a mile to the Police Station."[9]

Sally, a "shy, pleasant, self-conscious girl," was an underachiever at school, had been encopretic since childhood and enuretic until she was fourteen years old, and showed "no gross evidence of psychosis or organic deficits."[10] She was frequently teased at school because of her odor and "nervousness." Sally grew up in an intact but somewhat socially isolated family of modest means. Although she was apparently not abused by either parent, she was sexually abused by her grandfather, who lived next door and who—for two years prior to the killing—paid Sally weekly to provide him with oral sex.

Sally claimed amnesia for the period of time from the night before the shootings until just afterward. After neurological problems were ruled out and she was diagnosed as suffering a schizoid personality disorder, Sally was committed to a state institution for youth. At age eighteen, she was discharged from the institution, became pregnant out of wedlock, and thereafter "manage[d] a substandard existence for herself and her child and maintain[ed] a series of questionable relationships."[11]

In the second case reported by Russell, fifteen-year-old "Beckie" shot and killed a boy on her school bus, a youth who was part of a group of peers who had been teasing her earlier in the week. On the morning of the killing, another boy had given her the gun and threatened that "she would be killed if she did not kill the victim first."[12]

Beckie, "the product of violent rape when her mother was 15," was born in the West Indies but moved with her mother to inner-city Boston after a hurricane destroyed their home when Beckie was four years old.[13] Beckie's mother was "an irascible alcoholic" who abused her; her stepfather was "an irresponsible philandering man" with whom Beckie had a close relationship.[14] Over a period of several years prior to the killing, Beckie's home was twice destroyed by fire; she attempted suicide, was abducted at knife point by a man who tried to rape her, and became involved with a gang of delinquent girls and was charged with shoplifting and assault.

Beckie was a "potentially bright" child whose academic achievement was apparently limited by frequent moves and changes of school.[15] She demonstrated no evidence of psychosis or organic impairment. After being adjudicated a delinquent, Beckie was committed to state custody and remained there at the time of Russell's report. In assessing the dynamics in these two cases, Russell attached great significance to the fact that both girls had been neglected, abused, and dominated by their mothers, who demonstrated "a pervasive lack of support and caring . . ."[16]

In separate books about homicide, two other psychiatrists have also described cases in which teenage girls killed. Cassity discussed the case of Theresa Gresh, a fifteen-year-old who, having assisted her seventeen-year-old boyfriend in killing her mother, was convicted of murder.[17] Theresa, a "good student" and a "well spoken and well behaved child," was born out of wedlock and raised by her mother.[18] A lonely and obese girl, Theresa had never had any friendships with girls or boys until she met a seventeen-year-old Marine, became sexually involved with him, and made plans to marry him.

When her mother objected to their marriage plans, Theresa and her boyfriend killed the woman with a hammer and knife, stabbing her more than twenty times. The two then hid the body by covering it with plaster of paris in a bathtub. Psychiatric evaluation of Theresa after the killing revealed "no evidence of any major mental disturbance"; but the examiners pointed out that "she is very suggestible and immature, susceptible to influences brought to bear by stronger, more aggressive individuals."[19] Psychological testing put her IQ at 98, and she was diagnosed as suffering from a schizoid personality disorder without psychosis.

At trial, Theresa's attorney sought to blame her involvement in the killing on her boyfriend's overwhelming influence. A psychiatrist who had examined her testified that, at the time of the killing, Theresa was sane but that "Her will power was afflicted. She was not a free agent. She did not have the power to reflect and consider, and because of that she was unable to plan, design, contemplate, premeditate and form a judgment."[20] A jury convicted both Theresa and her boyfriend of murder. The boy was convicted of first-degree murder and sentenced to die in the electric chair. Convicted of the lesser charge of second-degree murder, Theresa was sentenced to serve from twenty years to life in prison.

In a more recent book, Gardiner described two girls, both of whom killed family members. In the first case, fourteen-year-old "Gloria" shot and killed her uncle.[21] Gloria, who had been physically and psychologically abused all her life by her mother and stepfather, went to live with her grandmother not long before the killing. Also living in her grandmother's home were some of her aunts and uncles, including Aunt "Ethel" and her husband, "Albert."

Gloria did not get along well with Ethel, who repeatedly suggested that Gloria be sent back to her abusive parents. On the day of the killing, Gloria and Ethel argued, and Ethel brandished a knife at Gloria. Gloria retreated, found a gun in a closet, loaded it, and went back to look into Ethel's window, where she saw Ethel pick up the knife and head toward the door. In Gardiner's words, "Gloria's fear and fury merged into a tempestuous frenzy, and she raised her gun. But it was Albert who came out first. Gloria shot. When she saw her uncle crumple to the ground, she dropped the gun."[22]

A psychiatrist who examined Gloria concluded that she suffered no mental illness and that "Her behavior stems largely from early conditioning when she was made to feel unwanted and severely deprived. . . . Her homicidal act was situational in character and it is my feeling that the killing occurred because of extreme provocation."[23] Gloria, sentenced to an indeterminate prison term, was incarcerated until age twenty-one, at which time she was paroled. After a relatively brief period of parole, she was released from state supervision. Her final parole report stated that she had made an excellent adjustment and was "a highly valued and respected community worker."[24]

In the second case described by Gardiner, seventeen-year-old Rose beat her younger brother to death with a bronze statuette.[25] When Rose was eighteen months old, her mother gave birth to another child. Rose showed "extreme jealousy" and overt aggression toward the younger child. By the time Rose was five years old, she was still acting aggressively toward her younger sister and was manifesting intolerable temper tantrums. Subsequently Rose was diagnosed as suffering from a heart condition and was placed in a "convalescent home" for sick children, where her parents seldom visited her and where she remained until she was eight years old.

Upon discharge from the convalescent home, Rose found that she now had a two-year-old brother who, in the eyes of her parents, "could do no wrong" and "was allowed his own way in everything."[26] When Rose complained to her parents because the boy urinated on her clothes and on the floor of her room, her parents placed her in foster care. For the next two years Rose was in three foster homes. At the age of twelve she returned home.

Shortly thereafter, Rose's parents sought to have her committed to a mental hospital—a plan opposed and obstructed by Rose's grandmother, who felt that it "would be a disgrace to the family."[27] Finally, however, after an incident in which Rose complained bitterly that her brother had chased a neighbor's dog with a red-hot poker . . . taken money from Rose's purse [and] again urinated on the floor of her room," Rose "was packed off to the mental hospital."[28] While hospitalized, Rose was found to be of average intelligence and was diagnosed as "without psychosis, primary behavior disorder, neurotic traits."[29] After two years of inpatient care, Rose was discharged with the notation: "Without psychosis. Prognosis guarded."[30] She returned immediately to her family's home.

The next two years were relatively uneventful. Rose did well at school and presented no behavioral problems. When Rose was sixteen, she had an altercation with her younger brother and knocked him momentarily unconscious with an iron candlestick. Her parents sought to have her placed in foster care again, but found that she was too old to be accepted.

Thereafter, Rose remained at home until one day, when she was seventeen, she was baby-sitting for her brother and killed him. Afterward, Rose told her boyfriend, without emotion, "I didn't hurt him. He didn't know what happened. And I was nice to him all evening. I gave him corned beef, and let him skip his bath and read his comic books. He was happy. And my father will never, never, never get over it."[31]

More recently, McCarthy, a psychologist, described the case of a seventeen-year-old girl, "B," who stabbed an older neighbor woman to death after a minor argument in which the neighbor criticized her.[32] Born out of wedlock, "B" had been raised by her mother and had little contact with her father. As a child, she was "depressed and isolated," but after reaching puberty, she became "outwardly aggressive and provocative" and had a history of violent, aggressive response to criticism.[33] Her homicidal reaction to the neighbor's criticism was attributed to a psychotic episode triggered by a "severe blow to her self-esteem."[34]

Most recently, Benedek and Cornell, a psychiatrist and psychologist respectively, described "Eve," a sixteen-year-old who, along with two older female friends, beat to death a fifty-year-old man, "who had a reputation in the community for cruising through town and picking up adolescent females for sexual favors."[35] Eve claimed that she had been "manipulated" by her older friends, but acknowledged that, after trying unsuccessfully to seduce the man, the three hit him with a hammer and chain, forced him into the trunk of his car, and then dumped him into an alley. Subsequently the man was admitted to a hospital and died from complications related to a broken collarbone and internal injuries.

Eve, the daughter of a "strict" mother and a disabled father who "didn't give me no trouble,"[36] had eight previous arrests, including two for violent offenses, one of which involved beating an elderly woman and stealing her money. Prior to the killing, Eve had dropped out of school in the tenth grade and had a history of alcohol and other drug abuse. Tried as an adult on charges of murder, kidnapping, and armed robbery, Eve was convicted and sentenced to prison.

Other Cases in Which Girls Killed

As these cases from the clinical and research literature suggest, homicides committed by girls involve a variety of dynamics. Some girls, such as "Sally," kill their abusive and/or neglecting parents or other family members. Some girls who kill, such as "B," appear to be seriously disturbed psychologically. Others, such as "Eve," kill in the course of committing other crimes such as robbery or larceny. And still others, such as "Beckie," commit what appear to be senseless killings.

Killings of all these types are further illustrated by other more recent cases, many of which provide additional insights into the dynamics of homicides committed by girls.

Intrafamilial Killings

When girls kill, they rarely kill strangers. For example, Rowley et al. examined FBI supplementary homicide data for one recent year and found that while only, 13.83 percent of male juveniles arrested for murder or non-negligent manslaughter had killed a parent, stepparent, or other family member, 44 percent of the female juveniles arrested for these crimes had killed a parent, stepparent, or other family member.[37]

Intrafamilial killings committed by girls differ from those committed by boys not only in incidence but also in at least a couple of other significant ways: (1) involvement of an accomplice or accomplices; and (2) relationship to victim.

Accomplices. The vast majority of intrafamilial killings committed by juveniles are committed by one person acting alone.[38] Where a juvenile acts with another to kill a family member, the juvenile perpetrator related to the victim is almost always a girl. Among the cases studied by Rowley and his colleagues, for example, "in 20 of the 21 intrafamilial homicides committed by more than a single offender, the identified juvenile perpetrator was female."[39] Two cases, briefly described in chapter 3, provide recent examples.

In the first, sixteen-year-old Cheryl Pierson, a popular high school cheerleader, offered Sean Pica, a seventeen-year-old classmate, $1,000 to kill her father, who had sexually and physically abused her for years. Sean bought a rifle, ambushed Cheryl's father, shot him five times, and killed him. Sean and Cheryl each pleaded guilty to manslaughter. Sean was sentenced to eight to twenty-four years in prison, while Cheryl received a sentence that allowed for her release after serving less than four months in jail.[40]

In the second case, another sixteen-year-old "begged" her nineteen-year-old boyfriend to kill her mother. The boyfriend responded with a love note ("To my dreamgirl . . . I will do the deed. I promise you."), then strangled the girl's mother with a stocking and dumped her body near a highway in another state.[41] Afterward, he explained his actions to two other teens who had accompanied him: "[She] kept begging me to do it. I had to do it."[42]

In other cases where girls act with accomplices to kill their parents, both the girl and the accomplice share in the actual killing. The case of fifteen-year-old Andrea Williams, also mentioned in chapter 3, is an example. Andrea (armed with a combat knife) and her eighteen-year-old boyfriend Mario Garcia (wielding a machete)—both apparently high on drugs—hacked Andrea's mother to death for trying to put an end to their romance. The couple then left the mother's body on the floor in her apartment while they continued to use the apartment for nine days until they were arrested. Both convicted, Andrea was sentenced to seven years to life while Mario received a sentence of fifteen years to life.[43]

Victims. At least some of the difference between male and female intrafamilial juvenile homicide seems attributable to one form of intrafamilial homicide committed almost exclusively by females: infanticide, especially the killing of newborns.

Infanticide is committed by both men and women of all ages,[44] but many, perhaps most, such killings, particularly killings of newborn infants, are committed by unwed teenage mothers—girls seeking to conceal the fact that they have given birth and/or trying to avoid the responsibilities of parenthood.

In one such case, a sixteen-year-old Wisconsin girl pleaded guilty to second-degree murder in satisfaction of first-degree murder charges stemming from the death of her baby, who was born after a pregnancy of seven to eight months. The newborn, who died from multiple stab wounds inflicted with a knife shortly after birth, was found in the garage of the girl's home, wrapped in a plastic bag. Neither the girl's parents nor school officials knew she was pregnant.[45]

In a similar case, a New York tenth-grader, fifteen years old, gave birth alone, then cleaned the baby, wrapped him in a towel, put him in a plastic garbage bag, and threw the bag down an eleven-foot embankment outside her home. The newborn suffered head injuries and died. According to the girl's aunt, no one in the girl's family knew she had been pregnant. After the killing, the girl told police that she had been motivated by concern that her mother would be upset if she learned that her daughter had given birth. The girl was charged with second-degree murder.[46]

In a California infanticide case, the teenage perpetrator's motives were different. A fifteen-year-old Latina girl, who had recently emigrated from Mexico, lived with her impoverished parents and was already the mother of one child. She did not speak English and had dropped out of junior high school at the age of fourteen, when her first child was born. Her parents told her that if she ever became pregnant again she would have to leave home because they could not support another child.[47]

Shortly thereafter, the girl did become pregnant. Nine months later she gave birth alone in her parents' home, placed the baby in a plastic bag, and threw the bag into a dumpster, where the baby was later found suffocated. The girl's lawyer described the girl and her motives, saying: "She is very young [and] unsophisticated. She sensed she had no options . . ."[48] The director of a nearby project for pregnant teenagers added that the girl was a victim of circumstances who found herself in a "no-win situation."[49] The girl was charged with murder and pleaded guilty. Despite the prosecutor's arguments for a sentence of up to seven years in prison, the court sentenced her to serve only a year in a juvenile detention facility.

Psychologically Disturbed Perpetrators

Even when girls kill people outside their own families, they are unlikely to act alone. Regardless of the victim–offender relationship, girls who kill generally do so in conjunction with an accomplice or accomplices.[50] Indeed, even psychologically disturbed girls who kill are unlikely to do so alone.

In some cases, psychologically disturbed girls play only a secondary role in homicides committed jointly with others. This seems especially likely where the girl's accomplice is a male. The dynamics of homicide committed by a boy-girl combination of perpetrators is illustrated by cases from Michigan and Mississippi.

In the Michigan case, a sixteen-year-old girl and her fourteen-year-old half-brother were charged in the deaths of a neighbor couple. The boy shot the victims in the head as they entered their home. Then he and his sister, who was later described by two psychologists as sometimes "out of touch with reality," hid the bodies in a crawl space near the kitchen of their home.[51]

In Mississippi, sixteen-year-old Attina Cannaday and her friends David Gray and Dawn Bushart kidnapped Attina's former boyfriend and his girlfriend after Attina reportedly caught the two in bed together. The three perpetrators forced the couple into a van at knife point and took them to an out-of-the-way area. David raped the woman. Then—depending upon which story one believes—either David or Attina forced the man into the woods and stabbed him nineteen times with a butcher knife.[52]

Attina, who ran away from home at age thirteen, married and divorced at fourteen, and worked as a dancer, barmaid, and prostitute before the killing, was found to have an IQ in the borderline mentally retarded range and a mental age of 9.8 years. She and David were both convicted of capital murder and sentenced to die.

In other cases, psychologically disturbed girls team up with other girls, who may or may not be psychologically disturbed, to kill. Such was the case with fourteen-year-old Shirley Wolf, who pleaded insanity in defense to charges that she and fifteen-year-old Cindy Collier brutally murdered an eighty-five-year-old woman.[53]

From infancy until age fourteen, Shirley was sexually abused by her father, uncle, and paternal grandfather. As early as kindergarten, she was identified as a child in need of psychiatric care. At the age of nine, Shirley was raped by her father. Thereafter, until she was fourteen, he repeatedly sexually assaulted her, sometimes as often as three times a day. Her father, who later pleaded guilty to child molestation, had even obtained birth control pills for Shirley once she reached puberty.

After serving 100 days in jail, her father was released on probation—on the condition that he have no contact with Shirley. The father then returned to live with Shirley's mother and two brothers. To meet this condition of probation, Shirley was placed in foster care and then a group home, from which she repeatedly ran away. She had met Cindy Collier at the group home only a few hours before the killing. Cindy Collier, though also from a troubled background, appeared more disturbing than disturbed. Prior to the killing, she had been arrested on burglary, theft, assault, and drug use charges.[54] Cindy told authorities that she had been beaten and raped as a child. As a result, she said, "I've hurt . . . stabbed [and] shot people."[55]

Hours after the two girls met for the first time, they went knocking randomly on apartment doors (asking for directions, water, use of a telephone, etc.) in a complex where Cindy had once lived. An eighty-five-year-old woman answered her door, invited the girls in, and talked with them for nearly an hour. After the woman received a call indicating that her son would soon pick her up and drive her to a bingo game, the girls attacked her. Shirley grabbed her by the throat and threw her to the floor. Cindy fetched a butcher knife from the kitchen and threw it to Shirley, who used it to stab the elderly woman twenty-eight times. Once it was clear that the victim was dead, the girls ransacked her apartment, tore the telephones from the walls, and tried unsuccessfully to steal the woman's car.

After receiving a psychiatric report on Shirley, her attorney attempted to explain the killing from her perspective, noting that while Shirley showed no remorse, it appeared that she had symbolically killed her own mother, whom she deeply hated.[56] The attorney further hypothesized that there was an "unfortunate chemistry" between Shirley and Cindy; each girl wanted to prove that she could do anything the other could do.[57]

Killings in the Course of Other Crimes

Females are in the minority not only among homicide perpetrators but also among perpetrators of almost all crimes. As one authority put it, "[M]ost crime is not committed by human beings in general. It is committed by men."[58] Just as they rarely kill, girls also rarely rob, burglarize, rape, or commit other crimes of the sort which occasionally end in homicide. The vast majority of these crimes are committed by men and boys.[59]

Occasionally, however, girls do kill in the course of committing another crime—usually robbery. But here, too, they rarely do so alone. Instead, girls who kill during the course of committing other crimes almost always act with accomplices. Interestingly, while homicides of this sort are quite rare, when they do occur they are likely to be among the most heinous of all juvenile killings.

In some cases, girls who kill during other crimes have male accomplices.

For example, two Pennsylvania girls, aged fifteen and sixteen, aided by an eighteen-year-old boy, robbed, bound, and gagged a ninety-one-year-old woman, then abandoned her. Twelve days later the woman died, and all three youths were charged with murder [60]

Often, however, robbery-related killings are committed by two or more girls acting together, without male accomplices. The notorious case of Paula Cooper, an Indiana teenager, is one example.[61] Paula was thirteen years old when she and three other teenage girls entered the home of an elderly Bible teacher on a pretext. After Paula stabbed the woman thirty-three times with a foot-long butcher knife, she and the three other teens fled with $10 and the victim's car.

Another example is an Illinois case in which four girls, ranging in age from thirteen to eighteen, met in a pinball parlor and "decided we should hitchhike and rob somebody."[62] They were picked up by a salesman, who they later alleged propositioned them for sex. According to the thirteen-year-old, who testified for the prosecution, one of her companions agreed to have sex with the man for $10, but then produced a gun and robbed him of $17 and his keys while another of the girls assisted by holding a knife to his throat. According to the witness, the man then chased the girls, demanding return of his keys. The girl with the gun, who was fifteen years old, responded by shooting the man in the forehead from a distance of 4 inches, killing him.

More recently, in what appeared to be a robbery-related slaying, three Los Angeles females, two fifteen-year-olds and a twenty-year-old, jumped from a car, confronted a woman walking on the street, and demanded her purse. When the victim resisted, one of the fifteen-year-olds pulled a gun from her waistband and shot the woman in the face, killing her. Police officials said they had "assumed" the killing was committed by a male and were "shocked" to learn that the killer was a girl.[63]

Senseless Killings

As was noted in chapter 5, while it might be argued that all juvenile homicides are senseless, some of these killings are at least understandable while others are almost entirely inexplicable. Most killings committed by girls—other than those committed by girls who are seriously disturbed psychologically—seem to fall in the "understandable" category, at least in the sense that these killings are arguably instrumental; that is, they are designed to help achieve some rational (though not socially acceptable) goal. Such goals include removing an abusive parent, concealing a pregnancy and/or avoiding responsibility for an unwanted newborn, and assisting in the commission of a robbery or other economic crime. Of course, even in some of these cases, such as the killings committed by Shirley Wolf and Paula Cooper, the girl's instrumental goal (obtaining money and a car) in no way explains or renders more understandable the degree of violence inflicted upon the victim.

Perhaps the two sorts of utterly senseless juvenile killings that most often involve girls are gang-related homicides and "romantic" murder-suicides of the sort described in chapter 5.

Gang-Related Killings. While girls are occasionally involved in organized gangs of their own, gang-related killings involving girls are generally the result of girls' relationships with boys who are members of male street gangs.[64] In most such cases, girls play a secondary accomplice role in the actual homicides and often receive much more lenient treatment from the criminal or juvenile justice system. Two recent cases in Boston and Los Angeles illustrate this phenomenon.

In Boston, members of a street gang—armed with guns, knives, clubs, and mace—waited near a dark stretch of highway, planning to flag down a car and steal it from the driver.[65] One of the male teens lay in the road, feigning injury, while female members of the gang flagged down a passing car. The driver stopped and got out of his car to help, but tried to flee when one of the boys confronted him with a gun. The youth with the gun then shot and killed the driver.

One of the girls, seventeen years old, admitted her involvement in the killing and agreed to testify against two of the boys in exchange for trial as a juvenile. The two boys, both tried as adults, were convicted of first-degree murder and sentenced to life in prison without parole.

More recently, in Los Angeles, two girls, aged seventeen and fifteen, were charged with murder along with two older males, twenty and twenty-seven, who were members of a street gang. All four were riding in a car allegedly driven by the seventeen-year-old girl. The car was chased by two police officers as it sped away from a drive-by shooting in which two rival gang members and a third person were shot and killed. Investigators said the car suddenly turned and "bore down" on the police vehicle. Shots were exchanged, and the twenty-seven-year-old man shot and killed one of the officers.[66]

"Romantic" Murder-Suicides. As was noted in chapter 5, teenage girls are sometimes parties to what appear to be murder-suicides—incidents in which a boy and girl, romantically linked to one another, are both found dead under circumstances suggesting that one killed the other and then killed himself/herself.[67] As the cases noted there suggest, however, it is not always clear what role a girl has played in such a case. The fact that both participants are dead frequently makes it difficult if not impossible to determine whether the girl was an initiator of the crime, a perpetrator, or simply a victim.

9
The Law's Response to
Juvenile Homicide

B y his own count, between the ages of nine and fifteen, Willie Bosket committed over 2,000 crimes, including twenty-five stabbings. Released from a state reform school at the age of fourteen, Willie ran away and started roaming the New York City subways, looking for drunks he could rob. During an eight-day crime spree, fifteen-year-old Willie Bosket brutally shot and killed two of his robbery victims.[1]

After his arrest, Willie said he had killed "for the experience."[2] When asked by police how he felt, Willie told them, "I shot people. That's all. I don't feel nothing."[3] Willie also reportedly boasted that he could have killed 100 people and would still have been incarcerated only until he reached the age of twenty-one.[4]

In that regard, Willie Bosket was correct. Under then-existing New York law, as a juvenile, he could only be tried in the Family Court and, if found guilty, committed to state custody for no more than five years.[5] Willie Bosket was found guilty of the two murders—that is, he was adjudicated a juvenile delinquent in the Family Court—and was given the maximum sentence allowed by law: placement in the custody of the New York State Division for Youth for a period of five years.[6]

Public outrage over the Bosket case, fueled by numerous critical media reports in an election year, spurred New York's Governor and State Legislature to immediate action. Within a month of Willie's sentencing, what came to be known as New York's "Willie Bosket Law" was drafted in a matter of days and presented to the Legislature in an "extraordinary session" called by the Governor. Introduced on July 14, 1978, the Governor's proposal encountered little opposition, was passed in both legislative houses by an overwhelming majority, and was signed into law by the Governor on July 20, 1978.[7]

New York's "Willie Bosket Law," formally known as the Juvenile Offender Law, provides that thirteen-, fourteen- and fifteen-year-olds charged with murder and those fourteen or fifteen charged with other violent felonies (manslaughter, kidnapping, arson, aggravated assault, rape, sodomy, attempted murder, attempted kidnapping, and first- and second-degree burglary) may be tried as adults in criminal court and, if convicted, subjected to lengthy terms of imprisonment.[8] Had Willie Bosket been tried and convicted under the Juvenile Offender Law, he could have been sentenced to serve from nine years to life in prison.

Although Willie Bosket was never subjected to the law his crimes helped create, his incarceration did not end with the five years he spent with the Division for Youth. Despite having assaulted two guards and escaping, he was released just days after his twenty-first birthday. Within four months he was arrested for attempted robbery and sentenced to serve between three and a half and seven years in prison for mugging an elderly blind man. Since then, Willie Bosket has set his cell afire seven times, attacked guards nine times, and tried several times to escape. After being declared a "persistent felon," he was sentenced to a term of twenty-five years to life in prison.[9]

Trial of Juvenile Killers in Adult Criminal Courts

While the case of Willie Bosket is unusual, if not unique, the law his crimes spawned is not. By 1978, every American jurisdiction except New York, Arkansas, Nebraska, and Vermont had enacted similar laws which allowed certain older juveniles to be prosecuted as adults.[10] Today all jurisdictions in the United States provide for the prosecution of some juveniles as adults.[11]

Crimes Subject to Adult Prosecution

These laws, variously known as transfer, waiver, or certification provisions, provide that older juveniles (generally those older than twelve) who commit the most serious personal crimes (e.g., homicide, rape, kidnapping, armed robbery, arson, sodomy, aggravated assault) may be prosecuted and, if convicted, punished as adult criminals. Punishment for juveniles convicted as adults may include lengthy prison terms and, in some jurisdictions, the death penalty.[12]

Minimum Age for Adult Prosecution

In murder prosecutions, the minimum age at which juveniles may be tried as adults varies across jurisdictions. Fifteen states (Alaska, Arizona, Florida, Kentucky, Maine, Maryland, Nebraska, Nevada, New Hampshire, Oklahoma, Pennsylvania, South Carolina, Washington, West Virginia, and Wyoming) set no age minimum.[13] The lower age limit for criminal prosecution of juveniles in murder cases is ten years in three states (Indiana, South Dakota, and Vermont), thirteen years in three states (Georgia, Illinois, and Mississippi), fourteen years in eleven jurisdictions (Alabama, Colorado, Connecti-cut, Iowa, Kansas, Massachusetts, Minnesota, Missouri, New Jersey, North Carolina, and Utah), fifteen years in ten other jurisdictions (Arkansas, District of Columbia, Idaho, Louisiana, Michigan, New Mexico, Ohio, Tennessee, Texas, and Virginia), and sixteen years in eight states (California, Delaware, Hawaii, Montana, North Dakota, Oregon, Rhode Island, and Wisconsin).[14]

Criteria for Trial as an Adult

In most states, in order to be "waived," "transferred," or "certified" from juvenile court to adult court, a juvenile must, in addition to meeting age and crime requirements, be found by the court not suitable for treatment as a juvenile. Although courts have wide discretion in making this decision, in most jurisdictions judges are directed by statute to consider certain factors. Specification of these factors varies from state to state, but most state laws include some variation or combination of the following, drawn from the United States Supreme Court's landmark 1966 decision in *Kent v. United States*:[15]

1. The seriousness of the alleged offense to the community and whether the protection of the community requires waiver.

2. Whether the alleged offense was committed in an aggressive, violent, pre-meditated, or willful manner.

3. Whether the alleged offense was against persons . . . greater weight being given to offenses against persons especially if personal injury is involved.

4. The prosecutive merit of the complaint, i.e., whether there is evidence upon which a Grand Jury may be expected to return an indictment . . .

5. The desirability of trial and disposition of the entire offense in one court when the juvenile's associates in the alleged offense are adults who will be charged with a crime . . .

6. The sophistication and maturity of the juvenile as determined by consideration of his home, environmental situation, emotional attitude, and pattern of living.

7. The record and history of the juvenile, including previous contacts with . . . law enforcement agencies, juvenile courts and other jurisdictions, prior periods of probation . . . or prior commitments to juvenile institutions.

8. The prospects for adequate protection of the public and the likelihood of reasonable rehabilitation of the juvenile (if he is found to have committed the alleged offense) by the use of procedures, services and facilities currently available to the Juvenile Court.

Several of these factors are clearly related to the juvenile's psychological makeup. For example: (1) the danger or threat posed to the community by the juvenile; (2) the degree of sophistication and maturity exhibited by the juvenile; and (3) the likelihood that the juvenile can be rehabilitated through the services available to—and prior to expiration of the jurisdiction of—the juvenile court.[16]

Given the clear relationship between these factors and the juvenile's psychological makeup and functioning, it is not surprising that forensic mental health professionals (primarily psychologists and psychiatrists) have come to play a major role in helping courts to determine whether or not a given juvenile should be tried as a juvenile or as an adult.[17] Juveniles charged with serious crimes and eligible for transfer, waiver, or certification are now routinely subjected to forensic mental health evaluations, and the courts routinely give great weight to these evaluations in determining whether to try a youngster as a juvenile or as an adult.[18]

Danger to the Community. Transfer, waiver, and certification laws vary in the ways they address the factor of danger to the community. Some, for example, direct the courts to consider the "prospects for adequate protection of the public," others refer to "the impact of [waiver] on the safety and welfare of the community," and still others specify consideration of "whether waiver is necessary to protect the public security."[19] Regardless of how these statutes are worded, however, virtually every court in every jurisdiction must decide whether or not, or to what extent, a juvenile being considered for waiver, transfer, or certification poses a danger to the community.

Consideration of the danger a juvenile poses to society is, of course, a reflection of incapacitation as a justification for criminal punishment. The assumption is that juveniles who pose no danger or only minimal danger to society may safely be treated as juveniles, while those who are more dangerous require longer and more secure incarceration for the protection of the public.

Maturity and Sophistication. Virtually all courts also consider the maturity and sophistication of the youth being considered for trial as an adult.[20] Consideration of this factor, too, is generally specified by statute. Some waiver, transfer, and certification laws make the point only generally, requiring, for example, consideration of the "history, character and condition" of the juvenile.[21] Most, however, speak in more specific terms—for example, "the sophistication and maturity of the juvenile as determined by consideration of his home, environmental situation, emotional attitude and pattern of living."[22]

What lies behind such concern over maturity and sophistication is society's long-standing notion that adult penal sanctions should be reserved for those mature enough to be held fully responsible for their crimes. Until waiver, transfer, and certification laws were enacted, it was legally presumed that all juveniles below a certain age (usually eighteen but sometimes sixteen) were not sufficiently sophisticated and mature to be held criminally responsible for their antisocial acts. Youths below this age were automatically treated as juveniles.[23] Under modern waiver, transfer, or certification laws, the presumption remains but is rebuttable. Where older juveniles have committed very serious crimes, including homicide, the state may attempt to rebut the presumption that these youngsters are too immature to be held criminally responsible.[24]

Amenability to Treatment. Some consider amenability to treatment "the overriding question in the [entire] juvenile process."[25] Certainly, amenability to treatment is considered at virtually every stage of the juvenile justice process from intake to disposition. Moreover, it is clearly the linchpin of the waiver/transfer/certification process. The clear bias in most waiver/transfer/certification law is in favor of retaining in the juvenile justice system those juveniles who are amenable to treatment in that system.[26]

In the context of deciding whether a given youth ought to be tried as a juvenile or as an adult, amenability to treatment is perhaps best thought of as presenting two questions: (1) Are the dispositions available to the juvenile court likely to rehabilitate the juvenile before that court's jurisdiction ends? (2) Are the services available to the juvenile in the criminal justice system appropriate to his/her needs?[27]

Application of the Criteria in Homicide Cases

As the cases reviewed throughout this volume indicate, some youngsters charged with homicide are tried as juveniles and others are prosecuted as adults. Although the courts are directed by statute to consider a number of criteria in deciding whether a juvenile charged with homicide should be tried as a juvenile or as an adult, it appears that certain factors are particularly predictive of adult prosecution of juveniles who kill. For example, Eigen studied all 154 cases in which juveniles were arrested for homicide in Philadelphia in one year.[28] Seventy-nine (51 percent) of these juveniles had their cases retained for trial in the juvenile court and the other sixty-five juveniles (49 percent) were waived for trial as adults.

Eigen found that four factors were especially predictive of whether a given juvenile homicide defendant would be retained in juvenile court or waived for trial as an adult. These factors included (1) the killing taking place during the commission of a felony; (2) the juvenile being seventeen years old at the time of the killing; (3) the juvenile being the principal assailant of the victim as opposed to an accessory; and (4) the juvenile having a prior criminal record.

Eigen found that where none of these factors was present, only 12 percent of the juvenile homicide defendants were waived to adult court; where one factor was present 33 percent were waived; where two factors were present 61 percent were waived; where three factors were present 83 percent were waived; and where all four factors were present 100 percent of the juveniles charged with homicide were waived for trial as adults. Eigen also found that the most powerful single predictor of waiver to adult court in these homicide cases was whether or not the juvenile in question was the principal assailant: even where no other factors were present, 56 percent of those juveniles who actually inflicted the fatal injury were waived for trial in adult criminal court.

In another study of waiver and disposition in juvenile murder and non-negligent manslaughter cases, U. S. Department of Justice staff examined 394 cases adjudicated in 1984 and 1985 in 15 states (Alabama, Arizona, California, Hawaii, Iowa, Maryland, Mississippi, Nebraska, New Jersey, North Dakota, Ohio, Pennsylvania, Tennessee, Utah, and Virginia).[29] Twenty-eight percent of these cases were waived to criminal court, 36 percent resulted in placement of the youth in a juvenile facility, 11 percent resulted in probation, 12 percent of the youths were released by the juvenile court, and 3 percent of the cases involved some "other" unspecified disposition.

More recently, Cornell and his colleagues have reported on the legal outcomes of the seventy-two juvenile homicide cases they studied in Michigan.[30] Forty-nine of these youths were above the age of sixteen and thus, under Michigan law, were all charged in adult criminal court. By law, the three youths who were under the age of fifteen had to be retained for trial in juvenile court. Thus, overall, twenty youths—all either fifteen or sixteen years old—were eligible for waiver from juvenile to adult court. Data on nineteen of these twenty youths were available, and eighteen of those nineteen had their cases waived for trial in adult court. The single eligible youth who was not waived for trial as an adult was a fifteen-year-old who shot and killed both his parents. Several years earlier, this boy had been sexually abused by his father.

The application of waiver criteria in juvenile homicide cases—and the tremendous discretion courts have in such application—is perhaps best illustrated by an actual case. Ricky Dale Mathis was sixteen years old when he was charged with murder and robbery in the death of a forty-year-old man, who had enticed Ricky, a runaway, into a sexual relationship at the man's mountain cabin. After performing oral sex on Ricky, the man tried to persuade Ricky to penetrate him anally. While pondering the man's request, Ricky grabbed a pocketknife and stabbed the man repeatedly in the back. When the man did not die from the stab wounds, Ricky beat him to death with a frying pan and hammer. Ricky then took the man's wallet and car keys, fled in the man's car, and turned himself in to authorities a short while later.[31]

The juvenile court waived Ricky's case for prosecution in the adult criminal court despite overwhelming evidence that Ricky should be tried as a juvenile. In affirming the juvenile court's decision to remand Ricky to adult court, the Court of Appeals quoted extensively from the juvenile court judge's decision:

> Ricky Dale Mathis is 16 years of age. . . . Mathis has had, from the beginning of formal schooling, a continuing inability to progress in school in . . . a normal manner. His principal problem appears to be an inability to master reading, and perhaps spelling . . .
>
> Mathis has had many advantages. It appears material needs (with at least reasonable wants) have been more than adequately provided . . .
>
> Mathis has not previously been referred to juvenile authorities. He has, however, experimented with some drugs, has drank [sic] alcoholics, he smokes, and uses profane and obscene language. He has on numerous occasions been a truant and a school discipline problem. He has been suspended and was transferred from a "progressive" school setting to "a more conventional" school. He has twice been a runaway, the last time ending in the present charge.
>
> Mathis' problems at schools caused him to be . . . referred for psychiatric help. He received evaluation and treatment by counseling on a weekly basis for about seven or eight months immediately prior to the offense alleged. This psychiatric therapy was given by an experienced doctor. . . . Another psychiatrist, engaged on behalf of Mathis, found him not to be mentally ill; however, found in addition to the aforementioned school problems, that Mathis had a progressive history of temper tantrums, depressions, runaway, truancy, lying, swearing, and resistance to authority.
>
> Paradoxically, Mathis was an active Boy Scout, excelling in achievement and scouting ability. . . . Mathis has been an exemplary inmate during his confinement in detention. . . .
>
> Both psychiatrists who testified estimate that Mathis will need counseling for three or four years. . . . Testimony has been received from Mathis' parents, treating psychiatrist, teachers and other associates. Most of these witnesses favor retention of juvenile court jurisdiction . . .
>
> It is urged on Mathis' behalf that he has not previously been adjudicated delinquent nor received the services available through counseling. His behavior pattern, however, is a familiar one. It seems most unlikely that any lack of prior juvenile court counseling service is of any persuasive significance in view of the extended efforts by schools to assist him, as well as the weekly psychiatric counseling he received over at least a seven months period of time. In this regard, Mathis' reaction to "crisis" (the truth of the charge being assumed) was of a kind and character weighing against retention of juvenile jurisdiction.
>
> Mathis is at the threshold of maturity. He was a juvenile heretofore; he will not be hereafter. He would, if retained in juvenile court, enter the only facility available to him above the average age of other inmates. From the

testimony, it is unlikely he would be retained beyond his 19th year, or, any more than three years. A longer period for any re-adjustment as well as a subsequent period of continued supervision seems clearly indicated. The public's interest cannot be otherwise reasonably recognized . . .[32]

To this rationale, the Court of Appeals added another reason for prosecuting Ricky as an adult rather than a juvenile:

From [the facts related by the arresting officer], we infer that the boy carried a springblade knife, and that under the stress of the situation, and desiring to acquire the victim's money, in a cool and calculated manner he proceeded with the assault.[33]

One Court of Appeals judge, who dissented, saw Ricky and his crime in a different light:

This case presents the always difficult problem of whether a child should be remanded for trial as an adult. The alleged crime was committed four days after his 16th birthday.

[T]his boy, not yet in high school, had never previously been referred to a juvenile court. His school difficulties were not of major dimensions and in the six months prior to the crime charged they had greatly improved, as a result of a change in schools combined with weekly treatment by a fully qualified child psychiatrist. Nothing in his history remotely hints at violent tendencies . . .

Nothing in this record indicates any prior involvement whatever of a homosexual nature in the boy's life, nor any indication of violence. Like *Cardiel* [a case in which this court reversed the juvenile court's decision to try a juvenile as an adult], this, too, was clearly "a one time thing." . . . Unlike *Cardiel*, this boy comes from a strong family background. His mother is and has been a school teacher for many years, holding a Master's Degree. His father, a college graduate, is a highly successful engineer and has worked for more than twenty years in a responsible position for a major corporation. . . . Thus unlike *Cardiel*, where the boy was completely emancipated and had no family strengths, this boy's family offers unusual strengths to aid in his rehabilitation. Here the trial court concluded that because of the viciousness of the crime it was unlikely that this boy could be rehabilitated before he is 21. No trained professional in either the social work, correctional or medical fields expressed such an opinion. Nor did anyone recommend that this boy should be remanded to the adult court or committed to an adult institution, or that either would be in the best interest of the public or of the boy.

From my examination of this record I conclude that the state has failed to establish . . . that it is in the best interests either of the public or of this child that he be remanded to adult court, let alone both of them, as [the law] requires.[34]

Punishment of Juveniles Who Kill

The major significance of the decision of where to try an alleged juvenile killer—juvenile court versus criminal court—lies in the law's response to the juvenile if he or she is found guilty of the crime.

Juveniles tried and convicted of murder or manslaughter in adult court may be sentenced to prison, detention in a juvenile facility, or both.[35] However, juveniles found guilty of these same crimes in juvenile court may not be sentenced to prison but only to detention in state juvenile facilities.[36] Moreover, in most states, while juveniles tried and convicted as adults may be sentenced to prison terms which greatly exceed the duration of their minority (i.e., extend well beyond their eighteenth or twenty-first birthdays), periods of detention imposed by juvenile courts are typically limited to the duration of the offender's minority or a relatively short period thereafter.[37]

Finally, in those states that impose the death penalty for certain murders, juveniles who are tried and convicted of murder in adult court are the only ones who are even eligible to be considered for capital punishment.[38] Thus, as is described in greater detail below, in some cases the transfer or waiver decision may mean the difference between life and death for a juvenile killer.

Incarceration of Juveniles Who Kill

When it comes to incarceration, juveniles convicted of homicide crimes in adult court are treated much more harshly than those found guilty of such crimes in juvenile court. For example, among the 154 juveniles arrested for homicide and studied by Eigen, 90 percent of those tried as adults were sentenced to prison, while fewer than half of those tried in juvenile court were incarcerated.[39]

Eigen also documented dramatic differences in the duration of incarceration between juvenile killers found guilty in juvenile court and those convicted in adult court.[40] In no case tried in juvenile court was the youth confined to a state institution beyond his or her twenty-first birthday. In those cases tried in criminal court, however, all of those youths convicted of felony-related murder and 84 percent of those convicted of murder not related to another felony were sentenced to terms of imprisonment ranging from one to two years to life in prison. One youth convicted in adult court was sentenced to die.

Cormier and Markus also reported similar differences in outcome in forty-one cases in which juveniles were charged with murder or manslaughter.[41] Among the twenty-five youths who had their cases retained in juvenile court, one was placed in the custody of his family while the other twenty-four were remanded to state custody until the age of twenty-one. Among the sixteen juveniles tried as adults, however, more than half received life sentences: "one was acquitted, nine were sentenced to life imprisonment, one was sentenced to 30 years, one was sentenced to two years, one received a ten year suspended sentence, two were found not guilty by reason of insanity, and one was found unfit to stand trial . . ."[42]

Cornell and his colleagues have also reported the legal outcomes among the sixty-seven juveniles in their sample who were tried on homicide charges in adult criminal court.[43] Twenty-five of these youths, all charged with first-degree murder (conviction for which carries a sentence of life imprisonment without parole), pleaded guilty to lesser charges. Thirty-four others went to trial and were convicted. In all, only eight of the sixty-seven youths were acquitted or had the charges against them dismissed.

Cornell and associates reported that of those youths who pleaded guilty or were convicted in adult court, one was sentenced to probation, while the others were all sent to prison.[44] Three quarters of the sample received prison sentences of ten or more years, including nineteen youths who were given the maximum sentence of life imprisonment.

Interestingly, Cornell et al. found no significant differences in sentences based upon either the youth's age or the general circumstances of the homicide—that is, whether the killing was one committed during the course of another crime (such as rape or robbery) or one committed against a victim (such as a relative or acquaintance) with whom the youthful killer had an ongoing and conflicted relationship. Offenders who were fifteen or sixteen were treated no more leniently than those who were seventeen or eighteen years of age. Indeed, "[i]f anything, there may have been a tendency for the younger youths to receive harsher sentences . . ."[45] More of the youths in the "conflict" group were convicted than in the "crime" group but the difference in rate of conviction was not significant.[46]

Rosner and his colleagues also reported the legal dispositions in the cases of forty-five juveniles charged with murder or manslaughter.[47] One of these youths was found not guilty by reason of insanity and another died prior to sentencing. Among the forty-three who were sentenced, nine received terms of probation up to five years, three were sent to "reform school," and the remaining thirty-one were sentenced to terms of imprisonment, including three sentences of fifteen years to life.[48] Unlike Cornell et al., Rosner and colleagues found a clear relationship between age and duration of sentence: "When adolescents become older, the sentences they receive become longer."[49]

Capital Punishment for Juveniles Who Kill

The United States is one of the few nations in the world that allow the execution of individuals for crimes committed while they were juveniles. Since

1979, Amnesty International has documented only eight executions of juvenile offenders in the world. Three of these executions took place in the United States. The remaining five occurred in Pakistan, Bangladesh, Rwanda, and Barbados.[50]

The execution of juvenile criminals in the United States, though relatively rare, is not new. Roughly 300 juveniles have been executed in the United States since 1642, when the first well-documented juvenile execution took place.[51] More than half of these juveniles were seventeen years old at the time of their crimes; more than 80 percent were sixteen or seventeen years old. From 1982 through 1988, a total of 2,106 death sentences were imposed in the United States, but only fifteen were imposed on persons for crimes committed when they were under the age of seventeen, and only twenty-four were imposed on individuals who were seventeen at the time of their crimes.[52] Currently, thirty juvenile killers—1.37 percent of the total U.S. death row population—are awaiting execution.[53] More than 90 percent of these inmates are males.

Capital punishment of juvenile killers is governed by statute and case law—primarily, three recent decisions of the United States Supreme Court.

Thirty-seven states have statutes permitting capital punishment.[54] Twelve of these states (California, Colorado, Connecticut, Illinois, Maryland, Nebraska, New Hampshire, New Jersey, New Mexico, Ohio, Oregon, and Tennessee) prohibit capital punishment for crimes committed while the offender was under the age of eighteen.[55] Three more states (Georgia, North Carolina, and Texas) forbid execution as a punishment for crimes committed before the age of seventeen.[56] Thus, overall, twenty-five states allow for the execution of juveniles convicted of murder, and twenty-two of these states (Alabama, Arizona, Arkansas, Delaware, Florida, Idaho, Indiana, Kentucky, Louisiana, Mississippi, Missouri, Montana, Nevada, Oklahoma, Pennsylvania, South Carolina, South Dakota, Utah, Vermont, Virginia, Washington, and Wyoming) allow the execution of juveniles convicted of murders committed before they were seventeen years old.[57]

In 1982, 1988, and 1989, the United States Supreme Court decided cases which challenged the constitutionality of state laws permitting the execution of persons for crimes committed while they were juveniles.

In 1982, in *Eddings v. Oklahoma*,[58] the Court was confronted with a case in which Monty Lee Eddings, a sixteen-year-old runaway who had been abused by his father, shot a state trooper through the heart with a sawed-off shotgun and then left him to bleed to death on the side of the road. Charged with first-degree murder, Monty pleaded no contest. At sentencing, the judge, who imposed a sentence of death, acknowledged that Monty's youth was a substantial mitigating factor but refused, as a matter of law, to consider Monty's disturbed family life and emotional problems as mitigating evidence.

Although Monty Lee Eddings challenged his sentence as a violation of the Eighth Amendment ban on cruel and unusual punishment, the Supreme Court vacated his death sentence on much narrower grounds. Justice Powell, joined by four other justices, held that in a capital sentencing proceeding, sentencing authorities may not "refuse to consider, as a matter of law, any relevant mitigating evidence."[59] Youth, the Court concluded, "is itself a relevant mitigating factor of great weight."[60]

In 1988, in *Thompson v. Oklahoma*,[61] the question was whether or not it was constitutionally permissible to execute a person for a crime he had committed while under the age of sixteen. On January 23, 1983, fifteen-year-old William Wayne Thompson left home with three older friends, explaining to his girlfriend that the trio was "going to kill Charles" Keene, Thompson's former brother-in-law.[62] Later that night, William and his companions brutally beat, shot, and killed Keene, apparently in retribution for abuse Keene had previously inflicted upon William's sister. William admitted that he had kicked Keene in the head, cut his throat and chest, and shot him in the head. William was certified to stand trial as an adult, tried and convicted of murder, and sentenced to die.

In *Thompson*, four Supreme Court justices held that execution of a person who was under the age of sixteen at the time of his or her offense constituted cruel and unusual punishment and was thus proscribed by the Eighth Amendment. Although a fifth justice, Justice O'Connor, concluded that "a national consensus forbidding the execution of any person for a crime committed before the age of 16 very likely does exist," she was "reluctant to adopt this conclusion as a matter of constitutional law without better evidence than we now possess."[63] Still, Justice O'Connor provided the fifth vote needed to vacate Thompson's death sentence, holding that those "below the age of 16 at the time of their offense may not be executed under the authority of a capital punishment statute [such as the Oklahoma law under which Thompson was sentenced] that specifies no minimum age at which the commission of a capital crime can lead to the offender's execution."[64]

While Justice O'Connor's decision spared William Wayne Thompson's life, it failed to resolve the controversy over the age at which capital punishment becomes a constitutionally valid penalty. A year later, in 1989, the Court confronted that question again in two cases decided together, *Stanford v. Kentucky* and *Wilkins v. Missouri*.[65] This time, the question was whether the Eighth Amendment forbade the execution of individuals for crimes they committed while either sixteen or seventeen years old.

Kevin Stanford and Heath Wilkins, whose cases were alluded to briefly in chapter 4, were both sentenced to die for their roles in separate homicides. At the age of seventeen years and four months, Kevin Stanford and an accomplice robbed a gas station, repeatedly raped and sodomized the female attendant, and then drove her to a secluded spot, where Kevin shot her "point-blank" in the head and face.[66] Kevin later reportedly told a corrections officer, "I had to shoot her, [she] lived next door to me and would recognize me."[67]

Emphasizing the nature of Kevin's offenses, his extensive history of delinquency, and the failure of the juvenile system to successfully rehabilitate him, the juvenile court determined that it would be in Kevin's best interest and the best interest of the community to try him as an adult. Kevin was tried in criminal court and convicted of murder, sodomy, robbery, and receiving stolen property. He was sentenced to death on the murder charge, and forty-five years imprisonment on the other charges.

Heath Wilkins was sixteen years and six months old when he and an accomplice decided to rob a convenience store and kill "whoever was behind the counter" because "a dead person can't talk."[68] In the course of committing such a robbery, Heath's accomplice held the store's clerk while Heath repeatedly stabbed her as she begged for her life. After taking cigarettes, liquor, rolling papers, and about $450 in checks and cash, the two left the clerk to die on the floor.

Focusing on the viciousness and violence of Heath's crime, on the failure of the juvenile justice system to rehabilitate him after past acts of delinquency, on the inability of that system to rehabilitate him within the seventeen months of remaining juvenile court jurisdiction, on Heath's experience and the maturity of his "appearance and habits," and on the need to protect the public, the juvenile court transferred Heath's trial to adult court.[69] There, Heath was charged with first-degree murder, armed criminal action, and carrying a concealed weapon.

Heath Wilkins waived counsel, pleaded guilty to all charges, declined representation at sentencing, presented no mitigating evidence, and told the judge he preferred to die rather than spend his life in prison. In his words, "one I fear, the other one I don't."[70] After hearing the state's evidence, the judge sentenced Heath to die.

As stated by Justice Scalia, writing for the Supreme Court:

> The thrust of both Wilkins' and Stanford's arguments is that imposition of the death penalty on those who were juveniles when they committed their crimes falls within the Eighth Amendment prohibition against "cruel and unusual punishments." Wilkins would have us define juveniles as individuals 16 years of age and under; Stanford would draw the line at 17.[71]

Justice Scalia, joined by four other justices, concluded that there is no national consensus against executing sixteen- and seventeen-year-olds convicted of murder, and the Supreme Court affirmed by a five-to-four vote the death sentences imposed upon both Kevin Stanford and Heath Wilkins.[72] In a strong dissent, Justice Brennan and three other justices pointed to psychological and psychiatric data indicating that juveniles lack the judgment and moral maturity necessary to hold them fully responsible for their crimes.[73]

After *Eddings, Thompson, Stanford,* and *Wilkins,* it is clear that there is no constitutional bar to imposing the death penalty upon juveniles who were at least sixteen years old at the time of their capital crimes. *Thompson* does not preclude imposing a death sentence upon a younger convicted murderer, so long as the statutory provisions under which the youth is sentenced explicitly set a minimum age for capital sentencing. *Eddings,* of course, requires that whatever the age of the juvenile, all mitigating evidence including the juvenile's youth be considered by the sentencing authority, whether judge or jury.

Thus, while rarely imposed, the death penalty remains a viable option for punishing juveniles who kill.

10
The Future of Juvenile Homicide

As the statistics cited in chapter 1 indicate, both the annual incidence and the rate of juvenile homicide in the United States—at least as reflected in arrests for murder or manslaughter—have shown a steady increase over the past several years. Indeed, in 1988 (the most recent year for which national arrest data are available), the number of juvenile homicide arrests was the highest in nine years and, for the first time, constituted more than 10 percent of the annual total of all homicide arrests.[1]

Any attempt to project the future incidence and rate of juvenile homicide is obviously speculative, but the confluence of a host of forces currently operating in American society suggests that the number and rate of juvenile homicides will continue to increase and may reach record proportions by the turn of the century. Among these forces are: (1) increasingly serious substance abuse among juveniles and adults; (2) apparently rising rates of child maltreatment; (3) expanding access to guns, including high-powered automatic weapons; (4) the growing number of juveniles living in poverty; and (5) the anticipated resurgence of the juvenile population. This final chapter briefly examines each of these forces and their likely relationship to juvenile homicide as the twentieth century ends and the twenty-first century begins.

Substance Abuse

Although the federal government estimates that overall casual drug abuse in the United States has decreased over the last five years, government estimates also indicate that frequent abuse of certain substances—most notably cocaine and its derivative crack—has significantly increased in the same time period.[2] For example, between 1985 and 1988, federally sponsored household surveys found that the number of weekly cocaine users went from 647,000 to 862,000 and the number of daily cocaine users rose from 246,000 to 292,000.[3] During the same time period, emergency room visits related to cocaine use jumped from 8,000 to 46,000.

For the most part, these increases seem attributable to the increased avail-ability and abuse of crack. As Dr. William Bennett, director of the National Office of Drug Policy, recently explained: "Drug crime is up, drug trafficking is up, drug deaths are up, drug emergencies in our hospitals are up, all since 1985. And much of this can be explained in one word, and that word is 'crack.'"[4]

At the same time, Dr. Frederick Godwin, director of the Alcohol, Drug Abuse and Mental Health Administration, reported another finding from the 1988 survey: "600,000 young people, aged 12 to 17, had used cocaine within the past year, which places them at heavy risk for continued use, addiction, and severe medical consequences as well as the potential social consequences [including] juvenile crime . . ."[5]

Substance abuse affects the number and rate of juvenile homicides in at least three ways: (1) most directly by altering the psychological functioning of juveniles in ways which make them more likely to kill; (2) less directly by creating an environment in which some juveniles have economic incentives to kill; and (3) indirectly, by contributing to the likelihood of child maltreatment.

Killings by Juveniles under the Influence of Drugs

When drug abuse increases, so too does homicide, and the correlation ap-pears to hold for both adults and juveniles. Recent data from New York City, for example, provide a striking illustration. In 1985, officials estimated that there were 97,000 drug abusers under the age of seventeen in all of New York State, including New York City.[6] In 1988, the overall estimated number of drug abusers under seventeen in New York City alone reached an all-time high of 140,000.[7] As juvenile drug abuse was reaching record highs, so too was juvenile homicide. In 1988, the number of murders in New York City reached an all-time annual high of 1,896, and the number of murders com-mitted by juveniles went from twenty-four in 1987 to fifty-seven in 1988, a 138 percent increase in a single year.[8]

While there are no definitive data regarding how many juvenile homi-cides are committed by youths under the influence of drugs, it appears from existing evidence that a substantial proportion of juvenile homicides fall into that category. For example, as noted in chapter 4, Malmquist found that five of twenty juvenile killers in his sample had used barbiturates, amphetamines, psychotomimetics, marijuana, and/or psychedelics prior to killing;[9] Sorrells found that eight of thirty-one juvenile killers in his sample were under the influence of alcohol and/or other drugs when they killed;[10] and Cornell and his colleagues found that twenty-seven out of thirty-seven juveniles who killed during the course of another crime (e.g., burglary, rape, or robbery) were suffering from alcohol and/or other drug intoxication at the time of their crimes.[11]

Drugs play a variety of roles in juvenile homicides. Some drugs, such as crack, appear to stimulate violent and/or irrational behavior. Others seem to create confusion, lower inhibitions, impair judgment, and/or make youngsters more susceptible to peer influence. But whatever the role played by drugs in facilitating or encouraging juvenile homicide, it seems apparent that drug abuse is one factor which often increases the risk of such homicide.

Economically Motivated Killings Related to Drugs

Some juvenile homicides are drug related not because the perpetrators are necessarily under the influence of drugs when they kill, but rather because these homicides were committed as part of the juvenile perpetrators' efforts to make or protect drug profits.[12] In recent years, the sale of cocaine and crack has become a multi-million-dollar industry. The drug trade, though lucrative, is also extremely competitive in many locales, and it has become increasingly common for dealers to battle one another for "turf"—that is, the "right" to sell their illicit substances without competition in a given geographic area.[13] Among the "soldiers" in these so-called drug wars—a number of which result in homicides—are many juveniles.[14] Numerous other drug-related juvenile homicides have also resulted from the efforts of youthful drug dealers to secure payment for their product or the product they are selling or delivering for others.[15] As drug trafficking increases and/or becomes more competitive, it seems likely that the number of juvenile killings of both types will increase.

Parental Drug Abuse and Child Maltreatment

Finally, it appears that the growing problem of serious drug abuse has had and will continue to have an indirect and long-term but significant impact upon the incidence of juvenile homicide by contributing to the incidence of child abuse and neglect. It is widely acknowledged that parental drug abuse is one of the major causal factors in child abuse.[16] And, as is described in more detail below, there is a strong correlation between child abuse and juvenile homicide; many, perhaps most, juveniles who kill are or have been victims of child abuse.

Although, as is also explained below, uncertainty exists as to whether child abuse and neglect is increasing, there seems to be little if any disagreement with the conclusion that a growing number of cases of child abuse and neglect involve parents who are drug abusers and/or addicts. Such cases often begin even before the child is born, as in the case of the growing number of "cocaine babies," children born to cocaine-addicted mothers.[17] Other forms of child maltreatment result less directly but just as clearly from parental drug abuse and addiction as the effects of substance abuse lead parents to neglect, abandon, abuse, or even kill their children.[18]

Child Maltreatment

As noted in chapter 2, probably the single most consistent finding in juvenile homicide research to date is that juveniles who kill have generally witnessed and/or been directly victimized by domestic violence.[19] The research and clinical literature is replete with statistical and anecdotal evidence of an extremely high incidence of child abuse victimization among juveniles who kill.[20]

The correlation between child abuse and juvenile homicide, though not well researched, makes sense intuitively. Some children who are abused and/or witness abuse of loved ones learn to be violent; their abusive parents provide a powerful role model. Other abused children undoubtedly suffer psychological and/or physical trauma, which leads to impaired functioning (e.g., brain damage, neurological dysfunction, psychosis, etc.) of the sort often associated with juvenile homicidal behavior. Still other abused children kill in direct response to their abuse: they kill their abusers, generally their mothers and/or fathers.

Given the correlation between child abuse and juvenile homicide, increases in the incidence and/or severity of child abuse are likely to be followed by corresponding increases in the number and rate of juvenile homicides. If, as many contend, the United States is experiencing an "epidemic" of child abuse,[21] this "epidemic" will undoubtedly affect the incidence of juvenile homicide for some time to come.

It is difficult to say for certain whether child maltreatment is increasing in incidence and severity, but a variety of indicators suggest that it is. Looking solely at national data on child abuse and neglect reports, one might readily conclude that the incidence of child maltreatment is steadily increasing. Virtually all available data indicate a tremendous and steady increase in the number of reported cases of child abuse over the past decade. For example, the American Association for Protecting Children (AAPC), a division of the American Humane Association, has surveyed all fifty states, the District of Columbia, and the U.S. territories, and has estimated the annual number of child abuse and neglect reports for the years from 1976 through 1987.[22] The AAPC's estimates, derived from these surveys, are displayed in Table 10–1.

A significant limitation to these data, however, is that an unknown but probably large number of cases of child maltreatment go unreported while, at the same time, not all reported cases are substantiated. Indeed, the majority of child abuse and neglect turn out to be unsubstantiated.[24] An unsubstantiated report does not necessarily mean that the reported abuse or neglect did not occur, only that the investigating authorities, for whatever reason, were unable to find the kind of substantiating evidence the law requires in order to justify state intervention.[25]

Table 10–1
National Estimates of the Number and Rate per 1,000 of
Child Abuse and Neglect Reports 1976–1987[23]

Year	Number of Reports (and Percentage Change)	Rate per 1,000 Children (and Percentage Change)
1976	669,000	10.1
1977	838,000 (25.26)	12.8 (22)
1978	836,000 (−0.24)	12.9 (0)
1979	988,000 (18.18)	15.4 (19)
1980	1,154,000 (16.80)	18.1 (17)
1981	1,225,000 (6.15)	19.4 (7)
1982	1,262,000 (3.02)	20.1 (4)
1983	1,477,000 (17.04)	23.6 (17)
1984	1,727,000 (16.93)	27.3 (16)
1985	1,928,000 (11.64)	30.6 (12)
1986	2,086,000 (8.20)	32.8 (7)
1987	2,178,000 (4.40)	34.0 (4)

Whether or not substantiated cases of child abuse are increasing is difficult to establish with existing data, but testimony given before the U.S. Senate Judiciary Committee in May of 1989 indicates that there was a 64-percent increase in the number of confirmed child abuse cases in the United States between 1980 and 1986.[26]

Regardless of whether overall incidence is increasing, there are data which suggest that child abuse is becoming more severe—that is, more violent and more physically damaging to its young victims. Perhaps the clearest indicator of this sort is the recent dramatic increase in child abuse fatalities—that is, the growing number of children who are killed by their abusers. For example, between 1985 and 1987, there was a 25-percent increase nationally in the number of children who died as a direct result of child abuse.[27] Between 1986 and 1987, child abuse deaths almost tripled in Utah and virtually doubled in Virginia and North Carolina.[28] At roughly the same time, during fiscal 1988, Illinois experienced ninety-seven child abuse deaths, an 80-percent increase over the preceding fiscal year.[29]

Even more recent national and state data indicate that the upward trend in child abuse fatalities is continuing. In 1988, the number of recorded deaths from child abuse reached 1,225, an increase of 5 percent over the national total for 1987.[30] In California in 1988, ninety-six children died as a result of child abuse, up by more than 15 percent from the state total of eighty-three in 1987.[31]

Guns

Most homicides, including those perpetrated by juveniles, involve the use of firearms. As the cases reviewed throughout this volume indicate, guns are used by juvenile killers in a wide variety of homicidal contexts, including but not limited to: the youngster who finds his or her parent's handgun and uses it to kill a playmate, the abused child who shoots and kills his or her abusive parent, the juvenile robber who panics and uses a handgun to kill the robbery victim, the teenage gang member who fires a gun out a car window into a crowd on the street in a drive-by killing, and the juvenile drug dealer who uses a semiautomatic assault rifle to assassinate a competitor.

What all these juvenile homicides have in common is the fact their perpetrators had access to guns. What many have in common is that they would not have occurred but for the juvenile perpetrators' access to a firearm. There can be little doubt that increased access to guns among juveniles increases the likelihood of juvenile homicide.

Solid data on gun ownership and accessibility in the United States are hard to come by—and the available data are often disputed or subject to differing interpretations. Still, several points seem beyond dispute: millions of guns ranging from small handguns to semiautomatic assault rifles are owned by Americans; and many of these weapons are either in the hands of or readily available to juveniles, at least some portion of whom use them to kill other people.

It is difficult to say with certainty whether gun ownership in the United States is currently increasing, but not difficult to conclude that more Americans than ever own guns or that a growing number of American juveniles have easy access to guns. In 1987, "gun imports [to the United States] hit a 10-year peak" while "domestic production [of firearms] reversed a five-year decline."[32] While more recent statistics are not available, firearm industry sources indicate that production and sales of guns have continued to increase.[33]

In 1989, a Harris poll found that virtually every other household in the United States has a gun.[34] The Federal Bureau of Alcohol, Tobacco and Firearms recently estimated that some 70 million Americans own approximately 140 million rifles and 60 million handguns—including 2 to 3 million semiautomatic assault weapons.[35] One group of Americans known to be increasing in their ownership of guns is women. A Gallup poll conducted for one of the nation's leading gun manufacturers found a 53-percent increase in female gun owners between 1983 and 1986.[36]

Given the number of guns in American society, it is hardly surprising that some percentage of these firearms end up in the hands of children and adolescents. The problem of juvenile gun possession and use has become so serious in the past few years that some school systems are now using hand-held metal detectors to help keep guns out of the school environment.[37]

Much but not all of the problem with juveniles bringing guns to school is limited to large cities such as New York, Washington, Detroit, and Miami where guns are regularly found on public school students.[38] For example, in the 1986–1987 school year, school officials in Jacksonville, Florida, found thirty-nine guns in the public schools there; halfway through the next academic year, they had already found forty-five guns in the schools.[39] While some of the guns brought into schools by juveniles has been attributed to the drug trade, especially sale of crack, at least one study has found that many juveniles bring guns to school for their own protection. Youths, aged nine to seventeen, told researchers that they "believe carrying weapons is the only way they can protect themselves" from others with guns.[40]

Another symptom of the growing access juveniles have to guns is the recent rash of accidental shootings of children by other children and the government's response to these accidents. For example, in Florida, where it is estimated that 60 percent of all households have at least one gun,[41] five children were shot during one two-week period in the summer of 1989.[42] All five shootings, three of which were fatal, involved young children, and all were committed with guns belonging to one of the children's parents.[43] Similarly, the summer of 1989 witnessed the accidental shooting deaths of four children in Connecticut and two in Virginia.[44]

All three states responded almost immediately with legislation aimed at making it a crime to leave loaded guns where they are accessible to children.[45] Indeed, in Florida, in the very same month as the rash of shootings there, the legislature was called into special session. There, legislation, signed into law by the Governor, was enacted, making gun owners guilty of a felony if their unsecured guns are used by a child to injure or kill someone, and guilty of a misdemeanor if they carelessly store a gun and that gun is used by a child in a manner which threatens others.[46]

Even the National Rifle Association (NRA), which vehemently opposes virtually any legal controls on gun ownership, has acknowledged the growing problem of juveniles' access to guns. Recently, the NRA began producing and distributing a children's coloring book. The booklet, "My Gun Safety Book," is designed for children from kindergarten through first grade and tells them that if they find a gun, they should leave it alone, leave the area, and tell an adult.[47]

Eventually, gun safety laws (such as that recently enacted in Florida) and educational campaigns (such as that contained in the NRA's coloring book) may help stem the tide of juvenile access to guns, or at least make that access less deadly. At this point and for the foreseeable future, however, it appears that juvenile access to guns will likely continue to grow, and thus continue to contribute to the growing problem of juvenile homicide.

Poverty

The link between poverty and crime in American society, including violent crime, is complex and not entirely understood, but almost universally recognized.[48] It is impossible to say what percentage of juvenile homicides are committed by economically impoverished youths, but that percentage is undoubtedly high, at least for certain types of killings such as gang killings, killings committed in the course of robberies, and drug-related killings. Youngsters living in poverty are more likely to become involved in juvenile gangs, more likely to commit economically motivated crimes such as robbery, and more likely to be exposed to the temptations of involvement in the drug trade flourishing in their communities. Thus, with increased poverty is likely to come increases in the number and rate of these kinds of juvenile homicides.

Between 1980 and 1987, the most recent year for which national data are available, the number of American juveniles (i.e., persons under the age of eighteen) living below the poverty level grew from 11 million to 13 million.[49] In 1987, the U.S. government's "official" poverty level was an income of $11,603 for a family of four.[50] The slow but steady increase in the percentage of American youngsters living below the poverty level over the past decade is depicted in Table 10–2.

Resurgence of the Juvenile Population

One final force bound to affect the incidence of juvenile homicide in the coming years is the expected expansion of the American juvenile population between now and the twenty-first century. The recent annual increases in the rate of juvenile homicide noted earlier are a function of two factors, annual increases in the number of juvenile homicides coupled with corresponding annual decreases in the number of juveniles in the American population. To put it another way, in recent years, despite a steady decline in the number of juveniles, the number of juvenile homicides has shown a steady increase.

According to recent estimates and future projections prepared by the U.S. Census Bureau, the United States is beginning to undergo a demographic shift in which the population of juveniles at risk for committing homicide will no longer be decreasing but instead will be increasing. Since the number of homicides committed by juveniles under the age of five is negligible, the relevant juvenile population at risk for committing homicide is that including youngsters between the ages of five and seventeen. The Census Bureau estimates that the number of juveniles aged five to seventeen dropped 3.4 percent between 1980 and 1990, but the Census Bureau projects that this same age group will increase in number by 7 percent between 1990 and the end of the century.[52]

Table 10–2
Percentage of Americans under Age 18 in Families below the Poverty Level 1978–1987[51]

Year	Percentage
1978	15.7
1979	16.0
1980	17.9
1981	19.5
1982	21.3
1983	21.8
1984	21.0
1985	20.1
1986	19.8
1987	20.4

If the Census Bureau projections are correct, and even if the annual rate of juvenile homicide only remains stable instead of continuing to increase as it has since 1984,[53] the final decade of the twentieth century will witness a roughly 7-percent increase in the annual number of juvenile killings. However, given the earlier described confluence of forces now at work in American society and likely to help drive up the rate of juvenile homicide in the foreseeable future—that is, increasing drug abuse, child abuse, access to guns, and childhood poverty—the rate of juvenile homicide is almost certain to continue growing over the next ten years. If that is the case, the number of juvenile homicides will expand much faster than the number of juveniles, and the 1990s will probably witness the highest annual number of juvenile homicides in American history.

Notes

Introduction: The Dynamics of Juvenile Homicide

1. Shulins, "Kids Who Kill—I," Associated Press [hereinafter AP], BC cycle, June 29, 1986.

2. Rawls, "Youth in Capital Murder Trial Hospitalized for Drug Overdose," AP, AM cycle, August 17, 1987.

3. "Parents Forgive Teen-Ager Convicted of Toddler's Death," AP, PM cycle, January 22, 1987.

4. "Georgia Sisters Indicted for Their Mother's Murder," *Jet,* November 1987 at 47; "Golden," United Press International [hereinafter UPI], AM cycle, December 7, 1987.

5. "Conner," UPI, BC cycle, March 20, 1986.

6. "Teen Killer Will Remain in Custody," UPI, PM cycle, July 3, 1987.

7. Quintana, "Teen Gang Member Arrested in Fatal Shooting of Boy in Park," *Los Angeles Times,* June 26, 1987, at 1, col. 1.

8. Jones, "Satanists' Trail; Dead Pets to a Human Sacrifice," *Los Angeles Times,* October 19, 1988, at 1, col. 1; Bryson, "Teenager Convicted in Beating Death of Classmate," AP, AM cycle, May 5, 1988.

9. "Babystab," UPI, AM cycle, February 27, 1986.

10. Shulins, *supra* note 1.

11. "Court Upholds Conviction of Witte in Slaying of Husband," UPI, BC cycle, December 9, 1987.

12. "Teenager Accused of Rape, Murder to Be Tried as Juvenile," UPI, AM cycle, January 7, 1986.

13. Cohen, "Teenage Murderer is One of 35 on Death Row Who Killed as Children," AP, BC cycle, January 18, 1987.

14. "Father Discusses 'Skinhead' Sons," UPI, BC cycle, March 6, 1988.

15. Feron, "Rockland Jury Hears Evidence in Murder Trial," *New York Times,* January 14, 1989, at 28, col. 6.

16. "Prosecutor to Seek Death Penalty," UPI, AM cycle, March 7, 1987.

17. "Second Suspect Caught in Decapitation Slaying," UPI, PM cycle, July 30, 1987.

18. In re K.S.J., 365 S.E. 2d 820, 821 (Ga. 1988).

19. "Teenager Charged with Five Slayings in Athens," UPI, AM cycle, August 17, 1987.

20. "Bat Slaying Trial Nearing a Close," UPI, BC cycle, March 8, 1988; "Matthews Lawyer Seeks Overturn of Life Sentence," *Boston Globe,* January 14, 1989, at 26.

21. "All We Want Is Something to Do," UPI, AM cycle, April 22, 1986

22. "Rivas," UPI, BC cycle, December 27, 1987.

23. Murphy, "Police Capture Youth Accused of Killing Three," AP, PM cycle, December 4, 1987; Langner, "LaPlante Convicted, Gets Life in 3 Killings," *Boston Globe,* October 26, 1988, at 1.

Chapter 1: A Statistical Overview

1. U.S. Department of Commerce, Bureau of the Census, *Estimates of the Population of the United States by Age, Sex and Race: 1980–1986* (1987).

2. U.S. Department of Justice, Federal Bureau of Investigation, *Uniform Crime Reports: Crime in the United States* [hereinafter *FBI Uniform Crime Reports*] (1979–1988).

3. Based upon calculations using data from *FBI Uniform Crime Reports* 1979 through 1988.

4. U.S. Department of Commerce, *supra* note 1.

5. Cornell, "Causes of Juvenile Homicide: A Review of the Literature," in E. P. Benedek & D. G. Cornell (eds.), *Juvenile Homicide* 3, 8–9 (1989).

6. *Id.*

7. *Id.* at 8.

8. *FBI Uniform Crime Reports* (1979–1988).

9. *Id.*

10. *Id.*

11. *See* LaFave & Scott, Criminal Law, 398–403 (1986).

12. *FBI Uniform Crime Reports* (1984–1988).

13. *Id.*

14. *Id.*

15. *Id.*

16. *Id.*

17. *Id. See also* Archer & Lloyd, *Sex and Gender* 102 (1982).

18. *FBI Uniform Crime Reports* (1985–1989).

19. *Id.*

20. *Id.*

21. *Id.*

22. *Id.*

23. *Id.*

24. *Id.*

25. U.S. Department of Commerce, *supra* note 1.

26. *FBI Uniform Crime Reports* (1983–1987).

27. *Id.*

28. *Id.*

29. *Id.*

30. Rowley, Ewing & Singer, "Juvenile Homicide: The Need for an Interdisciplinary Approach," 5 *Behavioral Sciences & The Law* 1 (1987).

31. *Id.*

32. *Id.*

33. *Id.*

34. *Id.*

35. *Id.*

36. Zimring, "Youth Homicide in New York: A Preliminary Analysis," 13 *J. of Legal Studies* 81, 90–91 (1984).

37. Rowley et al., *supra* note 30.

38. *Id.*

39. Zimring, *supra* note 36 at 91–92.

40. *FBI Uniform Crime Reports* (1985–1989).

41. *See*, e.g., Zimring, *supra* note 36 at 91.

42. Rowley et al., *supra* note 30.

43. Zimring, *supra* note 36 at 91.

44. *Id.* at 91–92.

45. New York State Division of Criminal Justice Services, Office of Justice Systems Analysis, *New York State Homicide* 1987 (1988).

46. *FBI Uniform Crime Reports* (1985–1989).

47. Zimring, *supra* note 36 at 92.

48. *Id.*

Chapter 2: Review of the Research

1. *See*, generally, Benedek & Cornell, "Clinical Presentations of Homicidal Adolescents," in E. P. Benedek & D. G. Cornell (Eds.), *Juvenile Homicide* 39–57 (1989).

2. King, "The Ego and the Integration of Violence in Homicidal Youth," 45 *Am. J. Orthopsychiatry* 134, 135 (1975).

3. Data listed in this table are derived from studies that specified actual diagnoses or at least categories of diagnosis, including psychosis.

4. Bender, "Children and Adolescents Who Have Killed," 116 *Am. J. Psychiatry* 510 (1959).

5. Stearns, "Murder by Adolescents with Obscure Motivation," 114 *Am. J. Psychiatry* 303–305 (1957).

6. Marten, "Adolescent Murderers," 58 *Southern Medical J.* 1217, 1217–1218 (1965).

7. Smith, "The Adolescent Murderer: A Psychodynamic Interpretation," 13 *Archives of General Psychiatry* 310, 316 (1965).

8. Hellsten & Katila, "Murder and Other Homicide by Children Under 15 in Finland," 39 *Psychiatric Quarterly* 54, 73 (1965).

9. Scherl & Mack, "A Study of Adolescent Matricide," 5 *J. Am. Academy of Child Psychiatry* 559 (1966).

10. Malmquist, "Premonitory Signs of Homicidal Juvenile Aggression," 128 *Am. J. Psychiatry* 461, 462 (1971).

11. Walsh-Brennan, "Psychopathology of Homicidal Children," 94 *Royal Society of Health* 274, 276 (1974).

12. Sendi & Blomgren, "A Comparative Study of Predictive Criteria in the Predisposition of Homicidal Adolescents," 132 *Am. J. Psychiatry* 423, 425 (1975).

13. King, *supra* note 2 at 135.

14. Tanay, "Reactive Parricide," 21 *J. Forensic Sciences* 76 (1976).

15. Sorrells, "Kids Who Kill," 23 *Crime & Delinquency* 312, 316 (1977).

16. Rosner, Wiederlight, Rosner & Wieczorek, "Adolescents Accused of Murder and Manslaughter: A Five-Year Descriptive Study," 4 *Bull. Am. Academy of Psychiatry & Law* 342, 345–346 (1978).

17. Russell, "Ingredients of Juvenile Murder," 23 *Int'l. J. of Offender Therapy & Comparative Criminology,* 65 (1979).

18. Petti & Davidman, "Homicidal School-Age Children: Cognitive Style and Demographic Features," 12 *Child Psychiatry & Human Development* 82, 85 (1981).

19. Russell, "Girls Who Kill," 30 *Int'l. J. of Offender Therapy & Comparative Criminology* 171, 173, 175 (1986).

20. Cornell, Benedek & Benedek, "Characteristics of Adolescents Charged with Homicide: Review of 72 Cases," 5 *Behavioral Sciences & the Law* 11, 18–19 (1987).

21. Cornell, "Causes of Juvenile Homicide," in E. P. Benedek & D. G. Cornell (Eds.), *Juvenile Homicide* 3, 15–16 (1989).

22. *Id.*

23. Schacter, "Amnesia and Crime: How Much Do We Really Know?" 41 *Am. Psychologist* 286 (1986); R. Rogers, *Conducting Insanity Evaluations* (1986).

24. *Id.*

25. McCarthy, "Narcissism and the Self in Homicidal Adolescents," 38 *Am. J. Psychoanalysis* 19 (1978); Lewis, Moy, Jackson, Aaronson, Restifo, Serra & Simos, "Biopsychosocial Characteristics of Children Who Later Murder: A Prospective Study," 142 *Am. J. Psychiatry* 1161, 1164 (1985).

26. Lewis, Pincus, Bard, Richardson, Prichep, Feldman & Yeager, "Neuropsychiatric, Psychoeducational, and Family Characteristics of 14 Juveniles Condemned to Death in the United States," 145 *Am. J. Psychiatry* 584, 587 (1988).

27. American Psychiatric Association, *Diagnostic and Statistical Manual of Mental Disorders,* Third Edition, Revised (1987).

28. Smith, "The Adolescent Murderer: A Psychodynamic Interpretation," 13 *Archives of General Psychiatry* 310, 311 (1965).

29. Rosner et al., *supra* note 16 at 345.

30. Russell, *supra* note 17.

31. Sorrells, *supra* note 15.

32. Sendi & Blomgren, *supra* note 12.

33. American Psychiatric Association, *supra* note 27.

34. Sorrells, *supra* note 15.

35. Fiddes, "A Survey of Adolescent Murder in Scotland," 4 *J. Adolescence* 47, 58 (1981).

36. *Id.* at 52.

37. Walsh-Brennan, *supra* note 11 at 276.

38. Brandstadter-Palmer, "Children Who Kill," paper presented at Annual Convention of the American Psychological Association (Toronto, August 1984).

39. Bender, *supra* note 4.

40. Corder, Ball, Haizlip, Rollins & Beaumont, "Adolescent Parricide: A Comparison with Other Adolescent Murder," 133 *Am. J. Psychiatry* 957 (1976).

41. Cornell et al., *supra* note 20.

42. Hays, Solway & Schreiner, "Intellectual Characteristics of Juvenile Murderers Versus Status Offenders," 43 *Psychological Reports* 80 (1978).

43. Petti & Davidman, *supra* note 18 at 85.

44. Solway, Richardson, Hays & Elion, "Adolescent Murderers: Literature Review and Preliminary Findings," in J. Hays, T. Roberts & K. Solway (Eds.), *Violence and the Violent Individual* 193 (1981).

45. Lewis et al., *supra* note 26.

46. Bender, *supra* note 4.

47. Patterson, "Psychiatric Study of Juveniles Involved in Homicide," 13 *Am. J. Orthopsychiatry* 125 (1943).

48. King, *supra* note 2.

49. Brandstadter-Palmer, *supra* note 38.

50. *See,* e.g., Scherl & Mack, *supra* note 9; Stearns, *supra* note 5; Hellsten & Katila, *supra* note 8; Sendi & Blomgren, *supra* note 12; Bernstein, "Premeditated Murder by an Eight-Year-Old Boy," 22 *Int'l. J. Offender Therapy & Comparative Criminology* 47 (1978).

51. *See,* e.g., King, *supra* note 2.

52. Lewis et al., *supra* note 26.

53. Patterson, *supra* note 47.

54. Bender, *supra* note 4.

55. Sendi & Blomgren, *supra* note 12.

56. King, *supra* note 2 at 136.

57. Brandstadter-Palmer, *supra* note 38.

58. Bender, *supra* note 4.

59. Woods, "Adolescent Violence and Homicide: Ego Disruption and the 6 and 14 Dysrhythmia," 5 *Archives of General Psychiatry* 528 (1961).

60. Kido, "An EEG Study of Delinquent Adolescents with Reference to Recidivism and Murder," 27 *Folia Psychiatrica et Neurologica Japonica* 77 (1973).

61. Lewis et al., *supra* note 25 at 1165.

62. Lewis et al., *supra* note 26.

63. *Id.* at 585.

64. *See,* e.g., Hellsten & Katila, *supra* note 8 at 60; Russell, *supra* note 19 at 172.

65. Petti & Davidman, *supra* note 18 at 85.

66. Walsh-Brennan, *supra* note 11 at 276.

67. Sendi & Blomgren, *supra* note 12 at 424.

68. Restifo & Lewis, "Three Case Reports of a Single Homicidal Adolescent," [letter] 142 *Am. J. Psychiatry* 388 (1985).

69. Thom, "Juvenile Delinquency and Criminal Homicide," 40 *J. Maine Medical Ass'n.* 176 (1949).

70. Stearns, *supra* note 5; Podolsky, "Children Who Kill," 31 *General Practitioner* 98 (1965).

71. Patterson, *supra* note 47.

72. Petti & Davidman, *supra* note 18.

73. Rosner et al., *supra* note 16.

74. McCarthy, *supra* note 25.

75. Sorrells, *supra* note 15 at 317.

76. Brandstadter-Palmer, *supra* note 38.

77. *See,* e.g., Bernstein, *supra* note 50; Woods, *supra* note 59; Easson & Steinhilber, "Murderous Aggression by Children and Adolescents," 4 *Archives of General Psychiatry* 27 (1961); Hellsten & Katila, *supra* note 8; Russell, *supra* note 19; Smith, *supra* note 7; Scherl & Mack, *supra* note 9; Tooley, "The Small Assassins," 14 *J. Am. Academy of Child Psychiatry* 306 (1975); Stearns, *supra* note 5.

78. King, *supra* note 2.

79. Fiddes, *supra* note 35.

80. Lewis et al., *supra* note 26.

81. Petti & Davidman, *supra* note 18 at 85.

82. Corder et al., *supra* note 40.

83. Sorrells, *supra* note 15 at 317.

84. Lewis, Shanok, Grant & Ritvo, "Homicidally Aggressive Young Children: Neuropsychiatric and Experiential Correlates," 140 *Am. J. Psychiatry* 148 (1983).

85. *See,* e.g., Hellsten & Katila, *supra* note 8; Podolsky, *supra* note 70; Russell, *supra* note 19.

86. Lewis et al., *supra* note 84 at 151.

87. King, *supra* note 2 at 135.

88. *See,* e.g., Bernstein, *supra* note 50; Woods, *supra* note 59; Lewis et al., *supra* note 84.

89. Corder et al., *supra* note 40.

90. *See,* e.g., Patterson, *supra* note 47; Malmquist, *supra* note 10; Duncan & Duncan, "Murder in the Family: A Study of Some Homicidal Adolescents," 127 *Am. J. Psychiatry* 1498 (1971); Tanay, *supra* note 14.

91. *See,* e.g., Malmquist, *supra* note 10; Sargent, "Children Who Kill—A Family Conspiracy?" 7 *Social Work* 35 (1962).

92. Lewis et al., *supra* note 26 at 587.

93. Lewis et al., *supra* note 84.

94. Sendi & Blomgren, *supra* note 12 at 425.

95. King, *supra* note 2 at 135.

96. Corder et al., *supra* note 40.

97. *See,* e.g., Scherl & Mack, *supra* note 9; Duncan & Duncan, *supra* note 90; Tanay, *supra* note 14; Malmquist, *supra* note 10.

98. Lewis et al., *supra* note 26.

99. Sendi & Blomgren, *supra* note 12 at 425.

100. Corder et al., *supra* note 40 at 959.

101. Fiddes, *supra* note 35.

102. Rosner et al., *supra* note 16.

103. Sorrells, *supra* note 15.

104. Cornell et al., *supra* note 20.

105. *Id.*

106. Rowley, "Comparing Kids Who Kill with Other Violent Offenders: An Institutional Sample," unpublished manuscript, State University of New York at Buffalo, 1987.

107. Brandstadter-Palmer, *supra* note 38.

108. McCarthy, *supra* note 25.

109. Malmquist, *supra* note 10.

110. Walsh-Brennan, *supra* note 11.

111. Patterson, *supra* note 47.

112. Zenoff & Zients, "Juvenile Murderers: Should the Punishment Fit the Crime?" 2 *Int'l. J. Law & Psychiatry* 533 (1979).

113. Corder et al., *supra* note 40.

114. Malmquist, *supra* note 10.

115. *Id.* at 463.

116. Corder et al., *supra* note 40.

117. Sorrells, *supra* note fifteen at 316.

118. Cornell et al., *supra* note 20.

119. *Id.* at 15.

120. *Id.*

121. Brandstadter-Palmer, *supra* note 38.

122. Smith, *supra* note 7.

123. Cornell et al., *supra* note 41.

124. *Id.* at 14.

125. Rowley, *supra* note 106.

126. *See,* e.g., Scherl & Mack, *supra* note 9; Tanay, *supra* note 14; Sadoff, "Clinical Observations on Parricide," 45 *Psychiatric Quarterly* 65 (1971); Russell, "Juvenile Murderers," 9 *Int'l. J. Offender Therapy & Comparative Criminology* 55 (1965).

127. American Psychiatric Association, *supra* note 27.

128. *See* Justice, Justice & Kraft, "Early Warning Signs of Violence: Is a Triad Enough?" 131 *Am. J. Psychiatry* 457 (1974).

129. Michaels, "Enuresis in Murderous Aggressive Children and Adolescents," 5 *Archives of General Psychiatry* 94 (1961).

130. *Id.* at 491.

131. Easson & Steinhilber, *supra* note 77.

132. Tooley, *supra* note 77.

133. Bernstein, *supra* note 50.

134. Russell, *supra* note 19.

135. Lewis et al., *supra* note 84.

136. Sendi & Blomgren, *supra* note 12.

137. Marten, *supra* note 6 at 1217–1218.

138. Zenoff & Zients, *supra* note 112 at 544.

139. Rowley, *supra* note 106.

140. *Id.*

141. Corder et al., *supra* note 40.

142. *Id. See also* Cornell et al., *supra* note 20.

143. *Id.*

144. Sendi & Blomgren, *supra* note 12.

145. Cormier & Markus, "A Longitudinal Study of Adolescent Murderers, 8 *Bull. Am. Academy of Psychiatry & Law* 240 (1980).

146. Russell, *supra* note 17.

147. Solway et al., *supra* note 44.

148. Fiddes, *supra* note 35.

149. Patterson, *supra* note 47.

150. Hellsten & Katila, *supra* note 8.

151. Duncan & Duncan, *supra* note 90.

152. Scherl & Mack, *supra* note 9.

153. Tanay, *supra* note 14.

154. *See,* e.g., Sadoff, *supra* note 126; Russell, *supra* note 17.

155. Cornell et al., *supra* note 20.

156. Solway et al., *supra* note 44.

157. Sendi & Blomgren, *supra* note 12.

158. Malmquist, *supra* note 10.

159. Cornell et al., *supra* note 20 at 17–18.

160. Solway et al., *supra* note 44.

161. Stearns, *supra* note 5.

162. Sorrells, *supra* note 15.

163. Patterson, *supra* note 47 at 126.

164. Duncan & Duncan, *supra* note 90 at 1500.

165. Sadoff, *supra* note 126.

166. Cornell et al., *supra* note 20 at 20–21.

167. Patterson, *supra* note 47.

168. Malmquist, *supra* note 10 at 464.

169. Hellsten & Katila, *supra* note 8 at 64.

170. Woods, *supra* note 59 at 529.

171. *Id.* at 530.

172. Patterson, *supra* note 47.

173. Schmideberg, "Juvenile Murderers," 17 *Int'l. J. Offender Therapy & Comparative Criminology* 240 (1973).

174. Cornell et al., *supra* note 20 at 21.

175. *See* Rowley, Ewing & Singer, "Juvenile Homicide: The Need for an Interdisciplinary Approach," 5 *Behavioral Sciences & the Law* 3 (1987).

176. *Id.*

Chapter 3: Intrafamilial Homicides

1. Tanay, "Adolescents Who Kill Parents—Reactive Parricide," 7 *Australian & New Zealand J. Psychiatry* 263, 273 (1973).

2. *See* Rowley, Ewing & Singer, "Juvenile Homicide: The Need for an Interdisciplinary Approach," 5 *Behavioral Sciences & the Law* 3 (1987).

3. *See FBI Uniform Crime Reports* (1984–1988).

4. Timmick, "Fatal Means for Children to End Abuse; Parricide Cases Evoke Conflict in Sympathy, Need for Punishment," *Los Angeles Times*, August 31, 1986, part 2 at 1, col. 1.

5. *FBI Uniform Crime Reports* (1983–1988).

6. Sadoff, "Clinical Observations on Parricide," 45 *Psychiatric Quarterly* 65 (1971).

7. *Id.* at 68.

8. Tanay, "Reactive Parricide," 21 *J. Forensic Sciences* 76 (1976).

9. *Id.* at 76.

10. Tanay, *supra* note 1.

11. *Id.*

12. Mones, "The Relationship between Child Abuse and Parricide: An Overview," in E. Newberger & R. Bourne (Eds.), *Unhappy Families* 31, 36 (1985).

13. *Id.* at 37.

14. *Id.*

15. Morris, *The Kids Next Door* 293 (1985).

16. Tanay, *supra* note 1 at 272.

17. Lessinger, "A Case of Justifiable Patricide?" *The Guardian,* May 25, 1983, at 17.

18. *Id.*

19. "Jahnke Conviction Upheld," *Denver Post,* December 13, 1984, at 1A and 28A.

20. Myers, "Deborah Jahnke Is Set Free," *Denver Post,* December 18, 1984, at 1A; Morris, *supra* note 15 at 148.

21. Holzberg, "A Tale of Suburbia: Bowling, Little League and Sex Abuse," *National Law Journal,* October 5, 1987, at 6; Kleiman, "Girl Says Hiring Father's Killer Seemed 'Like a Game' at First," *New York Times,* September 15, 1987, at B1–B2.

22. *Id.* at B1. *See also* "Youth Sentenced in Killing Classmate's Abusive Father," UPI, PM cycle, April 29, 1987.

23. *Id.*

24. "The Nation," *Los Angeles Times,* January 20, 1988, part 1 at 2, col. 5.

25. Kleiman, *supra* note 21; Holzberg, *supra* note 21.

26. *Id.*

27. Timmick, *supra* note 4.

28. *Id.*

29. *Id.* Galante, "Judge Mulls Proper Sentence for Killer of "Scum"; Public is Asked to Provide Suggestions," *National Law Journal,* February 13, 1984, at 9.

30. Mones, *supra* note 12 at 36.

31. Morris, *supra* note 15.

32. Hellsten & Katila, "Murder and Other Homicide by Children Under 15 in Finland," 39 *Psychiatric Quarterly* 54, 73 (1965).

33. Russell, "Juvenile Murderers," 9 *Int'l.J. Offender Therapy & Comparative Criminology* 50, 51 (1965).

34. *Id.*

35. Patterson, "Psychiatric Study of Juveniles Involved in Homicide," 13 *Am. J. Orthopsychiatry* 125, 126 (1943).

36. Benedek & Cornell, "Clinical Presentations of Homicidal Adolescents," in E. P. Benedek & D. G. Cornell (Eds.), *Juvenile Homicide* 52–53 (1989).

37. Ball, "Boy Three Kills Father Who Beat Mother," *Daily Telegraph,* October 6, 1988, at 3.

38. Rowley et al., *supra* note 2.

39. Sargent, "Children Who Kill—A Family Conspiracy?" 7 *Social Work* 35 (1962).

40. Russell, "Ingredients of Juvenile Murder," 23 *Int'l. J. of Offender Therapy & Comparative Criminology* 65 (1979).

41. Malmquist, "Premonitory Signs of Homicidal Juvenile Aggression," 128 *Am. J. Psychiatry* 461, 464 (1971).

42. *Id.*

43. Hellsten & Katila, *supra* note 32 at 73.

44. *Id.* at 62.

45. *Id.* at 64.

46. *Id.*

47. *Id.*

48. *Id.* at 65–66.

49. "Court Upholds Conviction of Witte in Slaying of Husband," UPI, BC cycle, December 9, 1987.

50. Testimony of Dr. Charles Patrick Ewing, *People v. Barnwell, Brown, and Small* (suppression hearing), September 4, 1986.

51. "Rainey, Police Say Boy 15 Just Snapped, Killed Stepfather," *Los Angeles Times,* July 19, 1988, part 2 at 3, col. 4.

52. *See* Morris, *supra* note 15 at 117–119 (1985).

53. Duncan & Duncan, "Murder in the Family: A Study of Some Homicidal Adolescents," 127 *Am. J. Psychiatry* 1498, 1500 (1971).

54. Basey & Thompson, "Honor Student Charged with Slaying Mother: Police Believe Argument Led to Fatal Beating," *Buffalo News,* June 26, 1988, at A1, A14.

55. Anzalone, "'Legend' Label for Teen Killer Outrages Neighbors," *Buffalo News,* June 26, 1989, at A1, A4; Andriatch. "Psychologist: Teen Showed Grief," *Niagara Gazette,* June 7, 1989, at 1A; Kurilovitch & Burch, "Shrubsall Pleads Guilty," *Niagara Gazette,* June 7, 1989, at 1A, 2A.

56. *See* Basey & Thompson, *supra* note 54; Anzalone, *supra* note 55; Andriatch, *supra* note 55; Kurilovitch & Burch, *supra* note 55.

57. Ferron, "Rockland Jury Hears Evidence in Murder Trial," *New York Times,* January 14, 1989, at 28, col. 6.

58. *See* Walsh, "Attorney Says Teen Accused in Mother's Slaying was Mentally, Sexually Abused by Her," *Rockland Journal-News,* June 15, 1988, at A1, A8.

59. Wertham, *Dark Legend: A Study in Murder* (1941).

60. Scherl & Mack, "A Study of Adolescent Matricide," 5 *J. Am. Academy of Child Psychiatry* 569 (1966).

61. *Id.* at 572.

62. *Id.* at 576.

63. *Id.* at 587.

64. "More Teens Attacking Parents," UPI, BC cycle, September 11, 1986.

65. "All We Want is Something to Do," UPI, AM cycle, April 22, 1986.

66. *Id.*

67. Benedek & Cornell, *supra* note 36.

68. Hamill, "A Crime That Defies Understanding," *Newsday,* February 1, 1989, at 18.

69. *Id.*

70. "Teenagers Arraigned in Mother's Killing," UPI, AM cycle, October 12, 1987.

71. "Georgia Sisters Indicted for Their Mother's Murder," *Jet*, November 1987, at 47.

72. Hellsten & Katila, *supra* note 32 at 66.

73. *See* notes 21–26 *supra* and accompanying text.

74. Hamill, *supra* note 68.

75. Yost, "Teen Begged Boyfriend to Kill Her Mother," UPI, AM cycle, November 13, 1987.

76. *Id.*

77. Harris, *Momslay,* UPI, AM cycle, December 19, 1985.

78. *Id.*

79. Klunder, "Youth Who Killed His Mother is Sent to CYA," *Los Angeles Times*, December 20, 1986, part 2 at 6, col. 1.

80. "Boy Kills Stepbrother, Wounds Parents," UPI, AM cycle, July 10, 1986.

81. "Warrant Issued for Son in Slayings," UPI, PM cycle, March 23, 1988.

82. *Id.*

83. "Brom," UPI, BC cycle, May 31, 1988.

84. "Teen Held in Killings," *Newsday*, March 23, 1989, at 16; "Teen Charged in Killings of Parents, Brother," *Buffalo News*, March 23, 1989, at A9; Foderaro, "Parents and a Brother Slain by Self-Styled 'Rambo'," 16, *New York Times*, March 23, 1989, at 16; "200 Mourn Three 'Rambo' Shooting Victims," *Buffalo News*, March 26, 1989, at A15.

85. "Teen Girl Sentenced to Life in Parents' Murder," UPI, PM cycle, January 30, 1987.

86. "Teenager Will Be Tried as Adult for Parents' Deaths," UPI, AM cycle, September 12, 1986.

87. Warner, "Jury Agonized Over Justice's State of Mind," *Buffalo News*, November 16, 1986, at 1, A11.

88. Knudson, "Expert Testifies Youth Killed Parents Because of 'Adopted Child Syndrome,'" *New York Times*, February 18, 1986, at B2, col. 1. *See also* "Boy 15 Convicted of Murder in Deaths of Adoptive Parents," *New York Times*, February 20, 1986, at B5, col. 4.

89. Ravo, "Small Town Has Sequel to Its 'Trial of the Century,'" *New York Times*, December 7, 1988, at B5, col. 1; "Youth is Imprisoned for Shooting Spree that Left Four Dead," *New York Times*, November 10, 1987, at B4, col. 6; Rimer, "Town is Stunned by Acquittal of Teenager in Killings of 4," *New York Times*, October 13, 1987, at B1, col. 2; "Right to Attorney Cited in Verdict," *New York Times*, October 8, 1987, at B5, col. 1; Rimer, "Slayings of Four Tied to a Game Using Fantasies," *New York Times*, December 20, 1986, at 30, col. 6.

90. "Psychologist Says Gates is not Faking Mental Illness," UPI, AM cycle, September 17, 1987.

91. "Tripleslay," UPI, AM cycle, August 25, 1987; "Wingfield," UPI, BC cycle, October 22, 1987.

92. Tooley, "The Small Assassins," 14 *J. Am. Academy of Child Psychiatry* 306 (1975).

93. *Id.* at 312.

94. Bender, "Children and Adolescents Who Have Killed," 116 *Am. J. Psychiatry* 510, 511 (1959).

95. "Eight-Year-Old Charged with Murder," *Newsday,* September 13, 1988, at 7; "Boy Eight Faces Murder Count in Fire," *Buffalo News,* September 14, 1988, at A14.

96. Shulins, "Kids Who Kill," AP, BC cycle, January 29, 1986.

97. Petti & Wells, "Crisis Treatment of a Pre-Adolescent Who Accidentally Killed His Twin," paper presented at Annual Meeting of the American Academy of Child Psychiatry (San Diego, 1978).

98. "Exorcise," UPI, BC cycle, April 29, 1987.

99. O'Connor, "Brother in Slaying Faces Test," *Chicago Tribune,* January 26, 1989 at, 6C; "Sixteen-Year-Old Charged in Brother's Death," *Chicago Tribune,* February 9, 1989, at 3.

100. "Judge Takes Defense Motion Under Advisement," UPI, BC cycle, January 30, 1988.

101. *Id.*

102. Caruso, "Troubled Teenager 'Confided Foster Tot Poisoning,'" *Boston Herald,* May 2, 1989, at 1, 18; Kindleberger, "Report of Confession Spurs Foster Deaths Probe," *Boston Globe,* May 3, 1989, at 32.

103. Leong, "Clinicolegal Issues for the Forensic Examiner," in E. P. Benedek & D. G. Cornell (Eds.), *Juvenile Homicide* 115, 123 (1989).

104. *Id.* at 125.

105. "Ohio News Briefs," UPI, PM cycle, September 30, 1987; "West Virginia News in Brief," UPI, AM cycle, January 25, 1988.

106. Patterson, *supra* note 35.

107. *Id.* at 126.

108. Woods, *Adolescent Violence and Homicide: Ego Disruption and the 6 and 14 Dysrhythmia,"* 5 *Archives of General Psychiatry* 528, 530 (1961).

109. *Id.*

110. *Id.* at 530–531.

111. Schmideberg, "Juvenile Murderers," 17 *Int'l. J. of Offender Therapy & Comparative Criminology* 240 (1973).

112. *Id.*

113. *Id.*

Chapter 4: Homicides Committed in the Course of Other Crimes

1. *See,* e.g., Cornell, Benedek & Benedek, "Characteristics of Adolescents Charged with Homicide: Review of 72 Cases," 5 *Behavioral Sciences & the Law* 11, 18–19 (1987).

2. *FBI Uniform Crime Reports* (1984–1988).

3. *Id.*

4. *Id.*

5. Cormier & Markus, "A Longitudinal Study of Adolescent Murderers," 8 *Bull. Am. Academy of Psychiatry & Law* 240 (1980).

6. Rowley, Ewing & Singer, "Juvenile Homicide: The Need for an Interdisciplinary Approach," 5 *Behavioral Sciences & the Law* 3 (1987).

7. *Id.*

8. *FBI Uniform Crime Reports* (1988).

9. *Id.*

10. *Id.*

11. *Id.*

12. *Id.*

13. *See FBI Uniform Crime Reports* (1984–1987).

14. Schacter, "Fourteen-Year-Old Pleads Guilty to Killing Elderly Neighbor," *Los Angeles Times*, June 25, 1986, Part 2 at 2, col. 5; Schacter, "Potential for Violence Cited: Stiffest Term Possible for Fourteen-Year-Old Killer," *Los Angeles Times*, August 5, 1986, part 2 at 2, col. 1.

15. Benedek & Cornell, "Clinical Presentations of Homicidal Adolescents," in E. P. Benedek & D. G. Cornell (Eds.), *Juvenile Homicide* 50 (1989).

16. Hellsten & Katila, "Murder and Other Homicide by Children under 15 in Finland," 39 *Psychiatric Quarterly* 54 (1965).

17. In the Matter of Anthony M, 63 N.Y. 270, 471 N.E.2d 447, 481 N.Y.S.2d 675 (1984).

18. *Id.*

19. *Id.*

20. *Magill v. Dugger,* 824 F.2d 879 (11th Cir. 1987).

21. Evans, "Court is Told Slain Editor was Sexually Assaulted," *New York Times*, July 16, 1980, at B2, col. 2; Putnam, "Youths Sentenced to Life in Death of Editor," AP, PM cycle, June 19, 1981.

22. *See,* e.g., Malmquist, "Premonitory Signs of Homicidal Juvenile Aggression," 128 *Am. J. Psychiatry* 461 (1971); Sorrells, "Kids Who Kill," 23 *Crime & Delinquency* 312 (1977); Cornell et al., *supra* note 1; Cornell, Benedek & Benedek, "A Typology of Juvenile Homicide Offenders," in E. P. Benedek & D. G. Cornell (Eds.), *Juvenile Homicide* 59 (1989).

23. Malmquist, *supra* note 22 at 463.

24. Sorrells, *supra* note 22 at 315.

25. Cornell et al., *supra* note 1.

26. *Id.*

27. "Convicted Teen to Be Sentenced in Two Weeks in Bugler Slaying," UPI, AM cycle, February 6, 1987.

28. Rosenbaum, "Too Young to Die?", *New York Times Magazine*, March 12, 1989, at 33–35, 58–61.

29. *Id.*

30. *Wilkins v. Missouri,* 57 U.S. Law Week 4973, 4984 (1989).

31. *See,* e.g., Esposito, "Teen Killed Mom over $200 to Pay Crack Bill," *Newsday*, January 7, 1989, at 5.

32. "Teenagers in Front Lines of Dallas Drug Wars," UPI, BC cycle, March 27, 1988.

33. *Id.*

34. *Id.*

35. *Id.*

36. "Second Suspect Caught in Decapitation Slaying," UPI, PM cycle, July 30, 1987.

37. *Id.*

38. Wilkinson, "Small Town in Disbelief over Elderly Man's Slaying for Jar of Pennies," AP, AM cycle, January 20, 1988.

39. *Id.*

40. "Youths Charged in Slaying of Elderly N.H. Woman," UPI, BC cycle, February 10, 1988; Testimony of Dr. Charles Patrick Ewing at sentencing hearing, State v. Demeritt (New Hampshire, April 14, 1989).

41. *Id.*

42. *See,* e.g., "Youth Gets Maximum Sentence for Slaying over Leather Coat," AP, AM cycle, January 16, 1987; "Youth Guilty of Murder in Newark Jacket Case," *New York Times,* March 12, 1987 at B2, col. 1; "Two Get 50-Year Terms in Murders of Priests in Buffalo Rectories," *New York Times,* November 3, 1988 at B6, col. 5; "Teenagers Held in Deaths of Two Priests in Buffalo," *Los Angeles Times,* March 9, 1987, part 1 at 2, col. 5; "Youths Charged in Killings Had Similar Backgrounds," AP, PM cycle, March 11, 1987; "Two Seized in Killing of Youth for Radio," *New York Times,* July 14, 1982 at B2, col. 6; "Juveniles," UPI, AM cycle, November 2, 1987.

43. Ressler, Burgess & Douglas, *Sexual Homicide* (1987).

44. *Id.* at xiii.

45. *Id. at 1.*

46. *Id.*

47. Stearns, "Murder by Adolescents with Obscure Motivation," 114 *Am. J. Psychiatry* 303 (1957).

48. *Id.* at 304.

49. *Id.*

50. *Id.* at 305.

51. Esposito, *supra* note 31.

52. *FBI Uniform Crime Reports* (1988).

53. *Id.*

54. Woods, "Adolescent Violence and Homicide: Ego Disruption and the 6 and 14 Dysrhythmia," 5 *Archives of General Psychiatry* 528, 529 (1961).

55. *Id.*

56. Patterson, "Psychiatric Study of Juveniles Involved in Homicide," 13 *Am. J. Orthopsychiatry* 125 (1943).

57. *Id.* at 129.

58. Ressler, Burgess & Douglas, "Rape and Rape-Murder: One Offender and Twelve Victims," 140 *Am. J. Psychiatry* 36 (1983).

59. "Teenager Accused of Rape, Murder to Be Tried as Juvenile," UPI, AM cycle, January 7, 1986; Reilly, "Juvenile Charged with Murder Must Stand Trial as Adult," UPI, BC cycle, July 8, 1986.

60. "Teenager Accused of Rape, Murder to Be Tried as Juvenile," *supra* note 59.

61. *Pinkerton v. State,* 660 S.W.2d 58 (Tex. Crim. App. 1983).

62. *Id.* at 62.

63. *Id.* at 60.

64. *See,* generally, Benedek & Cornell, *supra* note 15 at 48–49.

65. *Id.*

66. *Id.*

67. *Id.*

68. Woods, *supra* note 54 at 530.

69. "Youth Charged with Murder," UPI, BC cycle, February 26, 1987.

70. "Thirteen-Year-Old Found Guilty in Infant's Death," UPI, PM cycle, October 29, 1986.

71. Cassidy & Burks, "Teen-Age Boy is Charged in Death of 5-Year-Old," *Albuquerque Journal,* January 6, 1987; Burks, "Teenager to Remain in Custody," *Albuquerque Journal,* January 7, 1987.

72. Ressler, Burgess & Douglas, *supra* note 58.

73. Kramer, *At a Tender Age* 11–20 (1988).

74. *Id.* at 16.

75. Clarke, "Hamlin," UPI, AM cycle, May 11, 1982; Clarke, "Hamlin," UPI, AM cycle, May 12, 1982; Clarke, "Rape Victim Relives Crime," UPI, PM cycle, May 12, 1982; Clarke, "Hamlin," UPI, AM cycle, May 13, 1982; "Memories of a Murder Lingering in Vermont, *New York Times,* July 19, 1982 at A11, col. 4.

76. Clarke, "Hamlin," UPI AM cycle, May 12, 1982.

77. *Id.*

78. Clarke, "Hamlin," UPI, AM cycle, May 11, 1982.

79. "Police Arrest Teenagers in Killing on Expressway," AP, PM cycle, September 4, 1986.

80. "Roscetti," UPI, BC cycle, February 11, 1987.

81. "Prosecutor to Seek Death Penalty," UPI AM cycle, March 7, 1987.

82. "Beating," UPI, BC cycle, May 30, 1987.

83. *Magill v. Dugger,* 824 F.2d 879 (11th Cir. 1987).

84. *Id.* at 880.

85. Evans, *supra* note 21; Putnam, *supra* note 21.

86. Evans, *supra* note 21.

87. *Buchanan v. Kentucky,* 107 S.Ct. 2906 (1987).

88. *Id.* at 2910–2911, fn. 9.

Chapter 5: Senseless Homicides

1. Puig, "Fourteen-Year-Old is Sentenced to CYA Term in Sniper Shooting," *Los Angeles Times,* September 9, 1987, part 2 at 6, col. 4.

2. *Id.*

3. Kaplan, "Fourteen-Year-Old Snipers Convicted of Murder," *Los Angeles Times,* July 9, 1987, part 2 at 8, col. 2.

4. "Parents Forgive Teenager Convicted of Toddler's Death," AP, PM cycle, January 22, 1987.

5. "Bat Slaying Trial Nearing a Close," UPI, BC cycle, March 8, 1988; Murphy, "Thrill Killer, 15, Sentenced to Life Prison Term," *Buffalo News,* March 11, 1988, at 8; "Medicine Made Teenager Kill, His Lawyer Says," *Buffalo News,* March 9, 1988, at 9.

6. *Id.*

7. Burks, "Witness Says Friend Shot during Karate," *Albuquerque Journal*; Sanchez & Burks, "Teen Held on Charge of Murder," *Albuquerque Journal.*

8. *People v. Roe,* 1989 N.Y. Lexis 666 (Court of Appeals of New York, June 6, 1989).

9. *Id.*

10. *Id.*

11. "Karate," UPI, AM cycle, December 16, 1987; Fuentes, "Boy Gets 18 Years in Fatal Park Beating of Transient," *Los Angeles Times,* December 24, 1987, part 2 at 9, col. 3.

12. Bater, "Police Arrest Teens in Vagrant Beating Death," UPI, AM cycle, May 28, 1986.

13. "Youths Arrested in Fatal Stabbing of Homeless Man," UPI, AM cycle, October 6, 1986.

14. "Two Albany Teenagers Charged in Slaying of Gay Man," UPI, AM cycle, September 11, 1987.

15. *Id.*

16. *See* Lin & Hurtado, "Admission in Howard Beach Case; In Appeal, Lawyers Concede a Racial Motive in Attack," *Newsday,* April 11, 1989, at 7.

17. Goldman, "Youth Apologizes, Gets Shortest Term in Racial Death," *Los Angeles Times*, February 12, 1988, part 1 at 4, col. 1.

18. McDonnell, "Two Reputedly Hunted Targets for Slaying," *Los Angeles Times,* March 31, 1989, part 2 at 3, col. 4; McDonnell, "Youth to Be Tried as Adult in Killings of Two Migrant Workers," *Los Angeles Times,* April 28, 1989, part 2 at 1, col. 2.

19. *Id.*

20. McDonnell, "Companion Called Triggerman; One Accused of Killing Migrants Denies Guilt, *Los Angeles Times,* March 28, 1989, part 2 at 1, col. 5.

21. James, "Youths Convicted of Assault in Death of an Indian Man," *New York Times,* April 1, 1989, at 30, cols. 1–2; Walt, "A New Racism Gets Violent in New Jersey," *Newsday,* April 6, 1988, part 2 at 4.

22. *Id.*

23. "Conner," UPI, BC cycle, March 20, 1986.

24. "Photographer Found Dead," *Los Angeles Times,* October 13, 1987, part 2 at 2, col. 1.

25. "Goode," UPI, AM cycle, September 10, 1987.

26. "Rivas," UPI, BC cycle, December 27, 1987.

27. McCall, "The Fateful Odyssey of Three Teenage Runaways May Take Them to Florida's Death Row for Murder," *People,* January 10, 1983, at 67; "Three Arraigned in New York in Ritualistic Florida Slaying," *New York Times,* September 9, 1982, at B8.

28. Crawford and Sjostrom, "Elmhurst Teen Charged in Stabbings," *Chicago Tribune,* December 9, 1988, at 1C.

29. "Teasing Victim, 12, Kills Classmate, Then Himself in Schoolroom," *Buffalo News*, March 3, 1987, at D5, cols. 1–3.

30. Klunder, "'86 Homicides Reflect Domestic Turmoil," *Los Angeles Times*, January 4, 1987, part 2 at 4, col. 1.

31. "The State," *Los Angeles Times*, February 26, 1988, part 1 at 2, col. 6; Lindsey, "After Trial, Homosexuals Say Justice is Not Blind," *New York Times*, March 21, 1988, at A17, cols. 1–4;

32. *Id.*

33. *Id.*

34. Pessin, "Fourteen-Year-Old Indicted for Slaying Toddler," UPI, AM cycle, September 14, 1987.

35. "Father Discusses 'Skinhead' Sons," UPI, BC cycle, March 6, 1988.

36. *Id.*

37. *State v. Ryan*, 409 N.W.2d 579 (Neb. 1987). *See also* Robbins, "Murder Trial Starts for Survivalist and Son, Both Accused of Torture," *New York Times*, March 11, 1986, at A18.

38. *Id.* at 587.

39. *Id.*

40. "Suspect in Satanic Cult Murder Found Hanged in Cell," *Reuters*, North American Service, PM cycle, July 7, 1984; Hornblower, "Youths' Deaths Tied to Satanic Rite," *Washington Post*, July 9, 1984, at A1; "Grand Jury to Hear Testimony Beginning Today," AP, PM cycle, July 10, 1984.

41. Hornblower, *supra* note 40

42. *Id.*

43. *Id.*

44. "Grand Jury to Hear Testimony Beginning Today," *supra* note 40.

45. Hornblower, *supra* note 40.

46. "Murder and Suicide among Teens Caught Up in Dark World of Satanism," AP, BC cycle, February 14, 1988; Bryson, "Teenager Convicted in Beating Death of Classmate," AP, AM cycle, May 5, 1988; Jones, "Satanists' Trail: Dead Pets to Human Sacrifice," *Los Angeles Times*, October 19, 1988, part 1 at 1, col. 1; Jones, "Human Sacrifice: 'Fun' Killers Now Paying Devil's Dues," *Los Angeles Times*, October 20, 1988, part 1 at 1, col. 1.

47. Jones, *supra* note 46.

48. *Id.*

49. *Id.*

50. *Id.*

51. Bryson, *supra* note 46.

52. *Id.*

53. Jones, *supra* note 46.

54. Green, "A Boy's Love of Satan Ends in Murder, a death Sentence—and Grisly Memories," *People*, December 1, 1986, at 154.

55. *Id.*

56. *Id.*

57. "Youth Found Guilty in Grisly 'Vampire' Murder Case," *Reuters*, Library Report, AM cycle, September 24, 1988.

58. *Id.*

59. *Cult*, UPI, BC cycle, January 19, 1989; "Cult Slaying Victim Pleaded with Killers, Court Records Show," UPI, BC cycle, December 15, 1988.

60. Crawford & Sjostrom, *supra* note 28.

61. *Id.*

62. "Shotgun Slaying of Teen Linked to Satanic Worship," *Reuters*, North European Service, AM cycle, February 21, 1986; Kahane, *Cults That Kill* 183–195 (1988).

63. *Id.* at 184–185.

64. *Id.* at 185.

65. *Id.* at 190.

66. *Id.* at 187–188.

67. Benedek & Cornell, "Clinical Presentations of Homicidal Adolescents," in E. P. Benedek & D. G. Cornell (Eds.), *Juvenile Homicide* 39, 47 (1989).

68. "Murder and Suicide among Teens Caught Up in Dark World of Satanism," *supra* note 46.

69. "FTC Asked to Require Warnings before TV Show; Dungeons & Dragons," *Broadcasting*, January 28, 1985, at 88.

70. Maharaj, "Defense Based on Game Hasn't Won Many Juries," *Newsday*, June 16, 1988, at 27 (quoting Dr. Thomas Radecki).

71. *Id.*

72. Rawls, "Youth in Capital Murder Trial Hospitalized for Drug Overdose," AP, AM cycle, August 17, 1987.

73. "Sixteen-Year-Old Sentenced for Murder of His Playmate," *New York Times*, December 5, 1986, at 30, col. 4; "Sixteen-Year-Old is Convicted in Fantasy-Game Slaying of Boy, 11," *New York Times*, November 23, 1986, at 47, col. 1.

74. *Id.*

75. U.S. Dept. of Health & Human Services, *Helpful Information on Suicide* 4 (1986).

76. Pessin, "Sweethearts," UPI, AM cycle, April 29, 1986.

77. Lucadamo, "Two Teenagers Found Shot to Death," *Chicago Tribune*, November 28, 1988, at 8C.

78. "Pregnant Girl's Ex-Boyfriend Shoots Her and Kills Self," *New York Times*, April 12, 1987, at 41, col. 6.

79. Alexander, "N.H. Youth Shot Two Dead, Killed Self, Police Say," *Boston Globe*, June 18, 1989, at 37.

80. *See* notes 2–20 and accompanying text in chapter 2.

81. *See* Cornell, "Causes of Juvenile Homicide: A Review of the Literature," in E. P. Benedek & D. G. Cornell (Eds.), *Juvenile Homicide* 1, 15–16 (1989).

82. Benedek & Cornell, *supra* note 67 at 41–42.

83. "Boy, 15, Convicted of Murder in Deaths of Adoptive Parents," *New York Times*, February 20, 1986, at B5, col. 4; Knudson, "Expert Testifies Youth Killed Parents because of 'Adopted Child Syndrome'" *New York Times*, February 18, 1986, at B2, col. 1.

84. *Id.*

85. *Id.*

86. *Id.*

87. Warner, "Jury Agonized over Justice's State of Mind," *Buffalo News*, No-

vember 16, 1986, at 1, A11; Warner, "Justice Family Portrait a Troubled One," *Buffalo News*, September 22, 1985, at A1, A4, col. 1.

88. "Jury Finds Teenager Guilty of '85 Murder of His Mother," *New York Times*, November 1, 1986, at 14, col. 4.

89. King, "Jailing Dropped for Reporter in Murder," *New York Times*, April 4, 1982, at 25, col. 1.

90. "Coast Youth Who Boasted of Killing Girl Is Sentenced, *New York Times*, December 5, 1982, at 26, col. 1.

91. Sullivan, "Addict Guilty in Crack Rampage Killing," *New York Times*, February 28, 1989, at B3, cols. 3–6.

92. *Id.*

93. *Id.*

94. Cornell, *supra* note 81 at 15.

95. Benedek & Cornell, *supra* note 67 at 45.

96. *Id.*

97. *Id.*

98. *Id.*

99. *See* Smith, "The Adolescent Murderer: A Psychodynamic Interpretation," 13 *Archives of General Psychiatry* 310, 311 (1965); Menninger & Mayman, "Episodic Dyscontrol: A Third Order of Stress Adaptation," 20 *Bulletin of the Menninger Clinic* 153 (1956).

100. Cornell, *supra* note 81 at 14.

101. *Commonwealth v. Aulisio*, 522 A.2d 1075 (Pa. 1987); Robbins, "Death Sentence for Pennsylvania Boy Reflects Country's Mood, Judge Says," *New York Times*, June 14, 1982, at D10, col. 1; "Pennsylvania Teenager Is Given Death Sentence," *New York Times*, May 29, 1982, at 6, col. 6.

102. *Id.*

103. Robbins, *supra* note 101.

104. *Id.*

105. Quinn, "A Death in the Family," *Los Angeles Times*, May 18, 1986, part 2 at 10, col. 1.

106. *Id.*

107. "Teenager," *Reuters*, AM cycle, August 17, 1979; "Spencer," *Reuters*, AM cycle, April 4, 1980; Granberry, "Victims of San Diego School Shooting Are Forced to Cope Again 10 Years Later," *Los Angeles Times*, January 19, 1989, part 2 at 1, col. 1.

108. "Teenager,"*supra* note 107; "Spencer," *supra* note 107.

109. *Id.*

110. Granberry, *supra* note 107.

Chapter 6: Gang Killings

1. Yablonsky, *The Violent Gang*, 3 (1962).

2. *See* generally, Bosc, "Street Gangs No Longer Just a Big City Problem," *U.S. News & World Report*, July 16, 1984, at 108; Shapiro, "Kids Who Kill: In Detroit,

Teenage Violence Is an Epidemic," *Newsweek,* December 2, 1985, at 55; Tayler, "Gangs," *States News Service,* March 9, 1988; Raab, "Brutal Drug Gangs Wage War of Terror in Upper Manhattan," *New York Times,* March 15, 1988, at B1, col. 5; Reinhold, "In the Middle of L.A.'s Gang Wars," *New York Times Sunday Magazine,* May 22, 1988, at 30; Hearn, "Gang," *States News Service,* June 29, 1988; Reckten-wald & Blau, "Chicago Bucking National Trend in Big-City Slayings," *Chicago Tribune,* January 8, 1989, at C1; Overend & Baker, "Total Murders Down Despite Record High in Gang Killings," *Los Angeles Times,* January 10, 1989, part 2 at 1, col. 6; Jacobs & Cullen, "Gang Rivalry on the Rise in Boston," *Boston Globe,* March 26, 1989, Metro at 1; Hamilton, "Shooting of Youth Marks Escalation of Gang Violence to a Deadlier Level," *Los Angeles Times,* April 6, 1989, part 9 at 1, col. 6; "Gangs," *Reuters,* AM cycle, April 11, 1989; Lamar, "A Bloody West Coast Story: L.A.'s Police Fight against Crack-Dealing Street Gangs," *Time,* April 18, 1989, at 32; Ward, "Pasadena Police Plan Crackdown on Gangs," *Los Angeles Times,* May 21, 1989, part 9 at 1, col. 1; Ogintz, "Wounded Childhood: Many Youngsters Don't Need TV to Show Them the Face of Violence," *Chicago Tribune,* May 24, 1989, at C1.

3. Pitt, "Wolf Packs or Posses, Gang Violence Is Common," *New York Times,* May 9, 1989, at B1, cols. 3–6.

4. *See* sources cited in *supra* note 2.

5. *See* Reinhold, *supra* note 2.

6. *See,* e.g., Yablonsky, *supra* note 1; Campbell, *The Girls in the Gang* (1984); Moore, *Homeboys: Gangs, Drugs and Prison in the Barrios of Los Angeles* (1978).

7. For example, none of the clinical research reviewed in chapter 2 deals with gang-related juvenile killings. Even the very recently published edited volume, Benedek & Cornell (Eds.), *Juvenile Homicide* (1989) makes no reference to gang-related killings.

8. *See* Bosc, *supra* note 2.

9. *See,* e.g., Tayler, *supra* note 2; Reinhold, *supra* note 2.

10. *See* Hearn, *supra* note 2; Overend & Baker, *supra* note 2; "Gangs," *supra* note 2.

11. Hearn, *supra* note 2.

12. "House of Representatives Overwhelmingly Approves Juvenile Justice Bill," *PR Newswire,* June 1, 1988.

13. Overend & Baker, *supra* note 2.

14. Reiner, "Slain over a Baseball Cap," *New York Times,* May 18, 1989, at A31.

15. *Id.*

16. Based upon data provided in Overend & Baker, *supra* note 2.

17. *Id.*

18. *Id.*

19. *Id.*

20. Lamar, *supra* note 2.

21. Braun & Feldman, "Killings Related to Street Gangs Hit Record in '87," *Los Angeles Times,* January 8, 1988, part 2 at 3, col.4.

22. Reinhold, *supra* note 2.

23. Braun & Feldman, *supra* note 21.

24. Reinhold, *supra* note 2.

25. Baker, "Deeply Rooted in L.A.; Chicano Gangs: A History of Violence," *Los Angeles Times,* December 11, 1988, part 1 at 1, col. 1.

26. *Id.*

27. Horton, "Mothers, Sons and the Gangs; Four Parents and Their Struggles," *Los Angeles Times Magazine,* October 16, 1988, at 8.

28. Jacobs & Cullen, *supra* note 2.

29. *Id.*

30. *Id.*

31. Canellos, "Roxbury Activist Calls for Gang 'Cease-Fire'," *Boston Globe,* December 29, 1988, Metro at 17.

32. Jacobs & Cullen, *supra* note 2.

33. *Id.*

34. Hearn, *supra* note 2.

35. *See,* e.g., Recktenwald & Blau, *supra* note 2; Blau, "Gang Automatic Weapon Fire Kills Girl, Wounds Three," *Chicago Tribune,* April 18, 1989, at C6.

36. *Id.*

37. Recktenwald & Blau, *supra* note 2.

38. *Id.*

39. Ogintz, *supra* note 2.

40. Overend, "New LAPD Tally May Cut Gang-Killing Score," *Los Angeles Times,* October 20, 1988.

41. *Id.*

42. Bosc, *supra* note 2.

43. Raab, *supra* note 2.

44. *Id.*

45. *Id.*

46. *Id.*

47. *See* Pitt, "Gang Attack: Unusual for Its Viciousness," *New York Times,* April 25, 1989, at B1, B11, cols. 1–4; Pitt, *supra* note 3.

48. *Id.*

49. Ball, "Clockwork Orange Scourge Terrorizes the Big Apple," *Sunday Telegraph Limited,* May 21, 1989, International at 13. *See also* Pitt, *supra* note 47.

50. Pitt, *supra* note 3.

51. Pitt, *supra* note 47.

52. Overend, *supra* note 40.

53. Canellos, "Gang Links Suspected in Three Holiday Shootings," *Boston Globe,* December 28, 1988, at 13; Horton, *supra* note 27.

54. "Girl's Murder Attributed to School Drug Sellers," *New York Times,* December 13, 1983, at A22, col. 6.

55. "Two Youths Arrested in Drug-Related Slaying," *Los Angeles Times,* February 1, 1989, part 2 at 12, col. 1.

56. Horrock & Hundley, "Portrait of a Gun Culture: Schoolyard Killer's Arsenal Is Not Unique," *Chicago Tribune,* March 19, 1989, at C1.

57. "Two Arrested in Death of Man Hit by Train," *New York Times,* April 13, 1989, at B7, col. 1.

58. Stewart, "Gang Member Gets 97 Years for Role in Gang Rape, Burning," *Los Angeles Times,* April 15, 1988, part 2 at 3, col. 4; "Two Get Prison Terms for

Raping, Burning Women," *Los Angeles Times,* December 13, 1987, part 2 at 8, col. 1; "Two Gang Members Convicted in Rape," *Los Angeles Times,* June 26, 1987, part 1 at 2, col. 3; "Gang Rape Conviction," *Los Angeles Times,* March 25, 1988, part 2 at 2, col. 2.

59. *Id.*

60. Beene, "Trial in Murder of Church Elder to Begin Monday," *Los Angeles Times,* May 21, 1989, part 2 at 1, col. 5

61. Pristin, "Teen Gets 32 Years to Life for Murder of Church Elder," *Los Angeles Times,* July 2, 1988, part 2 at 3, col. 3.

62. Jones, "Two Gang Members Held in Drive-By Killing of Girl, 11," *Los Angeles Times,* March 1, 1989, part 2 at 3, col. 5; Jones, "Third Gang Member in Slaying of Girl Seized," *Los Angeles Times,* March 2, 1989, part 2 at 2, col. 3; Jones, "Youngsters' Fears and Nightmares Surface in Letters on Girl's Slaying," *Los Angeles Times,* March 3, 1989, part 2 at 1, col. 1.

63. "Girl, 16, Killed in Gang Shooting," *Chicago Tribune,* April 16, 1989, at C3; Blau, "Gang Automatic Weapon Fire Kills Girl, Wounds Three," *Chicago Tribune,* April 18, 1989, at C6.

64. Klein, "Gang Member Arrested in Killing of Pacioma Boy," *Los Angeles Times,* July 21, 1987, part 2 at 6, col. 1.

65. Feldman, "Convicts Dig Deep for Two Young Victims of Violence," *Los Angeles Times,* May 13, 1989, part 1 at 24, col. 1; Reiner, *supra* note 14.

66. "Two Youths Charged in Party Deaths of Three People," AP, PM cycle, November 10, 1986.

67. "Six Teenagers Held in Sun Valley Slaying," *Los Angeles Times,* May 9, 1989, part 2 at 2, col. 3.

68. "Teen Knifed in Gang 'Pay-Back' Dies," *Los Angeles Times,* April 7, 1989, part 2 at 2, col. 4.

69. Puig, "Violent Gang Loses Leaders, Identity," *Los Angeles Times,* December 5, 1987, part 2 at 10, col. 1.

70. *Id.*

71. *See,* e.g., Wolff, "Youths Rape Jogger on Central Park Road," *New York Times,* April 21, 1989, at B1, cols. 4–6.

72. *Id. See also* Pitt, *supra* note 3; Pitt, *supra* note 47; Kaufman, "Park Suspects: Children of Discipline," *New York Times,* April 26, 1989, at A1, col. 2.

73. Weiss, "'Grab Her'," *New York Post,* April 23, 1989, at 5, cols. 1–5.

74. Kaufman, *supra* note 72.

75. Pearl, Reyes & Phillips, "Rape Suspect: 'It was Fun'," *New York Post,* April 23, 1989, at 3, 33.

76. *Id.*

77. *See* Parascandola, Broderick, Weiss & Peyser, "Rampage Victim Clings to Life," *New York Post,* April 22, 1989, at 2–3.

78. *See* Wolff, *supra* note 71; Mustain & Marques, "Two Faced Pack," *New York Daily News,* April 22, 1989, at 4; Clark & Landa, "Rape Suspects Scoff," *New York Daily News,* April 23, 1989, at 5, 13.

79. *See* Ball, *supra* note 49; Pitt, *supra* note 47.

80. Kaufman, *supra* note 72.

81. *Id.*

82. "Manslaughter," UPI, BC cycle, May 2, 1986.

83. Kurtz, "Suspect in $20 Theft in N.Y. Beaten to Death by Crowd," *Washington Post*, March 22, 1988, at A3.

84. Awalt, "Teen Attacks on Parents Puzzle Authorities," AP, PM cycle, January 23, 1989.

85. *Id.*

86. *Id.*

87. Blau & Fegelman, "Three Charged with Murder in CTA Platform Stabbing," *Chicago Tribune*, June 14, 1989, at C1.

88. *Id.*

Chapter 7: Children Who Kill

1. *See FBI Uniform Crime Reports* (1985–1989).

2. *Id.*

3. *Id.*

4. *See* LaFave & Scott, *Criminal Law* 398–400 (1986).

5. *See FBI Uniform Crime Reports* (1985–1989).

6. Ball, "Boy, 3, Kills Father Who Beat Mother," *Daily Telegraph*, October 6, 1988, at 3.

7. *Id.*

8. *Id.*

9. "Eleven-Year-Old Girl to Appear in Juvenile Court on Murder Charge," UPI, PM cycle, April 23, 1987.

10. *Id.*

11. Meyer, "In Wheaton the Shock of a Family Tragedy," *Washington Post*, February 26, 1989, at D1, D11; "Mother Dead, Father Wounded; Boy Charged," *Chicago Tribune*, February 26, 1989, at C26; Hagigh, "Boy, 12, Feared Parents Would Punish Him," *Montgomery Journal*, February 28, 1989, at A1, A4; "Twelve-Year-Old 'Real Polite' Boy Guns Down Parents," *Reuters*, AM cycle, February 24, 1989.

12. *Id.*

13. *Id.*

14. Patterson, "Psychiatric Study of Juveniles Involved in Homicide," 13 *Am. J. Orthopsychiatry* 125 (1943).

15. Bender, "Children and Adolescents Who Have Killed," 116 *Am. J. Psychiatry* 510, 511 (1959).

16. *Id.*

17. Adelson, "The Battering Child," 222 *J. Am. Medical Ass'n.* 159, 160 (1972).

18. Tooley, "The Small Assassins," 14 *J. Am. Academy of Child Psychiatry* 306 (1975).

19. *Id.*

20. *Id.* at 307.

21. *Id.* at 316.

22. Easson & Steinhilber, "Murderous Aggression by Children and Adolescents," 4 *Archives of General Psychiatry* 27 (1961).

23. *Id.* at 29.

24. *Id.*

25. Carek & Watson, "Treatment of a Family Involved in Fratricide," 11 *Archives of General Psychiatry* 533 (1964).

26. Petti & Davidson, "Homicidal School-Age Children: Cognitive Style and Demographic Features," 12 *Child Psychiatry & Human Development* 82 (1981).

27. Shulins, "Kids Who Kill—I," Associated Press [hereinafter AP], BC cycle, June 29, 1986.

28. "Boy, 8, Faces Murder Count in Fire," *Buffalo News,* September 14, 1988, at A14; "Eight-Year-Old Charged with Murder," *Newsday,* September 13, 1988, at 7.

29. *Id.*

30. Dishneau, "Don't Say Murder, Judge Warns in Juvenile Case," AP, AM cycle, December 9, 1985.

31. Hicks, "Viet Boys, 12 and 13, Guilty in Murdering Praying Mother of 14," *Los Angeles Times,* July 30, 1986, part 2 at 1, col. 5.

32. *Id.*

33. Podolsky, "Children Who Kill," 31 *General Practitioner* 98, 101–102 (1965).

34. *Id.* at 102.

35. Thom, "Juvenile Delinquency and Criminal Homicide," 40 *J. Maine Medical Ass'n.* 176 (1949).

36. Podolsky, *supra* note 33 at 101.

37. Stearns, "Murder by Adolescents with Obscure Motivation," 114 *Am. J. Psychiatry* 303, 304 (1957).

38. *Id.*

39. Queen, "Tots Suspected in Baby's Death," *Buffalo News,* June 11, 1989, at A12.

40. Adelson, *supra* note 17.

41. *Id.* at 161.

42. *Id.*

43. "Child Killers," UPI, AM cycle, December 28, 1986.

44. Tackett, "Boys, 4 and 6, Accused of Attacking a Baby," *Chicago Tribune,* January 31, 1989, at C8.

45. *Id.*

46. Shulins, *supra* note 27.

47. *See* generally, Kohlberg, *The Philosophy of Moral Development* (1981); Kohlberg, "Moral Stages and Moralization: The Cognitive Developmental Approach," in T. Licona (Ed.), *Moral Development and Behavior* (1976); Damon, *Social and Personality Development* (1983).

48. Ziraldo, "Children Who Kill," *Los Angeles Times,* March 15, 1986, part 2 at 7, col. 1.

49. Palermo, "'Good Kids' Who Kill: Violent '80s to Blame?" *Los Angeles Times,* March 2, 1986, part 2 at 4, col. 6.

50. *Id.*

51. "Girl Charged with Murdering Ten-Year-Old," UPI, AM cycle, March 26, 1986.

52. *Id.*

53. "Teasing Victim, 12, Kills Classmate, Then Himself in Schoolroom," *Buffalo News,* March 3, 1987, at D5, cols. 1–3.

54. DePalma, "Ten-Year-Old Boy is Charged as Adult in Fatal Shooting of Seven-Year-Old Girl," *New York Times,* August 26, 1989, at 6, cols. 1–3; Blake, "Ten-Year-Old Pleads Innocent in Shooting," *Buffalo News,* August 27, 1989, at A13, cols. 1–2.

55. Russo, "Our Tough Gun Laws Are Not Enough," *New York Times,* April 17, 1988, Section 12NJ at 32, col. 2.

56. Rawls, "Investigation of Five-Year-Old in Fatal Shooting Stirs Controversy," *New York Times* October 10, 1981, at 8, col. 1.

57. *Id.*

58. "Boy, 6, Accidentally Kills Israeli Cabbie," *Los Angeles Times,* March 7, 1989, part 1 at 9, col. 3; "Dad Charged in Gun Mishap; Cabbie Killed," *Chicago Tribune,* March 7, 1989, at M5.

59. *Id.*

Chapter 8: Girls Who Kill

1. *See FBI Uniform Crime Reports* (1985–1989).

2. *Id.*

3. *Id.*

4. Rosner, Wiederlight, Rosner & Wieczorek, "Adolescents Accused of Murder and Manslaughter: A Five-Year Descriptive Study," 7 *Bull. Am. Academy of Psychiatry & Law* 342, 345 (1979).

5. Cornell, Benedek & Benedek, "Characteristics of Adolescents Charged with Homicide: Review of 72 Cases," 5 *Behavioral Sciences & the Law* 11, 18–19 (1987).

6. Solway, Richardson, Hays & Elion, "Adolescent Murderers: Literature Review and Preliminary Findings," in J. Hays, T. Roberts & K. Solway (Eds.), *Violence and the Violent Individual* 193 (1981).

7. Russell, "Girls Who Kill," 30 *Int'l. J. Offender Therapy & Comparative Criminology* 171 (1986).

8. *Id.*

9. *Id.*

10. *Id.* at 172.

11. *Id.* at 173

12. *Id.*

13. *Id.* at 174.

14. *Id.*

15. *Id.*

16. *Id.* at 175.

17. J. Cassity, *The Quality of Murder: A Psychiatric and Legal Evaluation of*

Motives and Responsibilities Involved in the Plea of Insanity as Revealed in Outstanding Murder Cases of this Century (1958).

18. *Id.* at 190.

19. *Id.* at 192.

20. *Id.* at 209–210.

21. Gardiner, *The Deadly Innocents: Portraits of Children Who Kill* 24–46 (1976).

22. *Id.* at 32.

23. *Id.* at 37–38.

24. *Id.* at 46.

25. *Id.* at 148–165.

26. *Id.* at 151.

27. *Id.* at 152.

28. *Id.*

29. *Id.* at 153.

30. *Id.* at 154.

31. *Id.* at 162–163.

32. McCarthy, "Narcissism and the Self in Homicidal Adolescents," 38 *Am. J. Psychoanalysis* 19, 24 (1978).

33. *Id.*

34. *Id.*

35. Benedek & Cornell, "Clinical Presentations of Homicidal Adolescents," in E. P. Benedek & D. G. Cornell (Eds.), *Juvenile Homicide* 39, 50 (1989).

36. *Id.* at 51.

37. Rowley, Ewing & Singer, "Juvenile Homicide: The Need for an Interdisciplinary Approach," 5 *Behavioral Sciences & the Law* 3 (1987).

38. *Id.*

39. *Id.* at 8.

40. *See* Holzberg, "A Tale of Suburbia: Bowling, Little League and Sex Abuse," *National Law Journal,* October 5, 1987, at 6; Kleiman, "Girl Says Hiring Father's Killer Seemed "Like A Game" at First," *New York Times,* September 15, 1987, at B1–B2.

41. Yost, "Teen Begged Boyfriend to Kill Her Mother," UPI, AM cycle, November 13, 1987.

42. *Id.*

43. Hamill, "A Crime That Defies Understanding," *Newsday,* February 1, 1989, at 18.

44. *See* Daly & Wilson, *Homicide* 62 (1988).

45. "Babystab," UPI, AM cycle, February 27, 1986.

46. O'Brien, "Teen Held in Death of Newborn Infant Tells Police of Fear," *Buffalo News,* July 12, 1988, at B1, cols. 1–5.

47. Hicks, "Girl Who Killed Her Baby Gets Year in Juvenile Hall," *Los Angeles Times,* April 13, 1988, part 2 at 14, col. 5; Reyes, "Release Denied for Girl, 16, Held in Death of Her Baby, *Los Angeles Times,* October 20, 1987, part 2 at 4, col. 5.

48. *Id.*

49. *Id.*

50. *See* Rowley, Ewing & Singer, *supra* note 37.

51. "Girl to Stand Trial as Juvenile in Slayings," UPI, AM cycle, March 26, 1987.

52. Cannaday v. State, 455 So. 2d 713 (Miss. 1984).

53. McCall, "A Grandmother is Murdered, Two Teenage Girls are Convicted—There the Questions Begin," *People,* August 29, 1983, at 63.

54. *Id.*

55. *Id.*

56. *Id.*

57. *Id.*

58. Archer & Lloyd, *Sex and Gender* 102 (1982).

59. *See* generally, *FBI Uniform Crime Reports* (1980–1989).

60. "Teen," UPI, BC cycle, April 19, 1988.

61. Cohen, "Teenage Murderer Is One of 35 on Death Row Who Killed as Children," AP, BC cycle, January 18, 1987.

62. "Salesman," UPI, AM cycle, December 17, 1980. *See also* "Thirteen-Year-Old Witness in Salesman Slaying to Get Protective Custody," AP, PM cycle, December 18, 1980; "Hopfner," UPI, AM cycle, November 10, 1981; "Two Women Acquitted of Murder," AP, PM cycle, November 18, 1981; "Teens Sentenced," AP, AM cycle, December 21, 1981.

63. Renwick, "Police Find Increasing Number of Girls Involved in Gang Crime," *Los Angeles Times,* September 22, 1988, part 2 at 3, col. 1.

64. *Id.*

65. "Two Teens Get Life in 'Good Samaritan' Slaying," UPI, PM cycle, September 30, 1987.

66. "Two Charged in Slaying of Police Officer," *Los Angeles Times,* September 8, 1988, part 2 at 2, col. 4; "Adult Trial Ordered for Girl in Slaying," *Los Angeles Times,* March 28, 1989, part 2 at 2, col.1.

67. *See* chapter 5, notes 76–79 and accompanying text.

Chapter 9: The Law's Response to Juvenile Homicide

1. Butterfield, "A Boy Who Killed Coldly Is Now a 'Prison Monster'," *New York Times,* March 22, 1989, at A1.

2. Bauder, "New York's Most Notorious Prisoner Keeps System on Edge," *Buffalo News,* July 10, 1988, at H8, cols. 1–5.

3. Butterfield, *supra* note 1.

4. Bauder, *supra* note 2.

5. Singer & Ewing, "Juvenile Justice Reform in New York: The Juvenile Offender Law," 8 *Law & Policy* 463, 468 (1986).

6. Butterfield, *supra* note 1.

7. Singer & Ewing, *supra* note 5.

8. *Id.*

9. Butterfield, *supra* note 1.

10. Hamparian, Estep, Muntean, Priestino, Swisher, Wallace, & White, *Youth in Adult Courts: Between Two Worlds* 96 (1982).

11. Bonnie, "Juvenile Homicide: A Study in Legal Ambivalence," in E. P. Benedek & D. G. Cornell (Eds.), *Juvenile Homicide* 185, 193 (1989).

12. *Id.*

13. *Id.* at 194.

14. *Id.*

15. 383 U.S.541 (1966).

16. *See* Ewing, "Juveniles or Adults? Forensic Assessment of Juveniles Considered for Trial in Criminal Court," forthcoming in *Forensic Reports*.

17. *Id.*

18. *Id.*

19. *See* Miller, Dawson, Dix & Parnas, *The Juvenile Justice Process* 383–488 (1985).

20. *Id.*

21. *Id.*

22. *Id.*

23. *See* Levine, Ewing & Hager, "Juvenile and Family Mental Health Law in Sociohistorical Context," 10 *Int'l. J. Law & Psychiatry* 91 (1987).

24. *Id.*

25. Melton, Petrila, Poythress, & Slobogin, *Psychological Evaluations for the Courts: A Handbook for Mental Health Professionals and Lawyers* 297 (1987).

26. Ewing, *supra* note 16.

27. *Id.*

28. Eigen, "Punishing Youth Homicide Offenders in Philadelphia," 72 *J. Criminal Law & Criminology* 1072 (1981).

29. Snyder, Finnegan, Nimick, Sickmund, Sullivan & Tierney, *Juvenile Court Statistics 1985* 84 (1989).

30. Cornell, Staresina & Benedek, "Legal Outcomes of Juveniles Charged with Homicide," in E. P. Benedek & D. G. Cornell (Eds.), *Juvenile Homicide* 165 (1989).

31. *State ex rel. Juvenile Department v. Mathis*, 537 P.2d 148 (Or. App. 1975).

32. *Id.*

33. *Id.*

34. *Id.*

35. *See* Bonnie, *supra* note 11; Hamparian et al., *supra* note 10.

36. *Id.*

37. *Id.*

38. *See Stanford v. Kentucky* and *Wilkins v. Missouri*, 57 U.S. *Law Week* 4973 (1989).

39. Eigen, *supra* note 28.

40. *Id.*

41. Cormier & Markus, "A Longitudinal Study of Adolescent Murderers," 8 *Bull. Am. Academy of Psychiatry & Law* 240 (1980).

42. *Id.* at 245.

43. Cornell et al., *supra* note 30.

44. *Id.*

45. *Id.* at 180.

46. *Id.* at 181.

47. Rosner, Wiederlight, Rosner & Wieczorek, "Adolescents Accused of Murder and Manslaughter: A Five Year Descriptive Study," 4 *Bull. Am. Academy of Psychiatry & Law* 342, 345–346 (1978).

48. *Id.* at 348–349.

49. *Id.* at 349.

50. Brief for Amnesty International as *Amicus Curiae, Thompson v. Oklahoma* (1988).

51. Streib, "Imposing the Death Penalty on Children, in K. Haas & J. Inciardi (Eds.), *Challenging Capital Punishment: Legal and Social Science Approaches* 245, 251 (1988).

52. Wolfe, Ogloff, Streib & Ewing, "Issues and Perspectives on Juvenile Capital Punishment: A Dying Debate?" Unpublished manuscript, University of Nebraska at Lincoln; State University of New York at Buffalo, 1988, Streib, *supra* note 51 at 255.

53. NAACP Legal Defense and Educational Fund, Inc., *Death Row U.S.A.* (March 1, 1989).

54. *See Stanford v. Kentucky,* 57 *U.S. Law Week* 4973, 4976 (1989).

55. *Id.*

56. *Id.*

57. *Id.*

58. 455 U.S. 104 (1982).

59. *Id.*

60. *Id.*

61. 455 S.Ct. 2687 (1988).

62. *Id.*

63. *Id.*

64. *Id.*

65. 57 *U.S. Law Week* 4973 (1989).

66. *Id.* at 4974.

67. *Id.*

68. *Id.* at 4975.

69. *Id.* at 4984.

70. *Id.*

71. *Id.* at 4975.

72. *Id.* at 4978.

73. *Id.* at 4983.

Chapter 10: The Future of Juvenile Homicide

1. *FBI Uniform Crime Reports* (1989).

2. *See* "Text of President's Speech on National Drug Control Strategy," *New York Times,* September 6, 1989, at B6, col. 1.

3. Statement of Dr. William Bennett, Director, National Drug Control Policy, July 31, 1989, Humphrey Auditorium, Department of Health and Human Services, Washington, D.C.

4. *Id.*

5. Statement of Dr. Frederick Godwin, Administrator, Alcohol, Drug Abuse and Mental Health Administration, July 31, 1989, Humphrey Auditorium, Department of Health and Human Services, Washington, D.C.

6. Kerr, "Young Crack Addicts Find There's No Help for Them," *New York Times,* May 2, 1988, at B1, col. 2.

7. Guttenplan, "Kids Called Losers in NY War on Drugs," *Newsday,* June 16, 1989, at 29.

8. Gelman, "Homicide, They Wrote, 1,896 Times," *Newsday,* August 14, 1989, at 5; Hartocollis, "Growing Up Behind Bars: A Wave of Violence Engulfs a Generation," *Newsday,* August 16, 1989, at 4.

9. Malmquist, "Premonitory Signs of Homicidal Juvenile Aggression" 128 *Am. J. Psychiatry* 461 (1971).

10. Sorrells, "Kids Who Kill," 23 *Crime & Delinquency* 312 (1977).

11. Cornell, Benedek & Benedek, "A Typology of Juvenile Homicide Offenders," in E. P. Benedek & D. G. Cornell (Eds.), *Juvenile Homicide* 61, 73 (1989).

12. *See, e.g.,* Baker & Cohn, "Crack Wars in D.C.," *Newsweek,* February 22, 1988, at 24; "Two New York Teens Arrested in Murder," UPI, BC cycle, August 2, 1988; "Teenagers in Front Lines of Dallas Drug Wars," UPI, BC cycle, March 27, 1988.

13. *Id.*

14. *Id.*

15. *Id.*

16. *See* Sonkin, *Domestic Violence on Trial: Psychological and Legal Dimensions of Family Violence* (1987).

17. Besharov, "Let's Give Crack Babies a Way Out of Addict Families," *Newsday* (Ideas), September 3, 1989, at 4.

18. *See, e.g.,* "Drug Abuse and Child Abuse," *Boston Globe,* June 10, 1989.

19. *See* chapter 2 *supra* notes 88–100 and accompanying text.

20. *Id.*

21. *See, e.g.,* Shapiro & Shapiro, "The Epidemic of Child Abuse Turns Deadly: Parents Who Kill Their Kids," *U.S. News & World Report,* April 11, 1988, at 35; McGraw, "Lawmaker Proposes Tougher Child Abuse Laws," UPI, BC cycle, February 14, 1988; "Children," UPI, BC cycle, September 29, 1984 (quoting Rep. Jim McNulty regarding Congress's plans for legislation dealing with "an epidemic of child abuse offenses").

22. American Association for Protecting Children, *Highlights of Official Aggregate Child Neglect and Abuse Reporting* (1987).

23. *Id.* at 5–6.

24. *Id.* at 10–11.

25. *Id.* at 14.

26. Moody, "Infant," *States News Service,* May 16, 1989.

27. Shapiro & Shapiro, *supra* note 21.

28. *Id.*

29. Karwath, "Child Abuse Deaths Highest in Seven Years," *Chicago Tribune,* November 30, 1988, at C1.

30. Statement of the National Committee for Prevention of Child Abuse, Washington, D.C., March 31, 1989.

31. McCune, "Abuse," *States News Service*, March 31, 1989.

32. Golden, "The Arming of America," *Boston Globe* (Sunday Magazine), April 23, 1989, at 16.

33. *Id.*

34. "Guns," *U.S. News & World Report*, May 8, 1989, at 20.

35. *Id.*

36. Golden, *supra* note 32.

37. Perlez, "New York Schools Consider the Use of Metal Detectors," *New York Times*, May 4, 1988, at B1, col. 4; Malkin, "Florida Schools Screen for Guns," UPI, BC cycle, March 7, 1988.

38. *Id. See also* Golden, *supra* note 32.

39. Malkin, *supra* note 37.

40. Fulham, "Youths Who Carry Guns Are Afraid, Panel Finds," *Boston Globe*, October 5, 1988, at 37.

41. Schmalz, "Children Shooting Children: The Move Is on for Gun Control," *New York Times*, June 18, 1989, at 20, col. 5.

42. *Id. See also* Bearak, "Careless Firearm Storage Could Mean Jail; Five Child Shootings in Week Spur Gun Safety in Florida," *Los Angeles Times*, June 16, 1989, part 1 at 1, col. 5.

43. *Id.*

44. Hatch, "Panel is Set to Consider Curbs on Guns," *New York Times*, September 10, 1989, Section 12CN at 1, col. 5; Miller, "Stallings to Introduce New Gun Legislation," UPI, BC cycle, July 31, 1989.

45. *Id.*; Hatch, *supra* note 44; Moline, "Governor Signs Bill," UPI, BC cycle, July 12, 1989.

46. *Id.*

47. Secter, "Dick and Jane Find a Gun; Critics Quick to Take Aim," *Los Angeles Times*, December 17, 1988, part 1 at 30, col. 1; Scott, "NRA Book Touts Safety," *Newsday*, February 10, 1989, at 7.

48. *See*, e.g., Wilson & Herrnstein, *Crime and Human Nature* 472–476 (1985).

49. Cocco, "Trying to Mend 'Safety Net'," *Newsday*, January 20, 1989, at 7A.

50. *Id.*

51. U.S. Bureau of the Census, *Statistical Abstract of the United States* (1987).

52. *Id.*

53. *See* chapter 1, *supra* notes 3–6 and accompanying text.

Index

About the Author

Charles Patrick Ewing, a clinical and forensic psychologist and attorney, is Professor of Law and Clinical Associate Professor of Psychology at the State University of New York at Buffalo. After receiving a Ph.D. from Cornell University, he was a postdoctoral fellow at Yale University and received a J.D. from Harvard University. Dr. Ewing is the author of *Crisis Intervention as Psychotherapy* (Oxford University Press, 1978) and *Battered Women Who Kill: Psychological Self-Defense as Legal Justification* (Lexington Books, 1987) and editor of *Psychology, Psychiatry and the Law: A Clinical and Forensic Handbook* (Professional Resource Exchange, 1985). He is also the author or co-author of numerous articles and chapters dealing with psychology and law, psychotherapy, professional ethics, and violent behavior, and serves as co-editor of the journal *Behavioral Sciences and the Law*. A Diplomate in Forensic Psychology (American Board of Professional Psychology), Dr. Ewing has examined many homicide defendants and testified as an expert in numerous murder trials.